Give this text a spin on CD-ROM!

Advantage Interactive: Tutorials for Windows® 95 places this text in a multimedia format for a fun spin on the traditional way of learning **Microsoft® PowerPoint® 7.0 for Windows® 95**. With this interactive CD-ROM, you just don't read the material—***you experience it***, through video, animated examples, and a narration option! Set your own pace as you listen, watch, and practice. If you get stuck, an animation will show you exactly what to do or where to click. Here's what else you'll discover on this exciting spin:

- **Advantage Interactive** corresponds directly with this printed text—you will learn the exact same skills with either product.
- The **Quick Reference** boxes in the text are illustrated and annotated.
- The **Key Terms** are all hyperlinked—with definitions only a click away.
- The **Session Opening Cases** are included as exciting video clips.
- Each **Hands-On** example is both narrated and animated. (Narration may be placed in a read-only mode if desired.)
- **Advantage Interactive** connects Internet-users to web sites relevant to the study of **Microsoft® PowerPoint® 7.0 for Windows® 95**.
- You can take **Quizzes** to measure how well you're grasping the material.

To show you our appreciation for buying this book, we have attached a coupon that takes 50% off the price of **Advantage Interactive**. You spend only $10 (plus tax, shipping & handling) for a spin on this CD-ROM!

Simply fill out the attached coupon, include a check or credit card number, and mail to:

Times Mirror Higher Education Group
Attn: Mary Long
2460 Kerper Boulevard
Dubuque, IA 52001

AF709330

Please Allow 2-3 weeks for delivery.

System Requirements: 486 Processor running Windows® 95, SVGA video adaptor and monitor, MPC II compliant double speed CD-ROM or better, 4MB RAM (8 MB recommended), 2MB hard disk space, soundcard and speakers (recommended but not required).

IRWIN

EXPLORE OUR Web Site
http://www.irwin.com

YES! Please send me Advantage Interactive at 50% off its regular price!

Name ______________________________

Address *(Sorry, No P.O. Boxes)* ______________________________

City ____________________ State __________ Zip __________

E-mail Address ____________________ Phone Number ____________________

School ______________________________

Course Name & Number ______________________________

Please add $4.00 for shipping, handling and tax.

Payment Method: **Total Price: $14.00**

❒ Check Amount enclosed $ __________

❒ Visa ❒ MasterCard ❒ American Express

Account # ____________________ Exp. Date __________

Signature ______________________________

COUPON

IRWIN

Advantage Interactive: Tutorials for Windows® 95

Version: **Microsoft® PowerPoint® 7.0 for Windows® 95**

ISBN 0256233268 Book No. 91439400

PLACE
POSTAGE
HERE

Times Mirror Higher Education Group
Attn: Mary Long
2460 Kerper Boulevard
Dubuque, IA 52001

Microsoft® PowerPoint 7.0 for Windows® 95

Microsoft® PowerPoint 7.0 for Windows® 95

Sarah E. Hutchinson

Glen J. Coulthard

THE IRWIN ADVANTAGE SERIES FOR COMPUTER EDUCATION

IRWIN

Chicago • Bogotá • Boston • Buenos Aires • Caracas • London • Madrid • Mexico City • Sydney • Toronto

Irwin Book Team

Publisher: *Tom Casson*
Sponsoring editor: *Garrett Glanz*
Developmental editor: *Kristin Hepburn*
Associate marketing manager: *Michelle Hudson*
Project editor: *Jane Lightell*
Production supervisor: *Pat Frederickson*
Art director: *Keith McPherson*
Assistant manager, graphics: *Charlene R. Perez*
Compositor: *Graphic Typesetting Service*
Typeface: *11/13 Bodoni Book*
Printer: *Webcrafters, Inc.*

Times Mirror
Higher Education Group

Library of Congress Cataloging-in-Publication Data

Hutchinson, Sarah E.
Microsoft PowerPoint 7.0 for Windows 95 / Sarah E. Hutchinson, Glen J. Coulthard.
p. cm. — (The Irwin advantage series for computer education)
Includes index.
ISBN 0-256-22051-4
1. Computer graphics. 2. Microsoft PowerPoint for Windows.
I. Coulthard, Glen J. II. Title. III. Series.
T.385.H88 1996
006.6′869—dc20 96-6164

Printed in the United States of America

1 2 3 4 5 6 7 8 9 0 WC 3 2 1 0 9 8 7 6

Contents

SESSION 1

Fundamentals 95

SESSION OUTLINE 2
INTRODUCTION 2
WHAT IS POWERPOINT? 3
- PowerPoint Viewer 4
- Presentations 4
- Slides 4
- Handouts 5
- Speaker's Notes 5
- Outlines 6

THE WINDOWS ADVANTAGE 6
FEATURES OF MICROSOFT POWERPOINT 7.0 7
WORKING WITH POWERPOINT 8
- How the Mouse Is Used 9
- How the Keyboard Is Used 10

STARTING POWERPOINT 10
- Loading Applications in Windows 95 11
- Loading Microsoft Powerpoint 7.0 12

THE GUIDED TOUR 14
- Application Window 15
- Presentation Window 16
- Menu Bar 18
- Shortcut Menus 18
- Toolbars 19
- Dialog Box 20
- The Windows Taskbar 21

GETTING HELP 22
OPENING A PRESENTATION 27
VIEWING A PRESENTATION 30
- Slide View 30
- Outline View 31
- Slide Sorter View 31
- Note Pages View 32
- Slide Show View 32
- For Practice 33

CLOSING A PRESENTATION 37
LEAVING POWERPOINT 38
SUMMARY 38
- Command Summary 39

KEY TERMS 39
EXERCISES 40
- Short Answer 40
- Hands-On 40

SESSION 2

Creating a Presentation

SESSION OUTLINE 46
INTRODUCTION 46
CREATING A PRESENTATION: AN OVERVIEW 47
- Using PowerPoint to Create a Presentation 48
- Reaching for the Dictionary 49

USING THE AUTOCONTENT WIZARD 50
USING A DESIGN TEMPLATE 57
SAVING A PRESENTATION 60
ADDING SLIDES 62
- Adding Text to a Slide 63
- Manipulating Bullets 66
- Formatting Text 67

REVIEWING YOUR PRESENTATION 71
EDITING A PRESENTATION 71
- Changing the Layout of a Slide 72
- Inserting Clip Art 74

USING THE STYLE CHECKER 76
PRINTING A PRESENTATION 78
SUMMARY 79
- Command Summary 80

KEY TERMS 80
EXERCISES 81
- Short Answer 81
- Hands-On 82

SESSION 3

Designing a Presentation

SESSION OUTLINE 90
INTRODUCTION 90
APPLYING TEMPLATES 91
USING THE SLIDE MASTER 95
  Editing the Slide Master 95
  Editing an Individual Slide 97
THE IMPORTANCE OF COLOR 99
  Editing the Current Color Scheme 100
VIEWING SLIDES IN BLACK AND WHITE 102
WORKING MORE WITH TEXT 104
  Text Bullets 104
  Manipulating Text in Outline View 107
  Using the Text Tool 110
SUMMARY 113
  Command Summary 113
KEY TERMS 114
EXERCISES 114
  Short Answer 114
  Hands-On 115

SESSION 4

Adding Visual Effects

SESSION OUTLINE 122
INTRODUCTION 122
WORKING WITH OBJECTS 123
INSERTING CLIP ART 125
  Finding the Art You Want 126
  Moving and Resizing Clip Art 130
INSERTING PICTURES 132
CREATING GRAPHS 132
CREATING ORGANIZATIONAL CHARTS 136
RUNNING SLIDE SHOWS 139
  Setting Timings 139
  Adding Transitions 141
  Creating a Build Slide 143
  Adding Animation 144
SUMMARY 146
  Command Summary 146
KEY TERMS 147
EXERCISES 147
  Short Answer 147
  Hands-On 148

SESSION 5

Notes, Handouts, and Printing

SESSION OUTLINE 156
INTRODUCTION 156
PUBLIC SPEAKING TIPS 157
SPEAKER'S NOTES 158
  Creating and Printing Speaker's Notes 158
  Modifying the Notes Master 161
AUDIENCE HANDOUTS 163
  Modifying the Handout Master 163
  Printing Audience Handouts 165
PRINT OPTIONS FOR SALES 166
  Setting Up the Slide Format 166
  35mm Slides 167
PACKAGING YOUR PRESENTATION 168
SUMMARY 168
  Command Summary 169
KEY TERMS 169
EXERCISES 169
  Short Answer 169
  Hands-On 170

APPENDIX
Toolbar Summary 175

INDEX 179

USING THIS GUIDE

Welcome to the Irwin Advantage Series! This tutorial is one in a series of learning guides that lead you through the most popular microcomputer software programs available. The following features are incorporated into each session of our guides to ensure that your learning experience is as productive and enjoyable as possible:

- Each session begins with a real-world ***case scenario*** that introduces you to a fictitious person or company and describes their immediate problem or opportunity. During the session, you obtain the knowledge and skills necessary to define and solve the problem or take advantage of the opportunity. At the end of the session, you are invited to solve problems directly related to the case scenario.
- ***Concepts, skills, and procedures*** are grouped into session topics and are presented in a logical and structured manner.
- ***In Addition boxes*** are placed strategically throughout the guide to provide information about topics related to the current discussion, but beyond the scope of the text.
- Commands and procedures are introduced using ***hands-on examples in a step-by-step format,*** and students are encouraged to perform the steps along with the guide.
- Each session concludes with ***short answer questions and hands-on exercises.*** These exercises are integrated with the session's objectives; they were not added as an afterthought. The exercises are comprehensive and meaningful, and they provide students with an opportunity to practice the session material. For maximum benefit, students should complete all the exercises at the end of each session.
- For each of the learning guides, an instructor's resource kit is available with suggested answers to the questions, exercises, and case problems appearing at the end of each session. In addition, the resource kit provides a test bank of additional questions and exercises.

The exercises and examples in this guide use several standard conventions to indicate menu options, keystroke combinations, and command instructions.

MENU INSTRUCTIONS

In Windows 95, all Menu bar options and pull-down menu commands have an underlined or highlighted letter in each option. When you need to execute a command from the Menu bar—the row of menu choices across the top of the screen—the tutorial's instruction line separates the Menu bar option from the command with a comma. Notice also that the word "CHOOSE" is always used for menu commands. For example, the command for quitting Windows is shown as:

CHOOSE: File, Exit

This instruction tells you to choose the File option on the Menu bar and then to choose the Exit command from the File pull-down menu. The actual steps for choosing a menu command are discussed later in this guide.

KEYSTROKES AND KEYSTROKE COMBINATIONS

When two keys must be pressed together, the tutorial's instruction line shows the keys joined with a plus (+) sign. For example, you can execute a Copy command in Windows by holding down CTRL and then pressing the letter **c**.

The instruction for this type of keystroke combination follows:

PRESS: CTRL +**c**

COMMAND INSTRUCTIONS

This guide indicates with a special typeface and color the data that you are required to type in yourself. For example:

TYPE: **Income Statement**

When you are required to enter unique information, such as the current date or your name, the instruction appears in italics. The following instruction directs you to type your name in place of the actual words "your name."

TYPE: ***your name***

ADVANTAGE DISKETTE

The Advantage Diskette provided with this guide or by your instructor contains the files that you use in each session and in the hands-on exercises. ***This diskette is extremely important to your success with the guide.*** If you are using this guide in a self-study program, we suggest that you make a copy of the Advantage Diskette. When the guide asks you to insert the Advantage Diskette, you insert and work with the copied diskette instead. By following this procedure, you will be able to work through the guide again at a later date using a fresh copy of the Advantage Diskette. If you want to copy the contents of the Advantage Diskette to a permanent storage device, such as a network drive, ensure that the storage device allows for Windows' long filenames.

ACKNOWLEDGMENTS

This series of learning guides is the direct result of the teamwork and heart of many people. We sincerely thank the reviewers, instructors, and students who have shared their comments and suggestions with us over the past few years.

We do read them! With their valuable feedback, our guides have evolved into the product you see before you. We also appreciate the efforts of the instructors and students from the Vernon Continuing Education division of Okanagan University College who classroom tested our guides to ensure accuracy, relevancy, and completeness.

We also give many thanks to Tom Casson from Richard D. Irwin for his skillful management of this text. Special recognition goes to Stacey Sawyer for her original design work on the series and for being just so talented! Finally, to the many others who weren't directly involved in this project but who have stood by us the whole way, we appreciate your patience, support, and understanding.

WRITE TO US

We welcome your response to this book, for we are trying to make it as useful a learning tool as possible. Write to us in care of Thomas Casson, Publisher, Richard D. Irwin, 1333 Burr Ridge Parkway, Burr Ridge, IL 60521. Thank you.

Sarah E. Hutchinson

Glen J. Coulthard

Microsoft PowerPoint 7.0 for Windows 95

Fundamentals

SESSION OUTLINE

What Is PowerPoint?
The Windows Advantage
Features of Microsoft PowerPoint 7.0
Working with PowerPoint
Starting PowerPoint
The Guided Tour
Getting Help
Opening a Presentation
Viewing a Presentation
Closing a Presentation
Leaving PowerPoint
Summary
Key Terms
Exercises

INTRODUCTION

Welcome to Microsoft PowerPoint 7.0 for Windows 95, a software program that helps you organize and present information to an audience. You can use PowerPoint to create overhead transparencies, 35mm slides, audience handouts and speaker's notes, and computer-based slide presentations. PowerPoint also provides tools that help you outline your thoughts, build a presentation quickly using professionally designed templates, and enhance your presentation with pictures, charts, sound, and video.

CASE STUDY VACATION VISTAS, INC.

Owned by Frank Muldanno, Vacation Vistas of Memphis is a tour operation specializing in Caribbean cruises. For the past eight months, business has been extremely slow. To increase demand for their cruises, Frank believes that he and his staff must direct more of their marketing to the local seniors community.

One of Frank's new marketing tactics was to hire Juanita Gomez, a local computer consultant and graphic designer, to produce a 35mm slide presentation that he could show at the neighborhood seniors' hall. Halfway through developing the presentation, Juanita accepted a job in Seattle but promised to send Frank the completed slides from the West Coast.

One week before the presentation, Frank receives a disk and a letter from Juanita with the following note: *"Dear Frank, please review the enclosed presentation and send the disk back to me for final production of the 35mm slides. By the way, the presentation was created using Microsoft PowerPoint. Good luck, Juanita."* Fortunately, Frank has recently purchased Microsoft Office, which includes PowerPoint, for his new office computer. Although he hasn't used the program before, he is relatively comfortable using Windows.

In this session, you and Frank will learn how to load and exit Microsoft PowerPoint and how to open and close an existing presentation. You'll also take a guided tour of the screen and learn how to access the Help facility. Lastly, you will experiment with the different methods of viewing a presentation in PowerPoint.

WHAT IS POWERPOINT?

Microsoft PowerPoint is a software program that enables you to produce high-quality output, such as overhead transparencies, 35mm slides, and computer-based displays, for presentation to an audience. Even if you don't consider yourself a speechwriter or graphic designer, you can still create informative and attractive presentations using PowerPoint. For those people who may question their creative and artistic talent, there is absolutely nothing to worry about—PowerPoint provides over 100 professionally designed templates containing proven layouts, color schemes, background textures, and typefaces. A **template** defines what your presentation will look like, where text and other objects will appear, and which foreground and background colors will be used. PowerPoint also provides **wizards** that can lead you step-by-step through creating different styles of presentations and performing other tasks.

POWERPOINT VIEWER

Microsoft PowerPoint includes a **run-time version** of the program called the PowerPoint Viewer. The Viewer is an entirely separate program from Microsoft PowerPoint contained on a single diskette, which you may legally copy and distribute along with your presentation files. It even comes with its own installation program. For example, you can create a presentation on your computer and then send it along on a diskette with the PowerPoint Viewer to your employees, clients, students, or other recipients who do not own Microsoft PowerPoint. As long as they have Microsoft Windows installed on their computers, the recipients of your diskettes will be able to view (but not change) your presentation using the Viewer.

The easiest way to prepare a presentation for delivery on another computer is to use the Pack And Go Wizard. This special wizard leads you through compressing your presentation onto one or more diskettes (or other storage device) and provides the option for packaging PowerPoint Viewer with the presentation.

PRESENTATIONS

In PowerPoint, a **presentation** is the collection of slides, handouts, speaker's notes, and outlines contained in a single disk file. As you create a presentation, focus on the overall design so that a cohesive theme is carried throughout. Your final product will be much more effective if you strive for and achieve a consistent look and feel for your presentation.

SLIDES

A PowerPoint **slide** is an individual page in your presentation. You progress through a presentation by flipping to the next slide (or returning to the previous slide). For computer-based presentations, there may be a transition effect between slides whereby the current slide dissolves or wipes from the screen before the next slide appears. A slide typically contains one or more of the following elements:

- Text titles or headings
- Body text, such as lists or phrases
- Tables, charts, or graphs
- Illustrations, including drawn or sketched art
- Shapes, such as lines, boxes, circles, or polygons
- Clip art or other pictures
- Output from other applications, such as a range of spreadsheet cells

Figure 1.1 shows a sample slide. You can output the slides on your printer as overhead transparencies or send your presentation file on a diskette to an outside service bureau to develop 35mm slides. A more fashionable option is to display your PowerPoint presentation on a computer monitor or use a projection unit (or LCD panel) and a large projection screen.

FIGURE 1.1 ONE EXAMPLE OF A PRESENTATION SLIDE

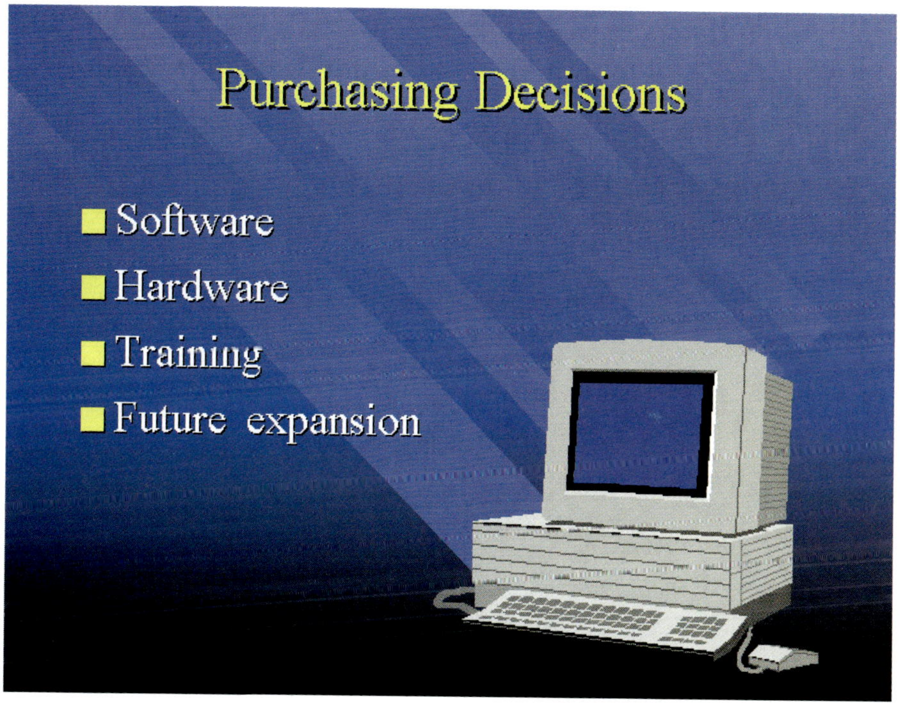

HANDOUTS

In addition to the actual slide presentation, PowerPoint enables you to create and print handouts for your audience. A **handout** consists of two to six slide images printed on a single page. Handouts help support your presentation by keeping the audience focused on what you are saying and by not requiring them to write down everything they see on the projection screen.

SPEAKER'S NOTES

To assist you in the actual delivery of a presentation, PowerPoint lets you enter and print a notes page for each slide. You can use these notes pages for prior studying, take them with you to the speaker's podium, or hand them out to the audience when supporting information for your slide show is necessary.

Speaker's notes pages are also invaluable if you've been given the task of preparing a presentation for someone else to deliver. The default format for a notes page places the slide image at the top of the page with the related text below.

OUTLINES

For brainstorming and organizing your thoughts, PowerPoint's outline feature is extremely valuable. In outline form, the text of your presentation—that is, headings and main body text—appears without the slide's background, colors, or graphics. Figure 1.2 shows the contents of the slide appearing in Figure 1.1 using the outline form. (*Note:* Figure 1.2 also shows the outline text for slides 4 through 6.)

FIGURE 1.2 VIEWING YOUR PRESENTATION USING THE OUTLINE FORM

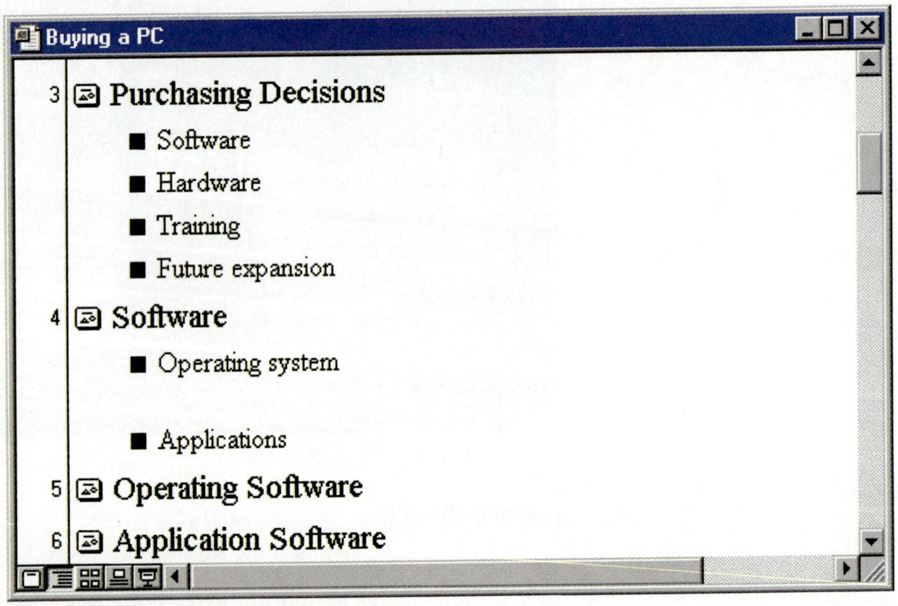

Now that you know the basic features of PowerPoint, let's review the general strengths of Microsoft Windows.

THE WINDOWS ADVANTAGE

As of this writing, the most recent version of Microsoft Windows is Windows 95. Windows 95 is a microcomputer operating system composed of software that runs the computer. Applications that have been written for Windows 95 have many features in common. Therefore, the knowledge you gain from learning one Windows application helps you to learn other Windows applications.

Some of the advantages of working in the Windows 95 environment include:

- *Programs that are easy to learn and easy to use.*
  Windows provides a standardized interface for all programs, whether they are word processing, spreadsheet, or database applications. As a result, you can use the knowledge acquired from one Windows product in working with other Windows products.
- *The ability to run more than one application at a time.*
  Windows 95 provides a **multitasking** environment whereby more than one application or program may be running at the same time. For example, multitasking allows you to simultaneously receive an electronic mail message, calculate a spreadsheet, and print a presentation.
- *The ability to exchange information among applications.*
  Windows provides a program called Clipboard that lets you copy and move information within an application or among applications. For example, it's easy to copy a budget from an Excel spreadsheet to the Clipboard and then paste that budget into a PowerPoint presentation.
- *The ability to display on the screen what you will get from the printer.*
  This feature is called **WYSIWYG** ("What You See Is What You Get"); it allows different fonts, borders, and graphics to be displayed on the screen at all times.

FEATURES OF MICROSOFT POWERPOINT 7.0

In the fall of 1995, Microsoft released Microsoft PowerPoint 7.0 for the Windows 95 operating system. To ensure its competitiveness in the marketplace, Microsoft introduced several significant features in PowerPoint 7.0. This section highlights some of these enhancements.

- Several "Auto" features make it easier for you to perform your work. AutoCorrect corrects your typing errors and capitalization mistakes, and AutoClipArt provides ClipArt suggestions that relate to your presentation topic. Also, the AutoContent Wizard has been enhanced to change your message depending on the size of your audience, type of audience, and time allotted for your presentation.
- After you've created a presentation, consider using the StyleChecker to scan your presentation for design problems such as spelling errors, incorrect and inconsistent use of capitalization or punctuation, and inconsistent use of font sizes and other style attributes. You can customize the StyleChecker to match the design rules you want your presentations to follow.
- The Pack And Go Wizard leads you step-by-step through preparing your presentation for delivery on another computer. Your presentation is automatically compressed onto one or more diskettes or other storage devices.

You're given the option of including the PowerPoint Viewer along with the presentation.

- Although most on-screen presentations are presented in color, audience handouts are often printed in black and white. To see how your presentation will look in black and white, use PowerPoint's Black and White View. In this view mode, all text is converted to black, the background is converted to white, and other objects are printed using a combination of white, black, and shades of gray. You can change the way objects appear if they don't show up well.
- Using the new Animation Effects toolbar, you can bring "life" and impact to your presentation by adding motion and sound effects to objects. For example, if you click the Laser Effect button, the text on a slide will appear from the upper-right corner of the slide and drop into position with an accompanied Laser sound effect.
- Meeting Minder, a new addition to PowerPoint 7.0, can help to improve communication during and after meetings. With Meeting Minder, you can include discussion notes on notes pages (described earlier) as the presentation is taking place, and then distribute them to the attendees after the meeting. Or, you can take the meeting's minutes and export them directly to Microsoft Word for printing. Additionally, Meeting Minder will automatically include any notes you take as action items on the final slide of your presentation.
- Similar to the concept of a conference call, PowerPoint 7.0 includes a new capability called Presentation Conferencing. With this capability, you can deliver a presentation or run a meeting from your computer onto a network of computers. PowerPoint provides a wizard to help you set up the presentation conference.

Now, let's begin our journey through Microsoft PowerPoint 7.0.

WORKING WITH POWERPOINT

Microsoft PowerPoint 7.0 is a complex yet easy-to-learn program. As you proceed through this guide, you will find that there are often three methods for performing the same command or procedure in PowerPoint:

- Menu — Select a command or procedure from the Menu bar.
- Mouse — Point to and click a toolbar button.
- Keyboard — Press shortcut keys (usually CTRL+letter).

Although this guide concentrates on the quickest and easiest methods, we recommend that you try the others and decide which you prefer. *Don't memorize all of the methods and information in this guide! Be selective.*

HOW THE MOUSE IS USED

The mouse is an essential tool for working with Microsoft PowerPoint. Regardless of whether your mouse has two or three buttons, you use the left or primary mouse button for selecting text and menu commands and the right or secondary mouse button for displaying shortcut menus.

The most common mouse actions used in PowerPoint are:

- Point — Slide the mouse on your desk to position the tip of the mouse pointer over the desired object on the screen.
- Click — Press down and release the left mouse button quickly. Clicking is used to position the insertion point and to choose menu commands.
- Right-Click — Press down and release the right mouse button. Right-clicking the mouse on text or an object displays a context-sensitive shortcut menu.
- Double-Click — Press down and release the mouse button twice in rapid succession. Double-clicking is often used to select and execute an action
- Drag — Press down and hold the mouse button as you move the mouse pointer across the screen. When the mouse pointer reaches the desired location, release the mouse button. Dragging is used to select a block of text or to move objects or windows.

You may notice that the mouse pointer changes shape as you move it over different parts of the screen. Each mouse pointer shape has its own purpose and may provide you with important information. Although Windows 95 lets you customize the mouse pointer, there are three primary mouse pointer shapes you should be aware of:

	left arrow	Used to choose menu commands, access the toolbars, and complete dialog boxes.
	hourglass	Informs you that PowerPoint is occupied with another task and requests you wait.
	I-beam	Used to modify and edit text and to position the insertion point.

As you proceed through this guide, other mouse shapes will be explained in the appropriate sections.

HOW THE KEYBOARD IS USED

Aside from being the primary input device for entering text in a presentation, the keyboard offers shortcut methods for performing commands and procedures. For example, several menu commands have shortcut key combinations listed to the right of the command in the pull-down menu. Therefore, you can perform a command by simply pressing the shortcut keys rather than accessing the Menu bar. Many of these shortcut key combinations are available throughout Windows applications.

STARTING POWERPOINT

This session assumes that you are working on a computer with Windows 95 (or Microsoft Windows NT 3.51 or later) and Microsoft PowerPoint 7.0 loaded on the hard disk drive. Because Windows is an operating system, it is loaded automatically into the computer's memory when you turn on the computer.

Perform the following steps on your computer.

1. Turn on the power switches to the computer and monitor. After a few seconds, the initial Windows 95 desktop will appear (Figure 1.3). (*Note:* The desktop on your computer may look different from Figure 1.3.)

FIGURE 1.3 THE WINDOWS 95 DESKTOP

2. If the Welcome to Windows 95 dialog box appears, do the following:
CLICK: Close button (☒) in the top right-hand corner of the window

QUICK REFERENCE
Loading Windows 95

Turn on your computer to load Microsoft Windows 95 (or Microsoft Windows NT 3.51 or later).

LOADING APPLICATIONS IN WINDOWS 95

Windows provides several methods for loading an application program, such as Microsoft PowerPoint. We describe the most common methods in this section.

- *Load a program by clicking the Start button (Start) on the taskbar and then choosing the Programs command.*
  After you choose Programs, click Microsoft PowerPoint on the Programs cascading menu. This method loads Microsoft PowerPoint.
- *Open a presentation file by clicking the Start button (Start) on the taskbar and then choosing the Documents command.*
  After you choose Documents, click the document that you want to open from the menu list. This method loads Microsoft PowerPoint and then displays the document that you selected. The Documents menu displays the last 15 files that you've worked with, regardless of the application you used to create them.
- *Open a presentation file by clicking the Start button (Start) on the taskbar and then choosing the Find command.*
  After you choose Find, click the Files or Folders command. Type the name of the file you want to locate and open, and then click the Find Now command button. Once a file is located, you may double-click its filename in the dialog box to load Microsoft PowerPoint and open the presentation. This method is useful when you know the name of the file, but don't know where it is located on the hard disk.
- *Open a presentation file from "My Computer" or from the Windows Explorer.*
  Once you know how to display files with one of these file-management models, you can simply double-click a document's filename to load the file with its source application, such as Microsoft PowerPoint.
- *If Microsoft Office is loaded on your computer, open a document or application directly from the Start menu.*
  If you have installed Microsoft Office on your computer, you will see two new menu items called New Office Document and Open Office Document on the Start menu. To load Microsoft PowerPoint, choose the New Office Document command and then select the Presentation tab. Double-click an appropriate presentation icon.

To load Microsoft PowerPoint and open a presentation you've worked with previously into the presentation window, choose the Open Office Document command. The Open dialog box will appear. We describe how to use the Open dialog box later in this session.

- *If Microsoft Office is loaded on your computer, open a presentation file or application from the Microsoft Office Shortcut Bar.*
  The Microsoft Office Shortcut Bar provides a Start a New Document button ( ) and an Open a Document button ( ). These two buttons perform the same functions as the two Start menu commands that we described previously.

LOADING MICROSOFT POWERPOINT 7.0

Perform the following steps to load Microsoft PowerPoint.

1. Point to the Start button (Start) on the taskbar and then click the left mouse button once. The Start menu appears as a pop-up menu.
2. Point to the Programs command using the mouse. Notice that a list of programs appears in a cascading menu to the right. Your screen should now appear similar to Figure 1.4. (*Note:* The list of programs may differ from those shown on your computer.)

FIGURE 1.4 THE PROGRAMS MENU

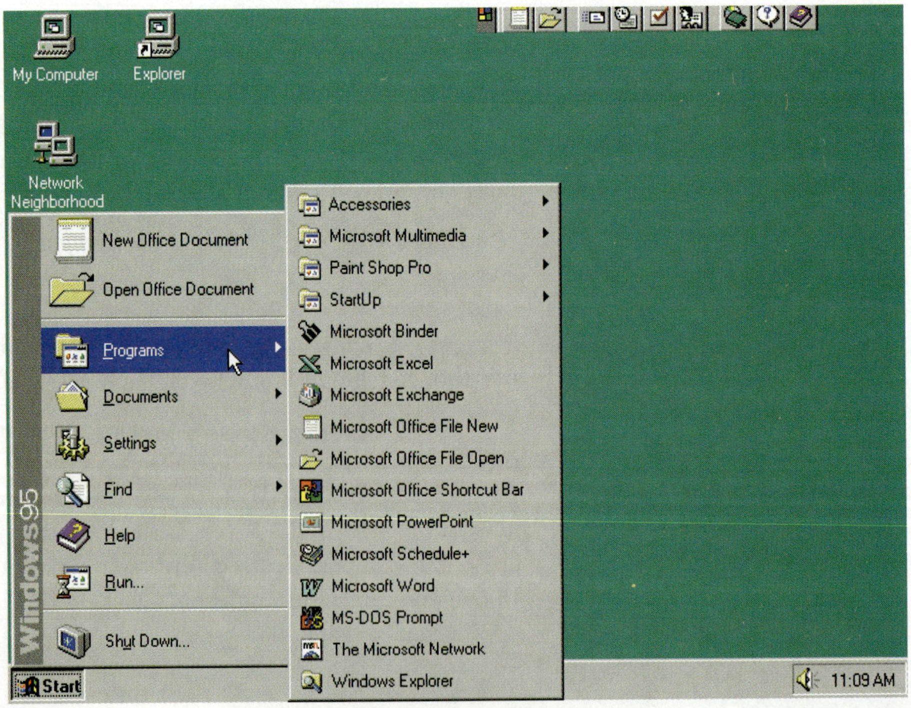

3. Point to the Microsoft PowerPoint command and then click the left mouse button once. After a few seconds, the Microsoft PowerPoint screen appears.

4. Each time you start PowerPoint 7.0, a Tip of the Day appears in a dialog box (shown in Figure 1.5). You can easily turn this feature off by removing the "✓" from the *Show Tips at Startup* check box. However, these tips provide a useful reminder of features that you may be underutilizing. Leave the check box selected for now and proceed to the next step:
PRESS: ENTER or CLICK: OK

FIGURE 1.5 TIP OF THE DAY DIALOG BOX

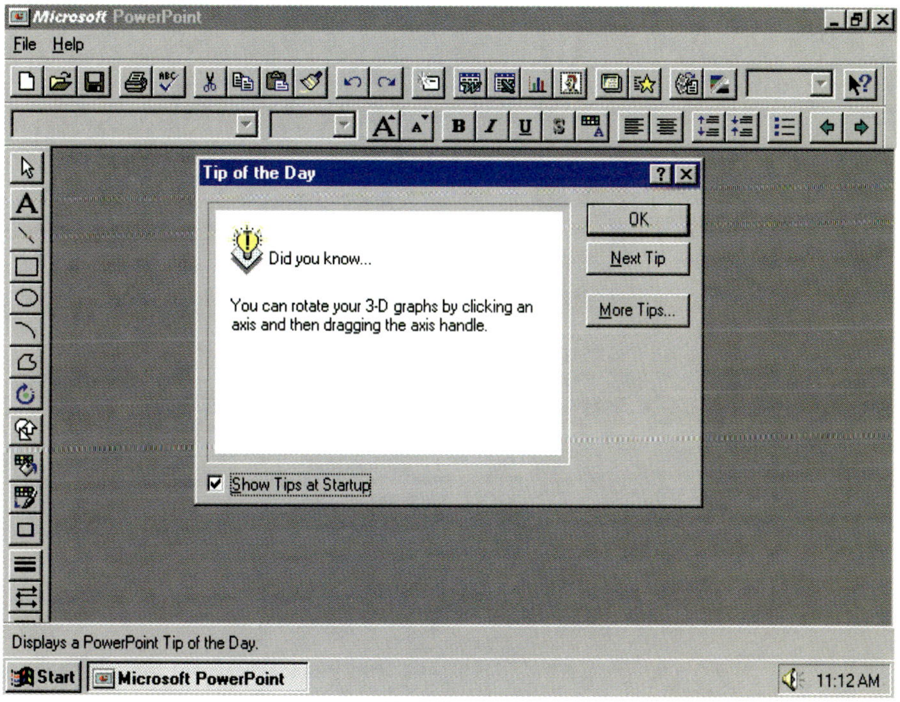

5. Next, the PowerPoint startup dialog box appears (Figure 1.6). You use this dialog box to determine how you want to proceed when PowerPoint is first loaded. (*Note:* Like the Tip of the Day dialog box, you can turn this feature off using the Tools, Options command. For this guide, we leave the startup dialog box displayed.)

FIGURE 1.6 THE POWERPOINT STARTUP DIALOG BOX

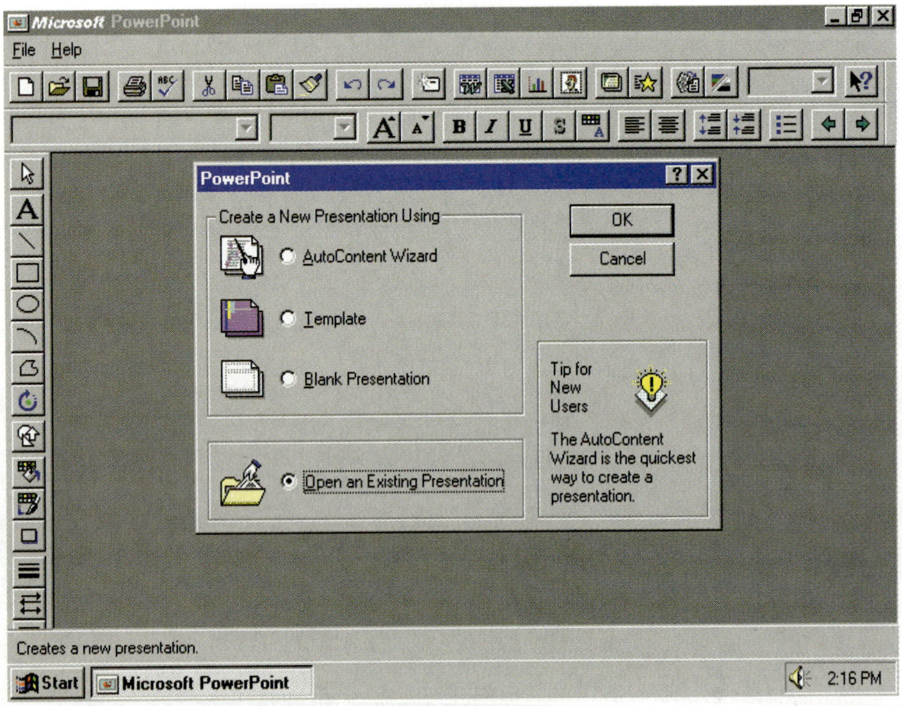

6. Before continuing, let's remove the startup dialog box so we can describe the components of PowerPoint in the next section. We will return to the options available in the startup dialog box later. Do the following:
   CLICK: Cancel command button
   (*Note:* The word CLICK means to point to the command button and then click the left mouse button once.)

> **QUICK REFERENCE**
> Loading Microsoft PowerPoint 7.0
>
> 1. **CLICK: Start button (Start) on the taskbar**
> 2. **CHOOSE: Programs, Microsoft PowerPoint**

THE GUIDED TOUR

Software programs designed for Microsoft Windows 95, such as PowerPoint, have many similarities in screen design and layout. Each program operates in its own application window, while the presentations, spreadsheets, and letters you create appear in separate document windows. In PowerPoint, the document window is referred to as the presentation window. This section explores the various parts of PowerPoint, including the tools for manipulating application and presentation windows.

APPLICATION WINDOW

The PowerPoint screen consists of the **application window** and the **presentation window**. The application window (Figure 1.7) contains the Title bar, Menu bar, Standard toolbar, Formatting toolbar, Drawing toolbar, Status bar, and Slide work area. Presentation windows contain the actual slide presentations that you create and store on the disk.

FIGURE 1.7 MICROSOFT POWERPOINT'S APPLICATION WINDOW

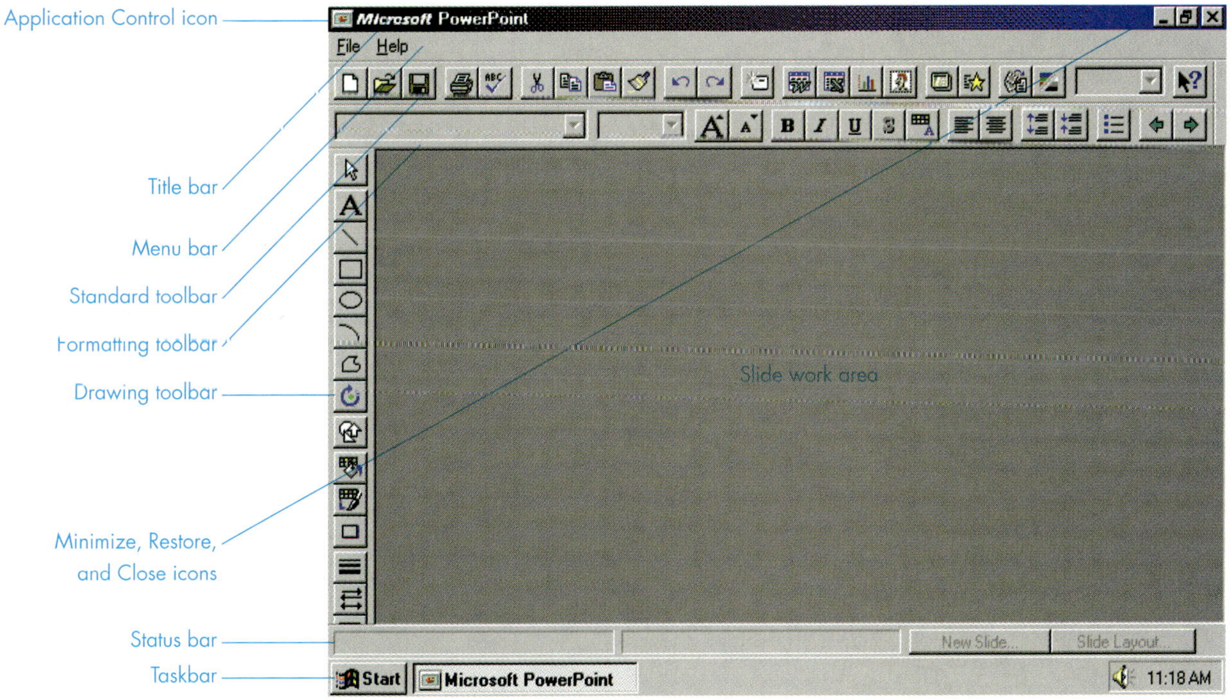

The primary components of the application window are:

Application Control icon (▣)	Used to size and position the application window using the keyboard. (*Note:* It is easier to use the mouse to perform the same options available in the Control menu.)

Minimize (▁) and Maximize (□), Restore (⧉), and Close (✕) icons	Located in the top right-hand corner of the application window, these icons are used to control the display of the application window using the mouse. (*Note:* The Maximize button doesn't appear in Figure 1.7.)
Title bar	The Title bar contains the name of the program or presentation file. Using a mouse, you can move a window by dragging its Title bar.
Menu bar	Contains the PowerPoint menu commands.
Standard toolbar	The Standard toolbar displays buttons for opening and saving presentations, editing text, and accessing special features using the mouse.
Formatting toolbar	The Formatting toolbar displays buttons for accessing character and paragraph formatting commands using a mouse.
Drawing toolbar	The Drawing toolbar displays buttons for drawing objects such as lines, circles, and boxes.
Status bar	Located at the bottom of the application window and above the taskbar, the Status bar displays the current slide number or presentation view, and a description of the highlighted menu command or toolbar button. There are also two hot buttons on the Status bar for adding a new slide and changing the layout of the current slide.
Slide work area	The Slide work area is where your presentation windows appear. You can work on more than one presentation at the same time in this work area.

Although typically maximized, you can size, move, and manipulate the PowerPoint application window on the Windows desktop to customize your work environment.

PRESENTATION WINDOW

The presentation window provides the viewing and editing area for a presentation. Figure 1.8 shows an example of a presentation window that is not maximized, as it would appear in the Slide work area of PowerPoint's application window. You will open and display a presentation window shortly.

FIGURE 1.8 THE PRESENTATION WINDOW

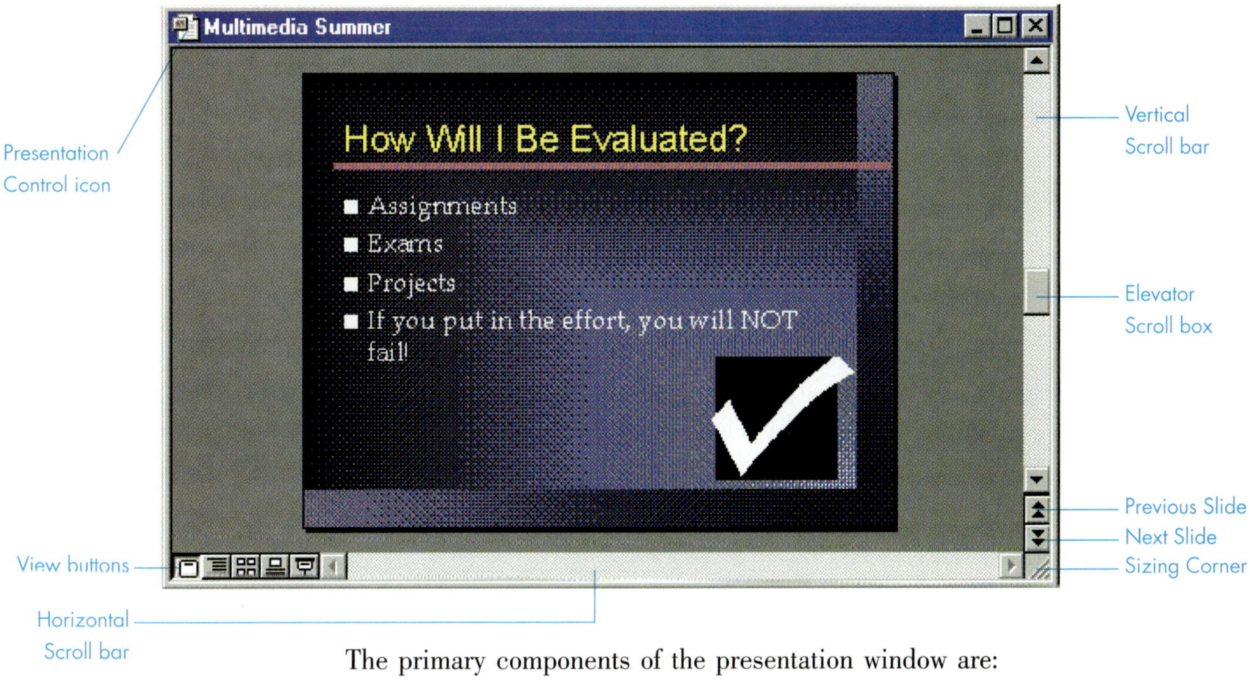

The primary components of the presentation window are:

Presentation Control icon (▣)	Used to size and position the application window using the keyboard. (*Note:* It is easier to use a mouse to perform the same options available in the Presentation Control menu.)
Scroll bar	Placed at the right border of the presentation window, the vertical scroll bar facilitates moving from slide to slide using the mouse. As you drag the scroll box or elevator up and down, the current slide number displays in a Slide number box along the scroll bar.
Previous slide (▲), Next slide (▼)	Use these buttons to display the previous slide or the next slide.
View buttons	Located at the bottom left-hand corner of the presentation window, the View buttons let you change the current view of the presentation.

You should recognize some familiar components in the presentation window that appear in all windows. For example, the Minimize and Maximize icons appear in the top right-hand corner of the presentation window. To restore a maximized presentation to a window, you click the Restore icon (▣). To maximize the presentation window, you click the Maximize icon (□). Before proceeding, make sure that your application and presentation windows are maximized.

MENU BAR

Like all Microsoft Windows programs, PowerPoint commands are grouped together on the Menu bar. Currently, only two commands—File and Help—appear on the Menu bar. After you open or begin a presentation, additional options become available, as shown below:

Commands in this guide are written in the following form: Edit, Copy, where Edit is the Menu bar option and Copy is the command to be selected from the pull-down menu. To execute a command, click once on the Menu bar option and then click once on the pull-down menu command. Commands that are not available for selection appear dimmed. Commands that are followed by an ellipsis (...) require further information to be collected in a dialog box.

To practice accessing the Menu bar, perform the following steps on your computer.

1. To choose the Help command, position the tip of the mouse pointer on the word Help in the Menu bar and click the left mouse button once. A pull-down menu appears below the Help option.
2. To see the pull-down menu associated with the File menu option, point to the File option on the Menu bar.
3. To leave the Menu bar without making a selection:
   CLICK: anywhere in the Slide work area
   (*Note:* Also, clicking the menu option twice, or clicking the Title bar, removes the pull-down menu.)
4. To again display the pull-down menu for the File option:
   CHOOSE: File
   This instruction tells you to click the mouse pointer on File in the Menu bar. (*Note:* All menu commands that you execute in this guide begin with the word "CHOOSE.")
5. To again leave the Menu bar without making a selection:
   CHOOSE: File

SHORTCUT MENUS

PowerPoint uses context-sensitive shortcut menus for quick access to menu commands. Rather than searching for commands in the Menu bar, you position the mouse pointer on text or an object, such as a graphic, and click the right mouse button. A pop-up menu appears with the most commonly selected commands for the text or object.

To practice accessing a shortcut menu, perform the following steps.

1. To display a shortcut or pop-up menu, position the mouse pointer over any button on the Standard toolbar and click the right mouse button. A shortcut menu should appear.
2. To remove the shortcut menu from the screen, move the mouse pointer away from the menu and click the right mouse button a second time. The shortcut menu disappears.

QUICK REFERENCE
Using Shortcut Menus

1. **Position the mouse pointer over an item, such as a toolbar button.**
2. **CLICK: the right mouse button to display a shortcut or pop-up menu**
3. **CHOOSE: a command from the menu, or**
   CLICK: the right mouse button away from the menu to remove it

TOOLBARS

Assuming that you haven't yet customized your PowerPoint screen, you will see the Standard and Formatting toolbars appear below the Menu bar. PowerPoint provides seven toolbars and hundreds of buttons and drop-down lists for quick and easy mouse access to its more popular commands and features. Don't worry about memorizing the button names appearing in the following graphics—the majority of these buttons are explained in subsequent sessions and all toolbars and their buttons are summarized in the Appendix. You can also point at any toolbar button and pause until a yellow ToolTip appears with the button name. With the ToolTip displayed, an extended description for the button appears in the Status bar.

The Standard toolbar provides access to file management and slide editing commands.

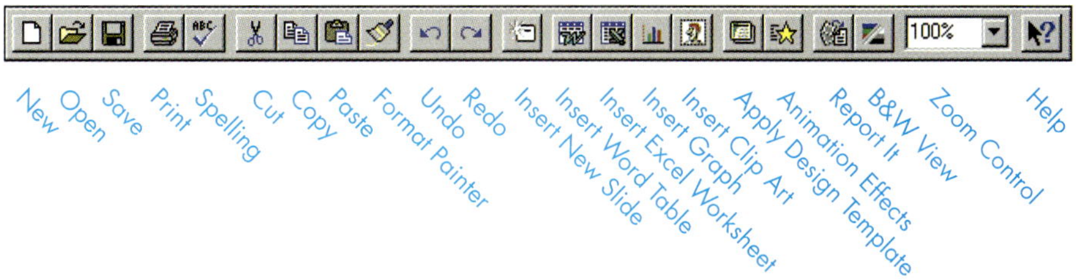

The Formatting toolbar lets you access formatting commands.

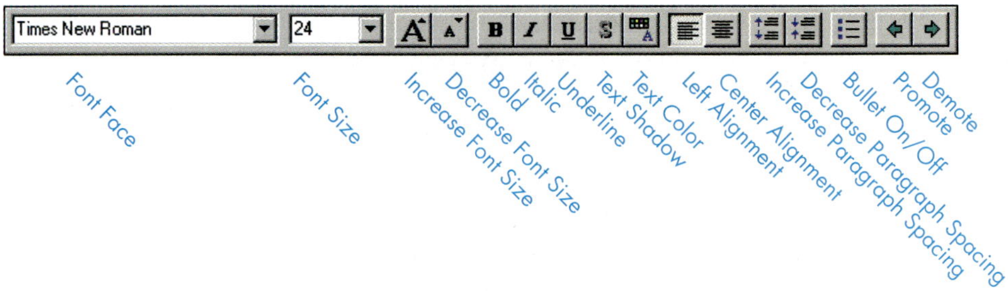

To display additional toolbars, you point to an existing toolbar and click the right mouse button. From the shortcut menu that appears, you can display and hide toolbars by clicking their names in the pop-up menu. If a toolbar is currently being displayed, a check mark appears beside its name. You can also choose the View, Toolbars command to display the Toolbars dialog box.

To practice displaying and hiding toolbars, perform the following steps.

1. Position the mouse pointer over any button on the Standard toolbar.
2. CLICK: right mouse button to display the shortcut menu
3. To display the AutoShapes toolbar:
   CHOOSE: AutoShapes
   The new toolbar appears in the Slide work area.
4. To remove the AutoShapes toolbar:
   RIGHT-CLICK: AutoShapes toolbar
   This instruction tells you to position the mouse pointer over the AutoShapes toolbar and click the right mouse button.
5. You will notice that the AutoShapes command on the shortcut menu has a check mark. To remove the AutoShapes toolbar:
   CHOOSE: AutoShapes
   The AutoShapes toolbar disappears from the application window.

DIALOG BOX

A dialog box is a common mechanism in Windows applications for collecting information before processing a command or instruction (Figure 1.9). In a dialog box, you indicate the options you want to use and then click the OK button when you're finished. Dialog boxes are also used to display messages or to ask for confirmation of commands.

FIGURE 1.9 A DIALOG BOX

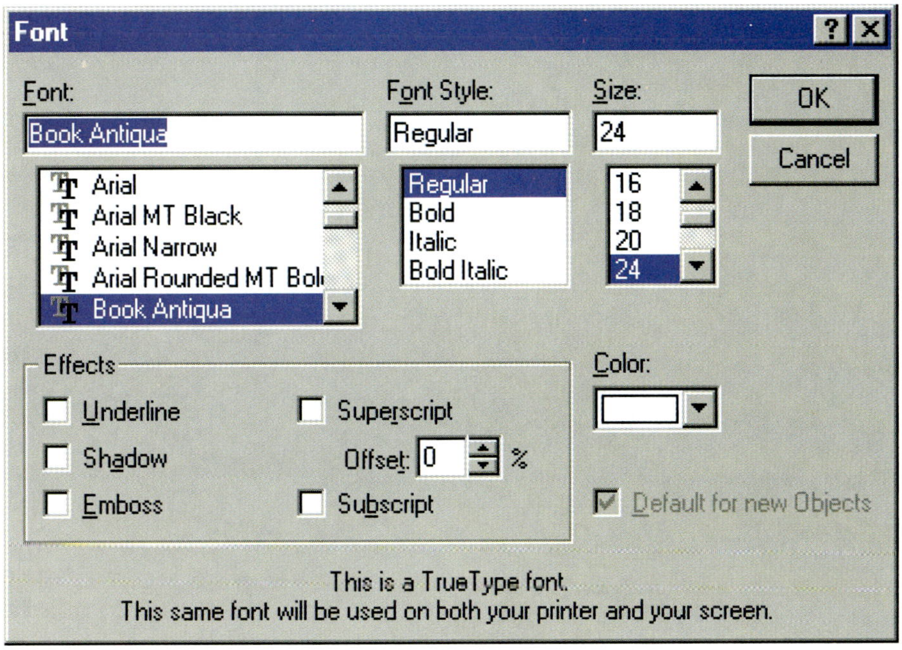

A dialog box uses several methods for collecting information, as shown in Figure 1.9 and described in Table 1.1.

Most dialog boxes provide a question mark button (?) near the right side of the Title bar. If you have a question about an item in the dialog box, click the question mark and then click the item to display some helpful information. You should also know that dialog boxes have a memory. For example, the tab that appears when you exit the dialog box will be selected the next time you open the dialog box.

THE WINDOWS TASKBAR

The Windows taskbar is usually located on the bottom of your screen below the Status bar. (*Note:* We say "usually" because you can move the taskbar on your desktop.) Each application that you are currently working with is represented by a button on the taskbar. To switch between applications, click the appropriate application button on the taskbar. At this point, you should see a button for Microsoft PowerPoint on the taskbar.

TABLE 1.1

Parts of a Dialog Box

Name	*Example*	*Action*
Check box		Click an option to turn it on or off. The option is turned on when an "×" appears in the box.
Command button		Click a command button to execute an action. You accept or cancel the selections in a dialog box by clicking the OK or Cancel command buttons, respectively.
Drop-down list box	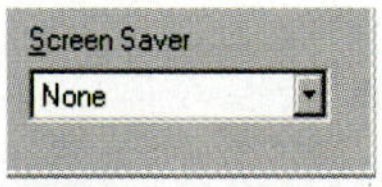	Make a choice from the list that appears when you click the down arrow next to the box; only the selected choice is visible.
List box	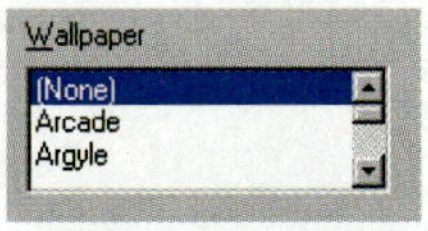	Make a choice from the scrollable list; several choices, if not all, are always visible.
Option button		Select an option from a group of related options.
Slide box	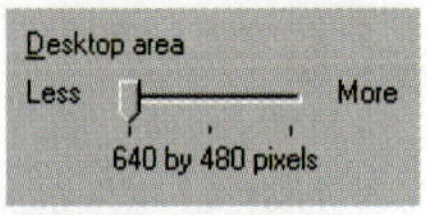	Drag the slider bar to make a selection, like using a radio's volume control.
Spin box		Click the up and down arrows to the right of the box, until the number you want appears.
Tab	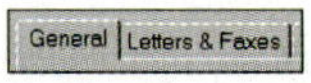	Click a named tab at the top of the window to access other pages of options in the dialog box.
Text box		Click inside the text box and then type the desired information.

GETTING HELP

Similar to most software programs, PowerPoint provides a comprehensive on-line Help facility. Table 1.2 describes the different methods you can use to access help while working in a presentation.

Many Help windows include buttons that look like . If you click this type of button, additional Help information or a wizard leads you through performing an activity. You may also notice that some words or phrases have a dotted underline. If you click a word or phrase that has a dotted underline, a definition box will appear.

TABLE 1.2

Displaying Help Information

To display . . .	*Do this . . .*
A description of a dialog box option	Click the question mark (?) icon in the dialog box's Title bar and then click an item in the dialog box. You can also right-click an item to display its description.
A description of a menu option	Click the Help button (?) on the Standard toolbar and then choose the desired command using the question mark mouse pointer.
A description of a toolbar button	Point to a toolbar button to display its ToolTip label; a full description of the toolbar button will appear in the Status bar. You can also click the Help button (?) and then click a toolbar button to display more detailed help information.
A list of help topics	Double-click the Help button (?), or choose Help, Microsoft PowerPoint Help Topics from the Menu bar. When the Help dialog window appears, select the Contents tab.
A search model for help topics	Double-click the Help button (?), or choose Help, Microsoft PowerPoint Help Topics from the Menu bar. When the Help dialog window appears, select the Index or Find tab. The Index tab enables you to search for text in the title of a Help topic; the Find tab enables you to search for text that appears anywhere in the Help topic.
A search model that lets you find help for questions entered using English phrases	Double-click the Help button (?) and then select the Answer Wizard tab, or choose Help, Answer Wizard from the Menu bar.

Perform the following steps to practice using the Help facility.

1. In the next few steps, you practice using the Help button (?) on the Standard toolbar to access Help for the File, New command and one of the toolbar buttons. Let's start with the File, New command. Position the tip of the mouse pointer over the Help button (?) on the Standard toolbar.
2. To activate the question mark mouse pointer:
   CLICK: Help button (?) once
3. CHOOSE: File, New
   Rather than executing the command, PowerPoint provides a description of the command.

4. After reading the description, close the window by clicking once in the description window.
5. To display information about a toolbar button:
   CLICK: Help button ( ) once
   CLICK: Save button ( ) on the Standard toolbar
6. After reading the description of the Save button, close the window by clicking once in the description window.
7. In the next few steps, let's practice displaying Help information as a list of topics. Do the following:
   DOUBLE-CLICK: Help button ( )
   (*Note:* You could have chosen Help, Microsoft PowerPoint Help Topics from the Menu bar.)
8. SELECT: Contents tab
   Your screen should now appear similar to Figure 1.10. (*Note:* When you first access Help, the Help Topics window will look the same as when you last accessed Help. That is, if the Index tab was displaying previously, it will appear when you access Help the next time.)

FIGURE 1.10 HELP TOPICS WINDOW: CONTENTS TAB

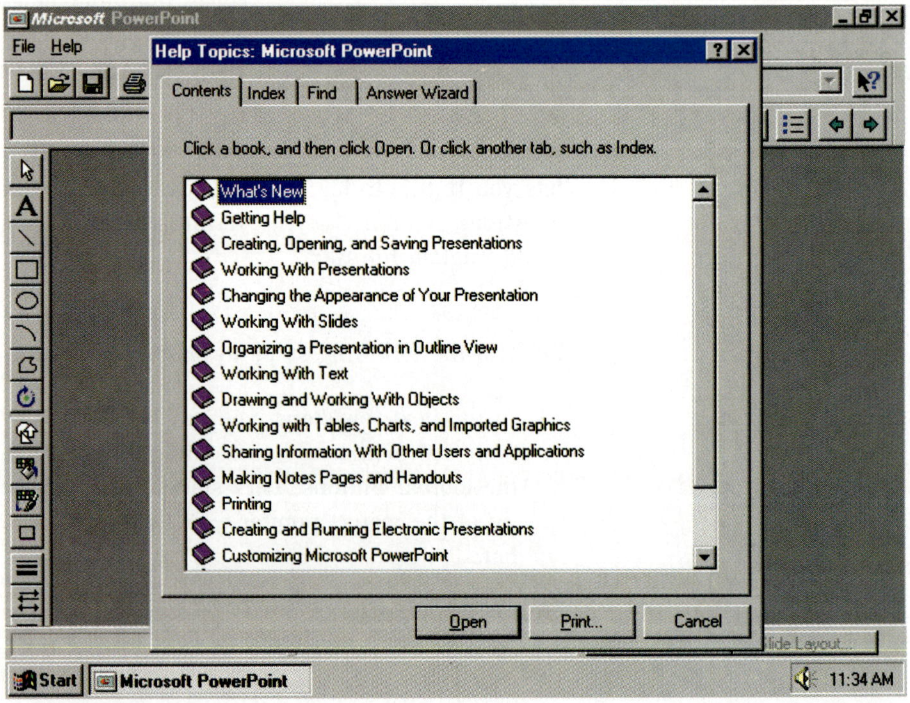

9. To display a book's contents:
   DOUBLE-CLICK: Printing topic
   DOUBLE-CLICK: Black and White Printing title
   Notice that a list of tasks or documents appears, each represented by a question mark. If you select a task or document, Word lists the steps necessary to perform the task. Sometimes Word will actually perform the procedure for you, as you'll see in the next step.
10. DOUBLE-CLICK: "Print slides, notes, outlines, or handouts in black and white" topic
11. A message appears informing you that the Answer Wizard will help you perform the task. To proceed:
    CLICK: Next >
    The wizard shows you the steps necessary to print a presentation in black and white. The Print dialog box appears with additional descriptive text.
12. To print the presentation, you could simply click the OK button. Since you don't have a presentation to print, do the following:
    CLICK: Cancel button
13. In the next few steps, you practice searching for Help topics. Do the following:
    DOUBLE-CLICK: Help button (?)
    SELECT: Index tab
    (*Note:* To select a tab, point to the tab name and then click the left mouse button once.)
14. To display information on clip art:
    TYPE: **clip art**
    Notice that "clip art" is highlighted in the topic area below.
15. To display a list of topics relating to clip art, do the following:
    CLICK: Display command button
    Your screen should now appear similar to Figure 1.11. An index of topics that relates to clip art is listed. To display a topic, you point to it and double-click.

FIGURE 1.11 HELP TOPICS WINDOW: INDEX TAB

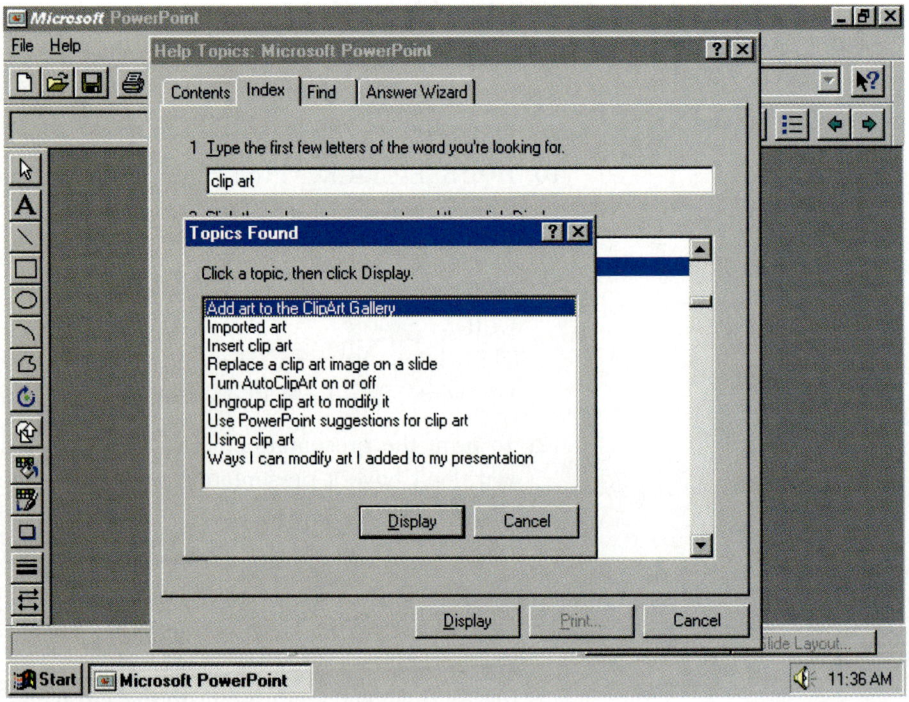

16. To leave the current window without selecting a topic:
    CLICK: Cancel button

17. The Help Topics window should still appear on the screen. To type in a question about clip art, perform the following steps:
    SELECT: Answer Wizard tab
    TYPE: **use clip art**
    CLICK: Search button
    Your screen should now appear similar to Figure 1.12. If you select a topic beneath the *How Do I* heading, the Answer Wizard responds by providing the steps for performing the task. If you select a topic beneath the *Tell Me About* heading, the Answer Wizard displays background information.

FIGURE 1.12 HELP TOPICS WINDOW: ANSWER WIZARD TAB

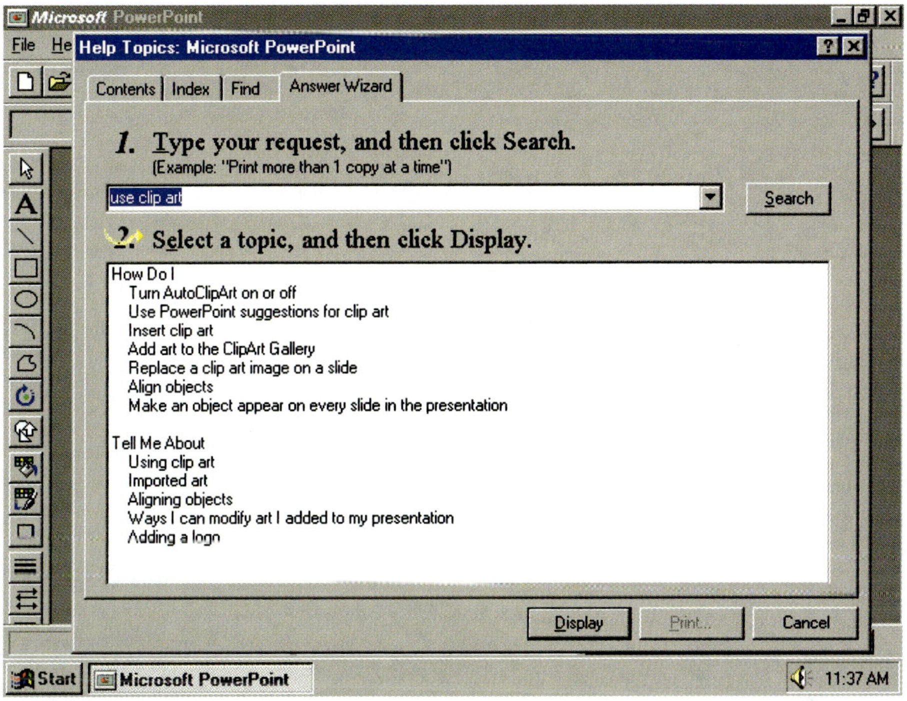

18. To close the Help Topics window:
    CLICK: Close button (☒) of the Help Topics window

QUICK REFERENCE
Displaying Help Information

- **To display Help information using the Help window:**
  DOUBLE-CLICK: Help button (?)
  CLICK: Contents, Index, Find, or Answer Wizard tab
- **To display a description of a menu option or toolbar button:**
  CLICK: Help button (?)
  CHOOSE: a menu option or CLICK: a toolbar button

OPENING A PRESENTATION

In this section, you open an existing presentation that is stored on the Advantage Diskette. Your first step is to display the Open dialog box by clicking the Open button (📂) on the Standard toolbar or choosing File, Open from the Menu bar. Once the Open dialog box appears, you select where the file is stored by clicking in the *Look in* drop-down list box and then selecting a file location. To load the presentation, you double-click the file's name appearing in the file area.

Perform the following steps.

1. Ensure that the Advantage Diskette is placed in the diskette drive.
2. To practice using the Open dialog box:
   CLICK: Open button (icon) on the Standard toolbar
3. To view the files on the Advantage Diskette:
   CLICK: down arrow beside the *Look in* drop-down list box
   SELECT: 3½ Floppy (where the Advantage Diskette is located)
   Your screen should now appear similar to Figure 1.13.

FIGURE 1.13 THE OPEN DIALOG BOX

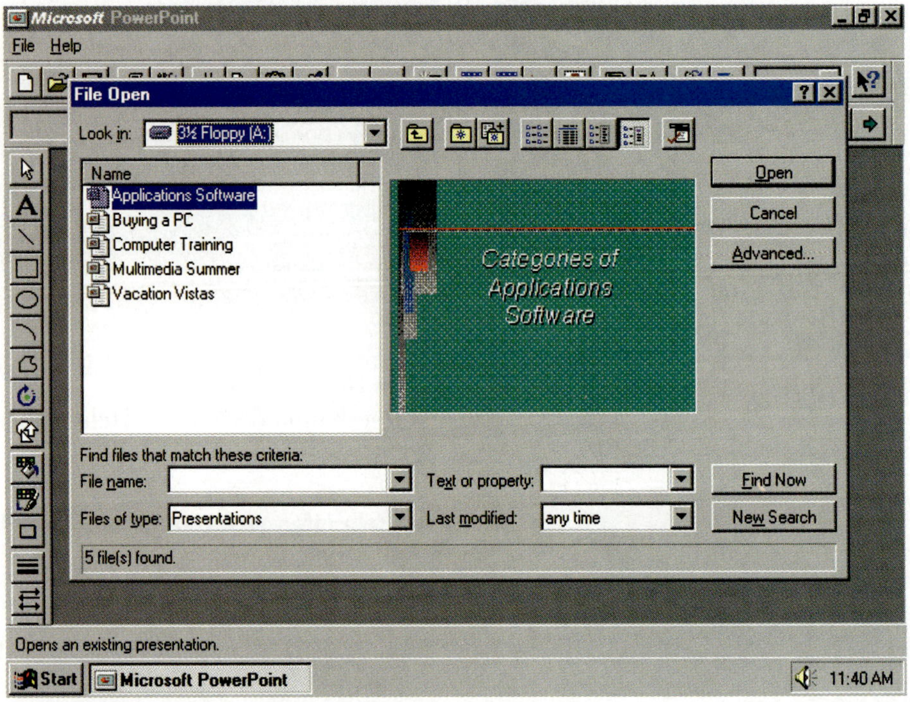

4. In the *Name* area of the Open dialog box:
   DOUBLE-CLICK: Buying a PC
   The presentation is loaded into the presentation window. Your screen should now appear similar to Figure 1.14.

FIGURE 1.14 THE "BUYING A PC" PRESENTATION FILE

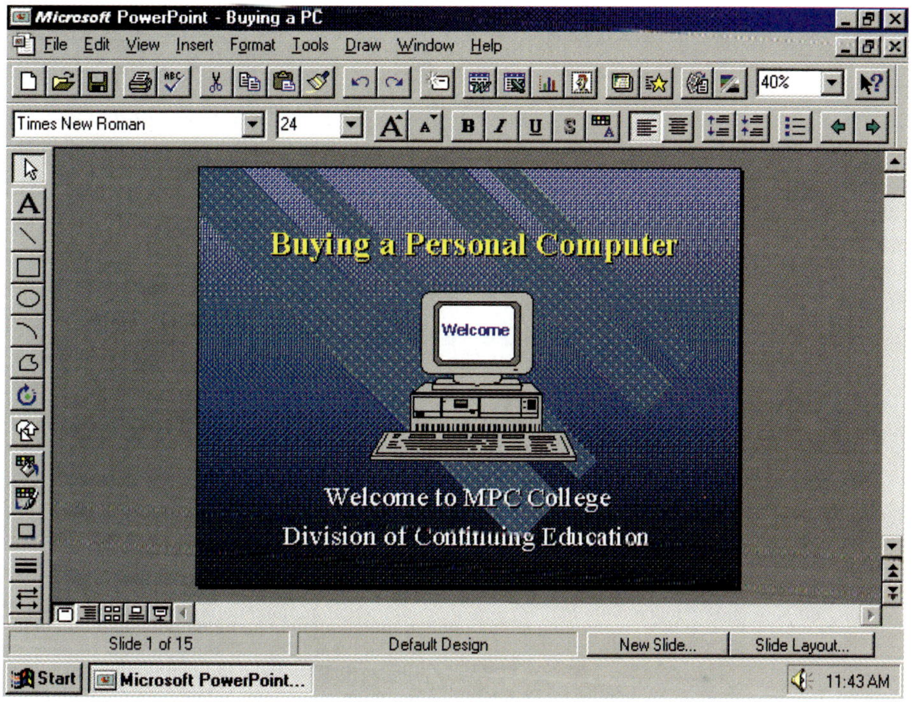

QUICK REFERENCE
Opening a Presentation

1. **CLICK: Open button (), or**
   CHOOSE: File, Open from the Menu bar
2. **SELECT: the desired file using the *Look in* drop-down list box**
3. **DOUBLE-CLICK: the desired file**

IN ADDITION

MODIFYING THE RECENTLY USED FILE LIST FOR OPENING PRESENTATIONS

Using the Tools, Options command, you can modify the number of entries that appear in the Recently Used File List at the bottom of the File pull-down menu. For example, you can have PowerPoint keep track of up to nine presentations, instead of the default four, that you've recently opened.

VIEWING A PRESENTATION

PowerPoint provides five different views of a presentation: Slide view, Outline view, Slide Sorter view, Notes Pages view, and Slide Show view. You switch among these views using the View command on the Menu bar or by clicking the View buttons located in the bottom left-hand corner of the presentation window. The active view of your presentation before being saved or closed becomes the default view when it is subsequently opened. Each view is described and illustrated in the following section.

SLIDE VIEW

The most common view to use for building or finalizing a presentation is Slide view. Similar to Page Layout view in Word for Windows, this view shows you how the slide will appear when printed or displayed. All text, graphics, and other media elements in your presentation appear in Slide view. You can perform the following tasks in Slide view:

- Insert, edit, and delete text
- Draw lines, squares, ovals, polygons, or other objects
- Add clip art, scanned photographs, or other media objects
- Add graphs, charts, or data from other applications
- Change the appearance of text and objects
- Change a template's style or color scheme

To select the Slide view, click the Slide view button (▣) or choose View, Slides from the menu. There are three toolbars, by default, that are available in Slide view—Standard, Formatting, and Drawing. As mentioned previously, you can add or remove toolbars using the shortcut menu, accessed by clicking the right mouse button over any toolbar button.

OUTLINE VIEW

Outline view is especially useful for organizing your thoughts and developing the textual content for a presentation. You can also use Outline view much as you would a word processor to enter, arrange, and edit textual information. You perform the following tasks in Outline view:

- Insert, arrange, and edit textual content (titles and main body text)
- Promote and/or demote textual content in your outline
- Display a slide's text with or without formatting
- Show a slide's titles only, or show titles and full text

To select the Outline view, click the Outline view button ( ) or choose View, Outline from the menu. In Outline view, the Outlining toolbar replaces the Drawing toolbar that is usually displayed in Slide view.

SLIDE SORTER VIEW

The Slide Sorter view provides a light table for viewing multiple slides. When selected, this view arranges small thumbnail representations of your slides, complete with text and graphics, in rows and columns. Slide Sorter view gives you an immediate feeling for the continuity or flow of a presentation. You perform the following tasks in Slide Sorter view:

- Manipulate the order of slides
- Add transitional effects from one slide to another
- Incorporate special "build effects" for a particular slide, such as highlighting each point in turn
- Hide slides from being displayed in a computer-based slide show
- Set timing options for rehearsing your presentation

To select the Slide Sorter view, click the Slide Sorter view button ( ) or choose View, Slide Sorter from the menu. In Slide Sorter view, the Slide Sorter toolbar replaces the Formatting toolbar.

NOTES PAGES VIEW

The Notes Pages view allows you to insert, edit, and delete reminder notes for yourself on each slide. You can also use a slide's notes page for creating extended notes as an audience handout. Whatever the purpose, this view lets you enter text and graphics in a Notes placeholder located below the image of the slide. You can perform the same tasks in Notes Pages view as in Slide view.

To select the Notes Pages view, click the Notes Pages view button ( ) or choose View, Notes Pages from the menu.

SLIDE SHOW VIEW

In Slide Show view, the presentation is displayed as an electronic computer-based slide show, complete with slide transitions and timing effects. The ability to switch quickly among the different views allows you to modify a slide's content in Slide or Outline view and receive immediate feedback in Slide Show view. This view is also called an *on-screen presentation.*

To select the Slide Show view, click the Slide Show view button ( ) or choose View, Slide Show from the menu. The most common methods for controlling a presentation in Slide Show view appear in Table 1.3.

TABLE 1.3

Controlling a Slide Show Presentation

Task Description	*Keyboard and Mouse Methods*
Go to the next slide	CLICK: left mouse button, or PRESS: PgDn, →, ↓, ENTER, Spacebar, or TYPE: **N**
Go to the previous slide	PRESS: PgUp, ←, ↑, or TYPE: **P**
Go to a specific slide	TYPE: **desired slide number**, and then PRESS: ENTER
Go to the first slide	TWIN-CLICK: left and right mouse buttons together and hold down for two seconds
Blank the screen to black	PRESS: **b** to blank screen to black PRESS: **b** again to unblank screen
Blank the screen to white	PRESS: **w** to blank screen to white PRESS: **w** again to unblank screen
Exit the slide show	PRESS: ESC

If you click the right mouse button in Slide Show view, a shortcut menu appears that provides options that are similar to those described in Table 1.3.

FOR PRACTICE

Let's practice switching among the views using the "Buying a PC" presentation.

1. To display the "Buying a PC" presentation in Outline view:
   CLICK: Outline View button (▤)
   Your screen should now appear similar to Figure 1.15.

FIGURE 1.15 "BUYING A PC" PRESENTATION IN OUTLINE VIEW

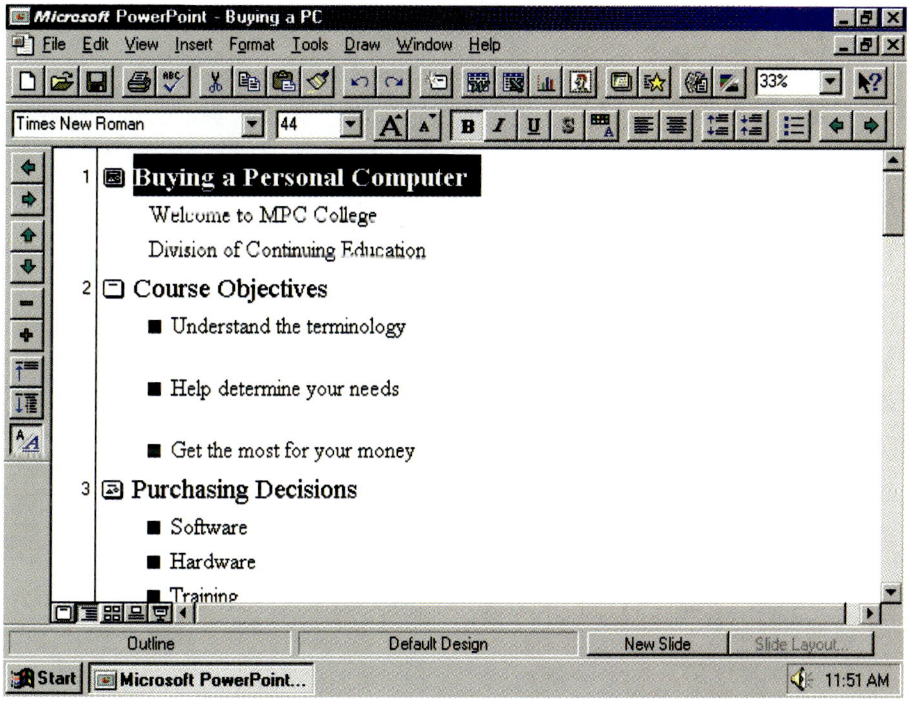

2. To display the "Buying a PC" presentation in Slide Sorter view:
   CLICK: Slide Sorter View button (▦)
   Your screen should now appear similar to Figure 1.16.

FIGURE 1.16 "BUYING A PC" PRESENTATION IN SLIDE SORTER VIEW

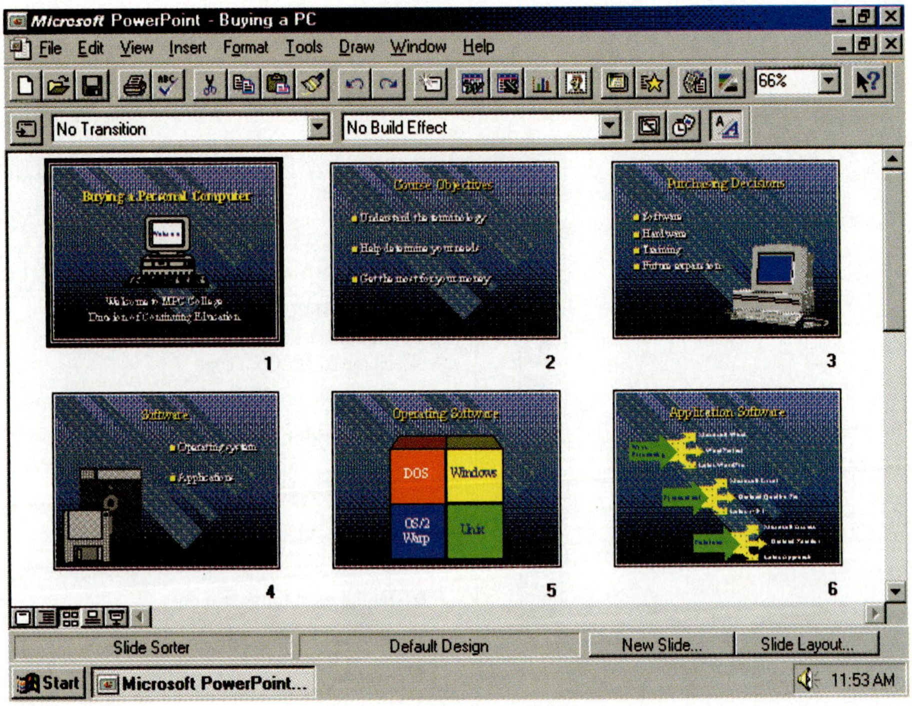

3. To display the presentation in Notes Pages view:
   CLICK: Notes Pages View button ( )
   Your screen should now appear similar to Figure 1.17.

FIGURE 1.17 "BUYING A PC" PRESENTATION IN NOTES PAGES VIEW

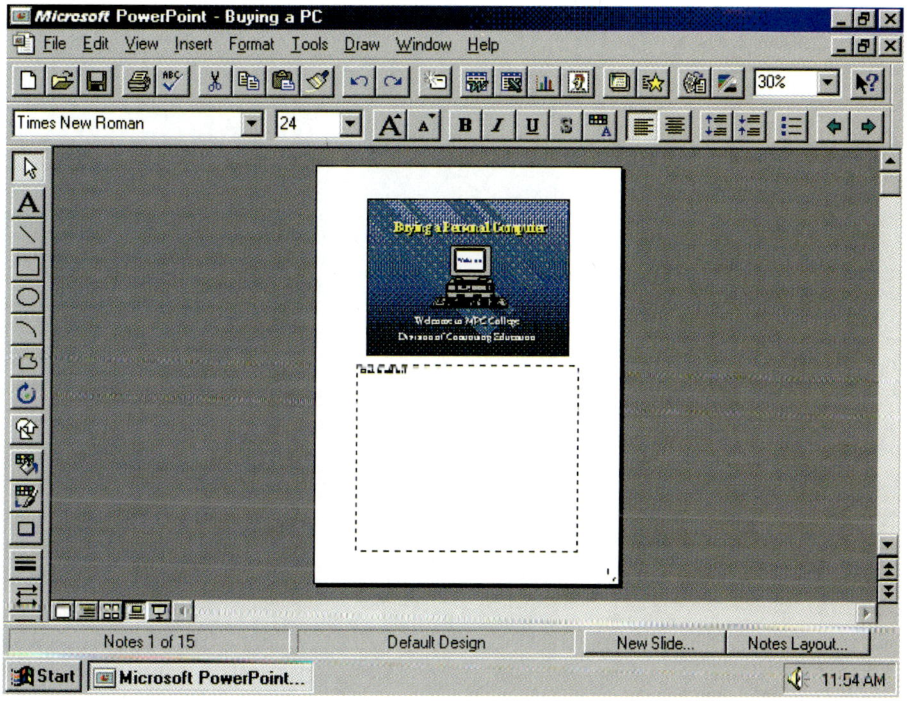

4. To display the presentation in Slide Show view:
   CLICK: Slide Show view button (![])
   Your screen should now appear similar to Figure 1.18.

FIGURE 1.18 "BUYING A PC" PRESENTATION IN SLIDE SHOW VIEW

5. To proceed to the next slide in the presentation:
   CLICK: left mouse button once
6. To display the next slide using the keyboard:
   PRESS: Spacebar
7. To return to the previous slide using the keyboard:
   PRESS: ↑
8. To return to the first slide in the presentation:
   TWIN-CLICK: left and right mouse buttons and hold for two seconds
   In most cases, you will hear a beep from your computer. Once the first slide appears, you then release the mouse buttons and the screen will show the first slide.
9. To exit the Slide Show view:
   PRESS: ESC
10. Return to Slide view before proceeding to the next section:
    CLICK: Slide view button (![])

QUICK REFERENCE
Changing the View for a Presentation

- **CLICK: [icon] to change to Slide view**
- **CLICK: [icon] to change to Outline view**
- **CLICK: [icon] to change to Slide Sorter view**
- **CLICK: [icon] to change to Notes Pages view**
- **CLICK: [icon] to change to Slide Show view**

QUICK REFERENCE
Navigating Through a Slide Show Presentation

- **CLICK: left mouse button to go to the next slide**
- **CLICK: right mouse button to go to the previous slide**
- **TWIN-CLICK: left and right mouse buttons and hold for two seconds to go to first slide**
- **PRESS: ESC to exit Slide Show view**

CLOSING A PRESENTATION

When you are finished working with a presentation, you should close the file to free up valuable computer memory. To close a presentation window, choose File, Close from the Menu bar or click the Close icon (☒) in the presentation window. If you've made changes to your presentation since you last saved it, you should save the presentation before you close the window. Let's close the "Buying a PC" presentation.

1. Since you haven't made any changes to the presentation:
   CHOOSE: File, Close
2. If there are any other presentations appearing in the slide area, repeat Step 1 to clear them from memory.

QUICK REFERENCE
Closing a Presentation

- **CHOOSE: File, Close, or**
- **CLICK: Close icon (☒) of the Presentation window**

LEAVING POWERPOINT

When you are finished using PowerPoint, save your work and exit the program by clicking the Close button (☒) that is located in the Title bar of the application window or choose File, Exit from the Menu bar. If you have made modifications to the presentation and have not saved the changes, PowerPoint asks whether the presentation should be saved or abandoned before exiting the program.

Perform the following step to finish working with PowerPoint.

1. CLICK: Close button (☒) of the application window
   Assuming that no changes were made to the document, the application is closed and you are returned to the Windows desktop.
2. To exit Windows 95:
   CHOOSE: Start, Shut Down
   SELECT: *Shutdown the computer?* option button
   CLICK: Yes command button

QUICK REFERENCE Exiting PowerPoint	• **CLICK: Close button (☒) of the application window, or** • **CHOOSE: File, Exit**

SUMMARY

PowerPoint provides you with powerful tools for creating presentations. A presentation can include one or more of the following: slides, handouts, speaker's notes, and outlines. In this session, after loading Microsoft Windows and PowerPoint, you were led on a guided tour of the program's major components. We also used the Help facility to retrieve information on menu commands and toolbar buttons.

Near the end of the session, you opened an existing presentation and practiced using the View buttons—located at the bottom of the presentation window—to display the presentation in five different views. These views included: Slide view, Outline view, Slide Sorter view, Notes Pages view, and Slide Show view. The session concluded when you closed the presentation and exited PowerPoint.

COMMAND SUMMARY

Many of the commands and procedures appearing in this session are provided in Table 1.4 below.

TABLE 1.4

Command Summary

Task Description	*Menu Command*	*Alternative Method*
Access the PowerPoint Help facility	Help, Microsoft PowerPoint Help Topics	
Access the Answer Wizard	Help, Answer Wizard	
Access context-sensitive help	F1	
Open an existing presentation file	File, Open	
Close a presentation file	File, Close	
Leave PowerPoint	File, Exit	

KEY TERMS

application window

In Microsoft Windows, each running application program appears in its own application window. These windows can be sized and moved anywhere on the Windows desktop.

handout

In PowerPoint, a handout which is given to audience members with two to six small images of the actual slides on each printed page.

multitasking

Activity in which more than one task or program is executed at one time.

presentation

In PowerPoint, a presentation is a collection of slides, handouts, speaker's notes, and outlines, all in one disk file.

presentation window

In PowerPoint, each open presentation appears in its own presentation window. These windows can be sized and moved anywhere within the Slide work area. (A presentation window represents your workspace.)

run-time version

A scaled-down version of the original software that includes a "player" for the application's data files, but does not usually allow the user access to any editing features.

slide
In PowerPoint, a slide is an individual page of a presentation.

template
A template defines how slide text will look, where the text and other objects will be positioned, and what colors will be used.

wizards
Wizards lead you through creating presentations and performing other tasks in PowerPoint.

WYSIWYG
Acronym for "What You See Is What You Get"; page description software feature that allows the user to see the final version of a document on the screen—including the results of formatting—before it is printed out.

EXERCISES

SHORT ANSWER

1. What is meant by the term *presentation?*
2. What are some of the output options for a presentation?
3. What is a template?
4. What is a dialog box?
5. How do you display the Help Topics window?
6. How do you open a presentation?
7. Describe the five different views that are available in PowerPoint.
8. In Slide Show view, how do you proceed to the next slide?
9. In Slide Show view, how do you return to the previous slide?
10. In Slide Show view, how do you return to the first slide?

HANDS-ON

(*Note:* Before working through the following exercises, make sure the Advantage Diskette is in the diskette drive.)

1. In this exercise, you practice accessing PowerPoint's Help facility.
   a. Load Microsoft PowerPoint.
   b. Remove the Tip of the Day dialog box when it appears.
   c. Remove the PowerPoint dialog box when it appears.

d. Using the Help button (?) on the Standard toolbar, retrieve help for the Open button ().

e. After reading the contents of the Help window, close the window.

f. After double-clicking the Help button (?), display the Index tab.

g. Search for information on "opening presentations."

h. Using the Answer Wizard, display help for "using color in presentations."

i. Display the Contents tab.

j. Browse through the Help topics by pressing the ↓ key repeatedly.

k. Close the Help Topics window before proceeding.

2. In this exercise, you open the presentation named "Computer Training" from the Advantage Diskette.

   a. Open the "Computer Training" presentation, stored on the Advantage Diskette.

   b. If the presentation isn't maximized in the presentation window, click its Maximize button ().

   c. Display the presentation in Slide Sorter view.

   d. Display the presentation in Outline view.

   e. Display the presentation in Notes Pages view.

   f. Display the presentation in Slide Show view.

   g. Let the slide show run on its own. (*Note:* You don't have to click the mouse button to display the next slide because transitions have been built into this presentation.) If you need to exit from the presentation before you've viewed all the slides, press ESC.

   h. Close the "Computer Training" presentation.

3. In this exercise, you open the presentation named "Multimedia Summer" from the Advantage Diskette.

   a. Open the "Multimedia Summer" presentation, stored on the Advantage Diskette.

   b. Display the presentation in Slide Show view.

   c. Practice navigating through the presentation using the keyboard and mouse methods.

   d. Move directly to slide number 3.

   e. Display the first slide in the presentation.

   f. Blank the presentation to a black screen.

   g. Unhide the presentation.

h. Blank the presentation to a white screen.

i. Unhide the presentation.

j. Return to Slide view.

k. Close the "Multimedia Summer" presentation.

CASE PROBLEMS — VACATION VISTAS, INC.

(*Note:* In the following case problems, assume the role of the primary characters and perform the same steps that they identify. You may want to re-read the session opening.)

1. Frank stares intently at the opened courier package in front of him. The letter from Juanita, which he has already read and is still digesting, has been placed neatly upon his desk. He now holds a disk labeled "Advantage Diskette" in his left hand and re-reads the sticky note attached to it. *"Frank, the presentation file on this diskette is called "Vacation Vistas." I recommend that you proof the textual and graphic content in the presentation. Bye for now, Juanita."*

   Not one to waste too much time sulking, Frank plans his approach. He loads the presentation into PowerPoint and gets an overall feel for the product using the Slide Sorter view. To proof the textual content, Frank switches to Outline view and finds two blatant mistakes. He writes down the two mistakes on a notepad that will later become his review letter to Juanita. To proof the graphic content, Frank uses the Slide view and again finds two obvious mistakes in the graphics that Juanita chose for the presentation. As before, Frank copies down the two mistakes on his note pad.

   Having closed the presentation, Frank must now write a letter to Juanita Gomez specifying the two textual errors and the two graphic errors in the "Vacation Vistas" presentation. He addresses it to her Seattle home at 1500 Country Club Lane, Seattle WA 98004. He'll include this review letter when he sends the disk back to Juanita for final production.

2. With only one week to go before his presentation at the local seniors' hall, Frank is getting a little nervous. As the expected attendance exceeds 100 seniors, he has rented a speaker's podium, a 35mm slide projector, and a large screen. Unfortunately, Frank isn't used to speaking in front of large groups and truly wanted some time to practice before the actual presentation.

   Having learned the fundamentals of PowerPoint, Frank remembers that he can use the Slide Show view to display and work through the presentation. He loads the "Vacation Vistas" presentation into PowerPoint and switches to Slide Show view. After progressing through four slides, Frank notices one of his staff passing by his office door with a client. Not wanting the client to see the unfinished presentation, Frank blanks the screen to black tcmporarily. When he unhides the presentation, he backs up a couple of slides to refocus his attention. With his train of thought interrupted, he decides to return to the first slide and start again. This time, he makes it all the way through the presentation.

3. Having finished practicing, Frank decides to close the "Vacation Vistas" presentation file and exit Microsoft PowerPoint. He doesn't save any changes that he may have made in the presentation. Before leaving his office for the evening, Frank writes down a summary of the five views and the primary methods for navigating a presentation in Slide Show view. He places the summary beside his monitor for easy reference.

Microsoft PowerPoint 7.0 for Windows 95

Creating a Presentation

SESSION OUTLINE

Creating a Presentation: An Overview
Using the AutoContent Wizard
Using a Design Template
Saving a Presentation
Adding Slides
Reviewing Your Presentation
Editing a Presentation
Using the Style Checker
Printing a Presentation
Summary
Key Terms
Exercises

INTRODUCTION

Compare electronic slide presentations with handwritten or typed overheads and you can immediately appreciate the value and impact of using presentation software like PowerPoint. But not only are electronic presentations more effective, they can take less time and effort to create. In this session, you learn how to improve the quality of your presentations while dramatically reducing your production timelines and budgets.

CASE STUDY BERKFORD COLLEGE, PENNSYLVANIA

Sharon Rheingold is a second-year law student at Berkford College in Pennsylvania. As a credit component toward her studies this semester, Sharon accepted a job teaching Public Speaking 101 to first-year business students. Given her goal of one day becoming a successful trial lawyer, Sharon saw this job as an opportunity to hone her communication skills on a captive audience. Little did she realize that Dr. Kirsten Antoski, the dean of Business Administration, had personally developed the course and expects each of her instructors to hand out professional presentation materials for each lecture. With an already suffocating course load, Sharon wonders how she can possibly meet Dr. Antoski's expectations and complete her own studies.

While discussing the situation with her roommate Walt, the two students thought of an especially good idea. Walt, a fourth-year student in the Faculty of Education, recommended Sharon use Microsoft PowerPoint to develop her lesson plans and course notes. Walt assured Sharon that with only a few tips she would be producing professional-looking handouts in hours instead of days. Furthermore, she could use PowerPoint to help teach her students some of the principles of public speaking.

In this session, you and Sharon learn how to use the AutoContent Wizard to create new presentations quickly and easily. You also learn how to use a design template, modify a slide's information, save a presentation to the disk, and print a presentation.

CREATING A PRESENTATION: AN OVERVIEW

Even if you haven't had much experience using PowerPoint, creating a new presentation is easy. You'll be amazed at how quickly you can organize content, select an output medium, and design the look of your slides. Though you may initially believe otherwise, the most time-consuming task involves gathering and writing the content for a presentation. It is important that you have a clear understanding of a presentation's objectives and can verbalize the information that you want to communicate to an audience. Anybody can choose background colors, apply fonts and styles, and insert graphics on a slide. Your goal is to create a presentation that communicates a message effectively—and that takes work.

USING POWERPOINT TO CREATE A PRESENTATION

The following steps provide an overview of the process for creating a presentation using Microsoft PowerPoint:

1. *Select a starting point for your presentation.*
   In the startup dialog box (Figure 2.1) that appears when you first load PowerPoint, the *AutoContent Wizard* and *Template* options can help you get started in creating a new presentation. The **AutoContent Wizard** provides the quickest and easiest method for creating a presentation by presenting you with a series of questions about the subject, visual style, length, and type of output for your presentation. If you just want to pick a subject or a visual style for a presentation, choose the *Template* option. For the greatest flexibility, you can create a presentation from scratch using the *Blank Presentation* option.

FIGURE 2.1 THE POWERPOINT STARTUP DIALOG BOX

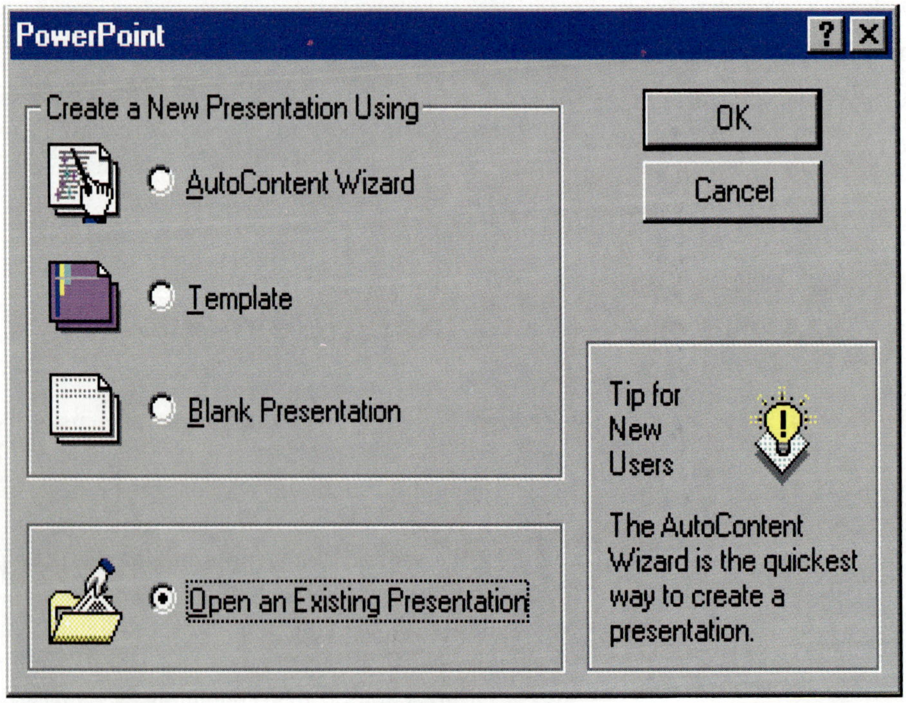

2. *Create the individual slides for your presentation.*
   After you select the starting point for your slide presentation, you must create the individual slides by adding, editing, and deleting text and graphics for each slide page. You typically use the Outline view to enter a slide's textual content and the Slide view to finalize the colors, typefaces, and placement of graphics, charts, and other objects. If you started creating a presentation using the AutoContent Wizard or by picking a presentation template, many of the slides for your presentation are automatically added to the presentation file. You simply edit the titles and body text on the slides to ensure their appropriateness for the topic. When you create a blank presentation, PowerPoint provides you with the first slide; you must create any additional slides from scratch.
3. *Review and refine your presentation in its entirety.*
   Once you've created the individual slides, you use Slide Sorter view and Slide Show view to review the presentation. While working in Slide Sorter view, you can manipulate the linear order of the slides, set the timing for rehearsing a presentation, hide slides, and add special effects to your presentation. For example, PowerPoint provides you with the ability to create **build slides** for computer-based presentations. On a build slide, you can make bullets appear on the screen one at a time and even dim previous points on the slide to draw further attention to the current bullet. Also, in Slide Sorter view you can incorporate transitions into your presentation. A **transition** is the visual effect you see when you go from one slide to the next in a computer-based presentation. For the acid test of previewing your work as it would be presented live, you use the Slide Show view.
4. *Save and print your presentation.*
   Not to tempt fate, you should save your presentation regularly as you work. Also, print your presentation for others to review. It's always wise to let your friends and co-workers find the errors before your audience has the opportunity! A second benefit of printing a presentation is that you will have a paper copy in case your computer files are deleted accidentally or become corrupted by a virus.

REACHING FOR THE DICTIONARY

Before you create a presentation in the next section, let's introduce and define some important terms:

Design template	Defined briefly in the last session, a design template is a presentation whose background, color scheme, typefaces, and other formatting options can be applied to another presentation. By using templates, you need not reinvent the wheel each time you create a presentation. PowerPoint provides 32 professionally

	designed templates from which you can choose. You can also design your own custom templates, using your corporate or school colors for example, and then apply them to the new presentations you create.
Presentation template	A presentation template is a presentation whose subject outline can be applied to another presentation. PowerPoint provides over 22 presentation templates that you can choose from to match your subject.
Default presentation format	PowerPoint provides a default presentation format—complete with a background design, color scheme, typefaces, and so on—that is applied when you choose the *Blank Presentation* option from the startup dialog box.
Masters	Each presentation you create contains a master for each output option in the presentation; that is, one for slides, one for the outline, one for the notes pages, and one for the audience handouts. Whatever you place on a master page will print on each page in the presentation, whether a slide page or a notes page. For example, to have a graphic of your company or school logo appear on each slide in the presentation, you place it on the Slide Master.

These terms will be explained further in later sections, but now we move on to learning by doing rather than by reading!

USING THE AUTOCONTENT WIZARD

If you're finding it difficult to organize and write down your thoughts, select the *AutoContent Wizard* option button from the startup dialog box or after choosing File, New from the Menu bar. After progressing through six dialog boxes, you'll have a skeletal framework for building a complete presentation.

To practice using the AutoContent Wizard, perform the following steps on your computer.

1. Make sure that you've loaded Microsoft PowerPoint and that the Advantage Diskette is inserted into drive A: or drive B:.

2. If the Tip of the Day dialog box appears on your screen, do the following to remove it (otherwise, proceed to Step 3):
   PRESS: ENTER or CLICK: OK

3. If the PowerPoint startup dialog box appears on your screen, do the following (otherwise, proceed to Step 4):
   SELECT: *AutoContent Wizard* option button
   PRESS: ENTER or CLICK: OK
   Now proceed to Step 5.

4. If the startup dialog box does not appear on your screen and you are certain that Microsoft PowerPoint is loaded, do the following to initiate the AutoContent Wizard:
   CHOOSE: File, New from the Menu bar
   SELECT: Presentations tab
   DOUBLE-CLICK: AutoContent Wizard icon

5. After reading the introductory text, proceed to the next step:
   CLICK: Next >

6. In this step, you enter the information you want to appear on the opening slide such as your name, the title of your presentation, and any personal information such as your company name. Use the mouse to move the cursor and to select text. (*Note:* You can also press TAB to move the cursor to the next text box and SHIFT + TAB to move to the previous text box.) After positioning the cursor, type the text you want to appear in the text box.

   Before continuing to the next step:
   TYPE: ***your name*** into the *What is your name?* text box
   (*Note:* Your name may already appear in this area.)
   TYPE: **Starting My Own Business** into the *What are you going to talk about?* text box
   TYPE: ***your school or company name*** into the third text box
   Your screen should now appear similar to Figure 2.2.

FIGURE 2.2 AUTOCONTENT WIZARD: DEFINING THE FIRST SLIDE

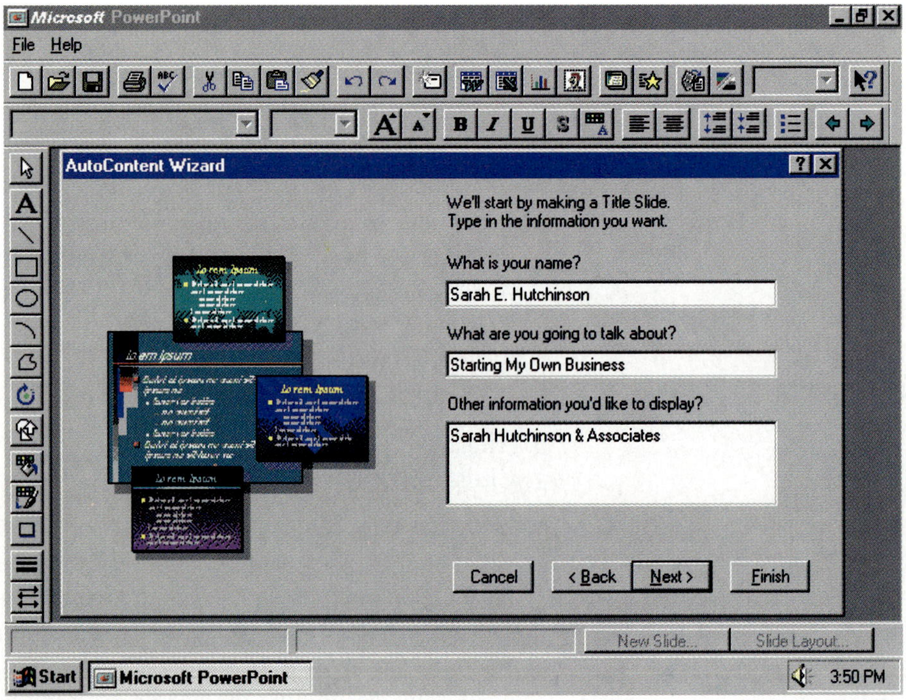

7. To proceed to the next step:
   CLICK: Next >
   Your screen should now appear similar to Figure 2.3. Here you specify the type of presentation that you want to create. A description of the selected presentation displays to the right.

FIGURE 2.3 AUTOCONTENT WIZARD: CHOOSING A PRESENTATION TYPE

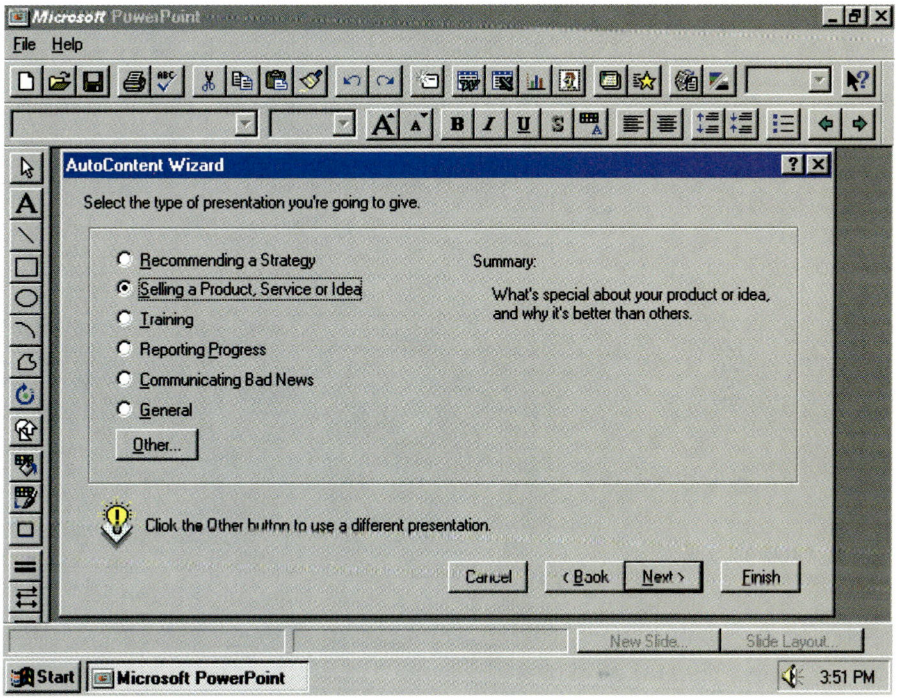

8. You're not limited to the current list of presentation types. To display additional presentation types, do the following:
   CLICK: Other command button
   A list of presentation templates appears in the *Name* list box.
9. Drag the vertical scroll bar downward to see additional presentation types. In this window, you select a presentation type by double-clicking its name. To return to the previous AutoContent window:
   CLICK: Cancel command button
10. SELECT: *Selling a Product, Service or Idea* option button
    CLICK: Next > to proceed
    Your screen should now appear similar to Figure 2.4.

FIGURE 2.4 AUTOCONTENT WIZARD: CHOOSING A VISUAL STYLE AND PRESENTATION LENGTH

11. Make the following selections (if they are not selected already):
    SELECT: *Default* option button for the visual style
    SELECT: *Haven't decided* option button for the presentation length
    CLICK: Next > to proceed
    Your screen should now appear similar to Figure 2.5.

FIGURE 2.5 AUTOCONTENT WIZARD: CHOOSING THE OUTPUT MEDIUM

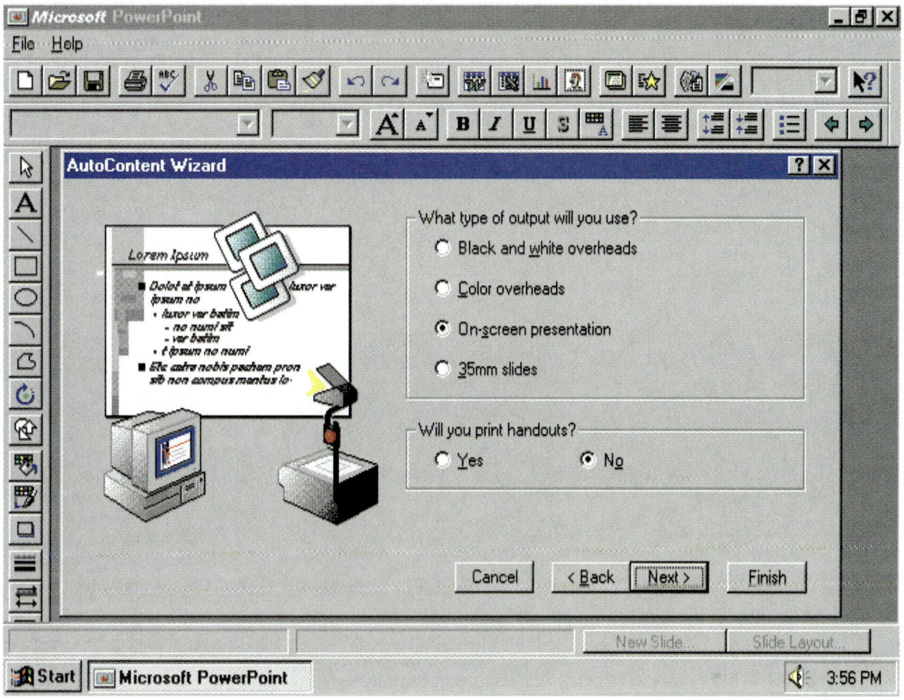

12. In this step, you choose how you want to output the presentation. Do the following:
    SELECT: *On-screen presentation* option button for the output
    SELECT: *No* option button for printing handouts
    CLICK: Next > to proceed
13. To finish using the AutoContent Wizard:
    CLICK: Finish
    The presentation is compiled and the first slide appears in Slide view (Figure 2.6).

FIGURE 2.6 THE FIRST SLIDE IN SLIDE VIEW

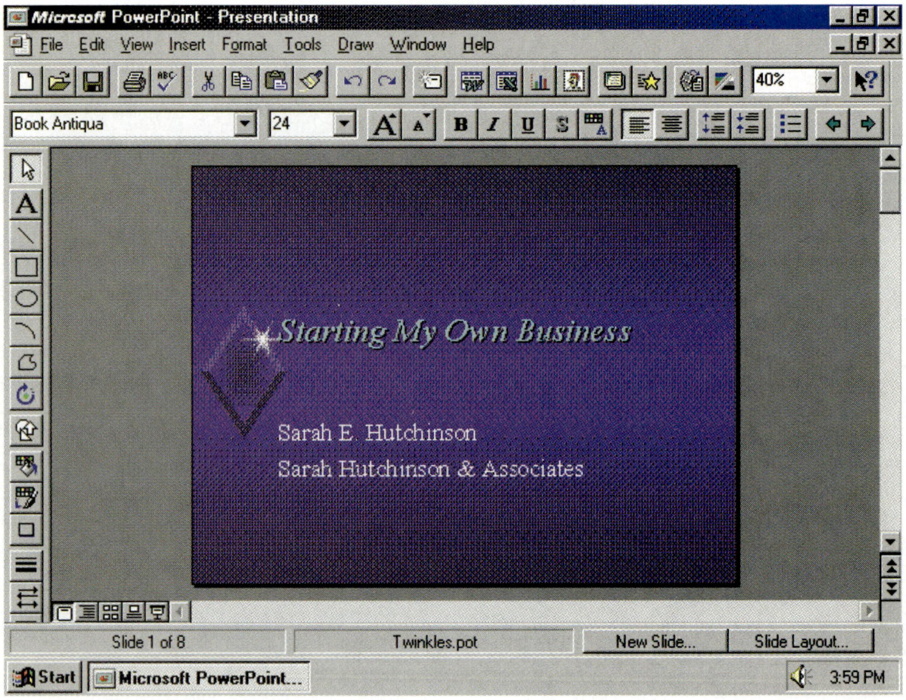

14. To display the new presentation in Slide Show view:
    CLICK: Slide Show button ( )
15. To advance through the presentation:
    CLICK: left mouse button continuously until you reach the end of the presentation and are returned to Slide view
16. Let's close the presentation and move on to the next section, where you will learn more about design templates. Do the following:
    CHOOSE: File, Close
    CLICK: No when asked whether you want to save the presentation

QUICK REFERENCE
Using the AutoContent Wizard

1. **Load PowerPoint and remove the Tip of the Day dialog box.**
2. **SELECT: *AutoContent Wizard* option button in the startup dialog box**
   PRESS: ENTER or CLICK: OK
   (*Note:* You can also choose File, New and select the AutoContent Wizard from the Presentations tab.)
3. **Proceed through the AutoContent Wizard dialog boxes, replying to questions and clicking Next >.**
4. **When you see the checkered flag in the AutoContent Wizard:**
   CLICK: Finish

USING A DESIGN TEMPLATE

One of the problems with the advent of presentation software programs like PowerPoint is that the presentation author has been hurled into the role of graphic designer. Many people who are highly skilled writers and content researchers find it difficult to take on the additional role of art director. Fortunately, PowerPoint provides 32 design templates to help those of us who consider themselves artistically challenged.

In this section, you create a presentation entitled "The Future of Computer and Communications Technology" for a class project. The objective of the presentation is to inform your classmates of three primary technology trends: connectivity, online information access, and interactivity.

To practice picking a design template, perform the following steps on your computer.

1. Make sure the Advantage Diskette is inserted into the diskette drive.
2. Your first step is to display the New Presentation dialog box:
   CHOOSE: File, New
3. To select a design template:
   SELECT: Presentation Designs tab
4. To view the design templates in a list:
   CLICK: List button ()
   Your screen should now appear similar to Figure 2.7. (*Note:* You may not have the same design templates stored on your hard drive as those shown in Figure 2.7.)

FIGURE 2.7 NEW PRESENTATION DIALOG BOX: PRESENTATION DESIGNS TAB

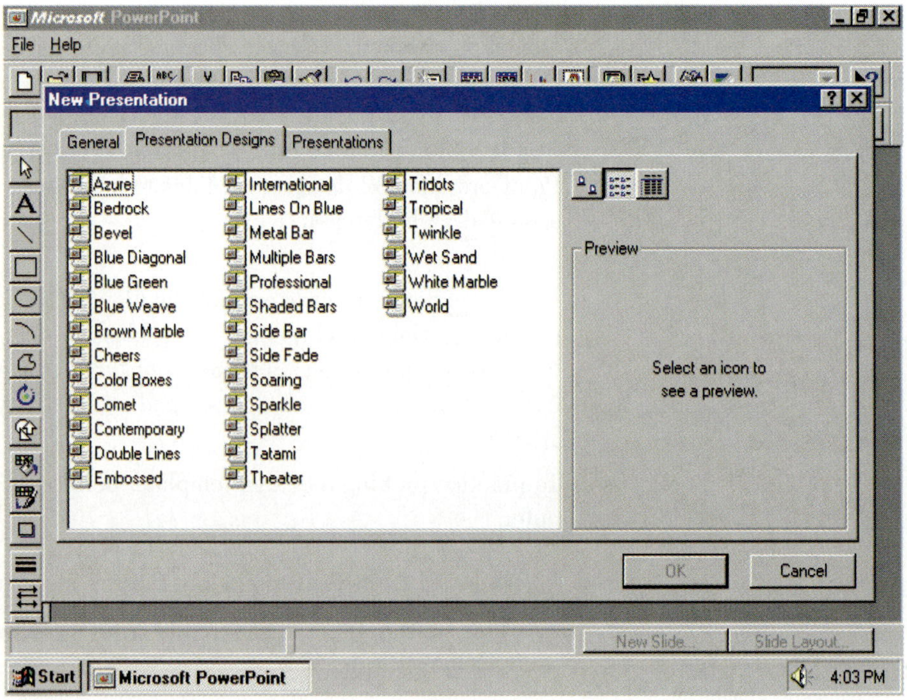

5. To preview a design template, you single-click the template name. An example of the design will appear in the Preview window. On your own, preview at least five design templates.

6. In this step, you will pick the "Lines on Blue" design template:
   DOUBLE-CLICK: Lines on Blue

7. PowerPoint needs to know what layout you want to use for the first slide (Figure 2.8). Do the following:
   SELECT: Title Slide layout (located in the upper-left corner)
   PRESS: ENTER or CLICK: OK
   Your screen should now appear similar to Figure 2.9.

FIGURE 2.8 NEW SLIDE DIALOG BOX

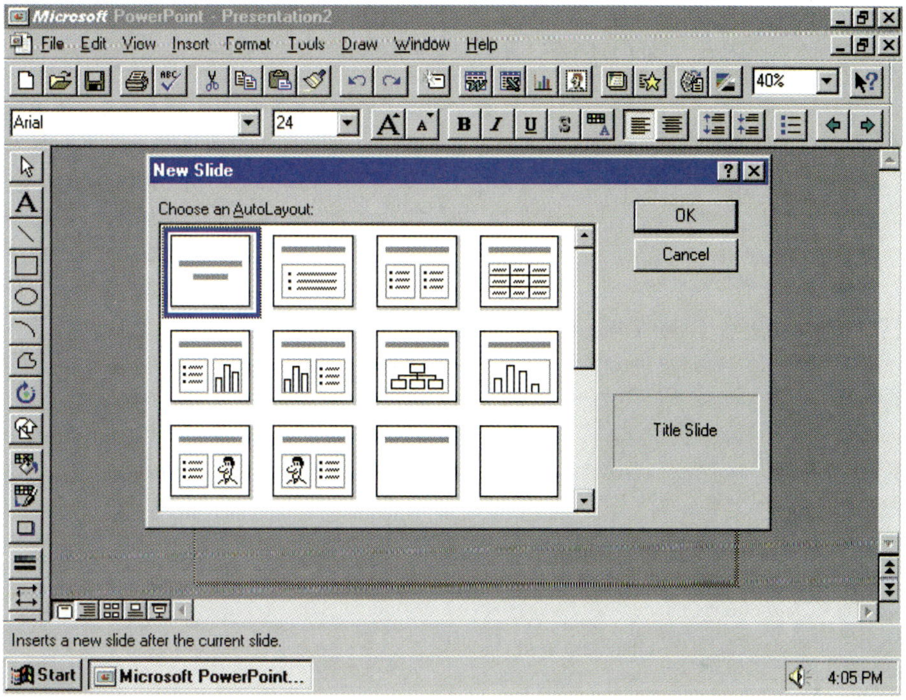

FIGURE 2.9 A TITLE SLIDE

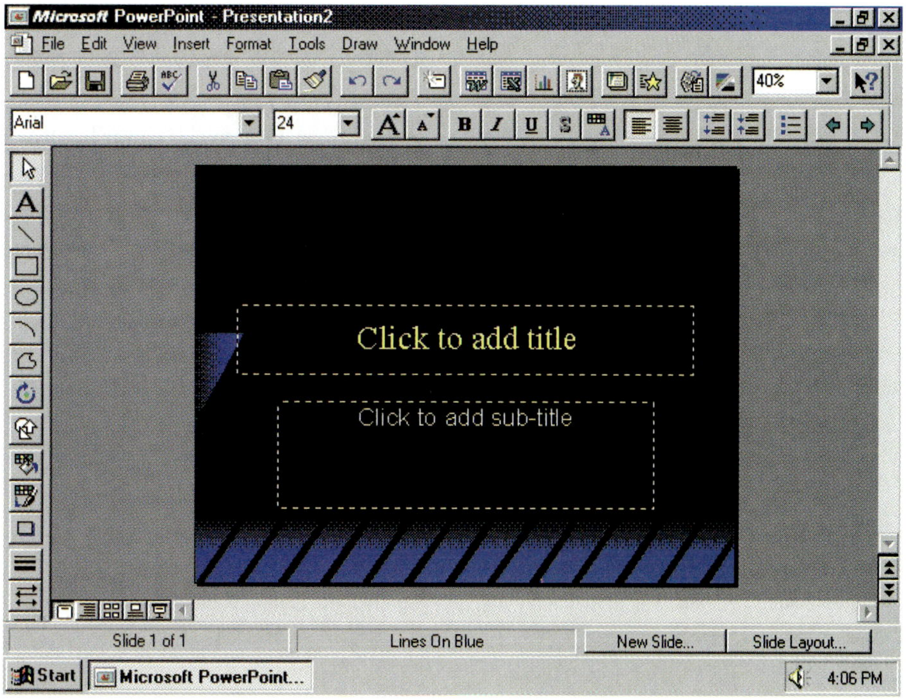

8. Before you modify this new presentation, let's continue to the next section to learn how to save it to disk.

SAVING A PRESENTATION

When you work on a presentation, it exists only in the computer's memory which is highly volatile. To permanently store your work, you must save the presentation to the hard disk or to a diskette. Saving your work to a disk is similar to placing it into a filing cabinet. To be safe, you should save your work every 15 minutes, or whenever you're interrupted, to protect against an unexpected power outage or other catastrophe.

To save a presentation to a disk, you click the Save button ( ) on the Standard toolbar or you select the File, Save command from the menu. If you haven't saved the presentation before, a dialog box appears where you specify the save location and name for the file. When naming a file, you can use up to 255 characters, including spaces. You can't use the following characters in filenames:

\ / : * ? " < > |

When you are finished typing the filename, press ENTER or click the Save command button. As the presentation is being written to the disk, the Status bar displays its progress.

Perform the following steps to save the current presentation.

1. Ensure that the Advantage Diskette is placed in the diskette drive.
2. CLICK: Save button ( )
   Your screen should now appear similar to Figure 2.10.

FIGURE 2.10 THE FILE SAVE DIALOG BOX

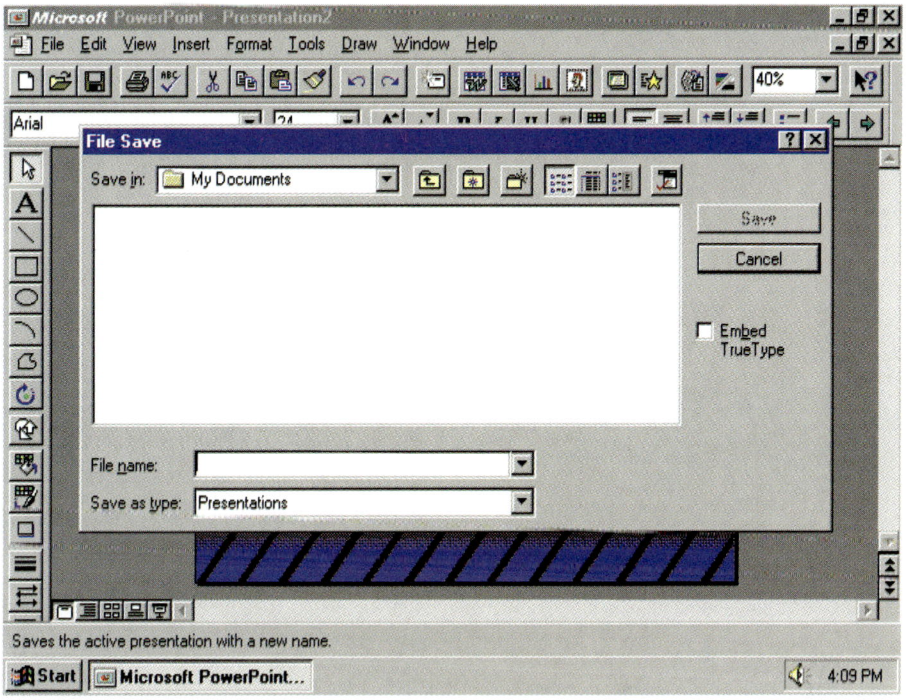

3. To choose where you want to save the file:
   CLICK: down arrow beside the *Save in* drop-down list box
   SELECT: 3½ Floppy (where the Advantage Diskette is located)

4. To save the file as "Future Trends":
   CLICK: anywhere in the *File name* text box
   TYPE: **Future Trends**
   CLICK: Save command button or PRESS: ENTER

There are times when you'll want to save an existing presentation under a different filename. For example, you may want to keep different versions of the same presentation on your disk. Or, you may want to use one presentation as a template for future presentations that are similar in style and format. Rather than creating an entirely new presentation, you can retrieve an old presentation file, edit the information, and then save it under a different name using the File, Save As command. If you want to update or replace an existing file, you use File, Save or click the Save button (▣).

QUICK REFERENCE
Saving a File

- **CLICK: Save button (▣) on the Standard toolbar, or**
- **CHOOSE: File, Save, or**
- **CHOOSE: File, Save As to save a file under a different name**

ADDING SLIDES

It's not just what you say, it's *how* you say it. As the old Chinese proverb has it, "Tell me and I'll forget; show me and I may remember; involve me and I'll understand." Involving an audience in your presentation means making it visually interesting, aesthetically pleasing, and relevant. Although we won't teach you writing skills in this guide, we will provide some pointers for communicating effectively using PowerPoint. To begin, your presentations should include some, if not all, of the following slides in addition to the body of the presentation:

- Use a *Title slide* to act as the backdrop for people entering the room or auditorium at the beginning of your presentation
- Use an *Introduction slide* to set the stage for your presentation and convince the audience that it will be a worthwhile use of their time
- Use an *Agenda* or *Objectives slide* to prepare the audience for what's coming up ahead in the presentation
- Use a *Closing slide* to reiterate and summarize your main ideas, to draw conclusions, and to revisit the presentation's objectives

Now that the "look" is defined for your presentation, let's create some slides. It's very easy; the instructions are right on the slide! As you proceed, you'll see that PowerPoint automatically creates **placeholders** on new slides for your text and graphics. There are three primary types of placeholders: Title or Sub-title, Text, and Object. While the first two are self-explanatory, an Object placeholder contains such items as clip art, graphs, and organizational charts. To edit a Title or Text placeholder, you click the mouse once in the placeholder and then type the desired text. To edit an Object placeholder, you double-click the mouse in the placeholder and create or pick the desired object.

When you add a new slide to your presentation, PowerPoint displays a dialog box with several **AutoLayout** options, which are formats for positioning text and graphics using placeholders. These AutoLayouts include slide formats for title slides, bulleted lists, graphs, two-column text slides, tables, and slides with clip art or graphics. AutoLayouts provide a great starting point for creating new slides in your presentation.

ADDING TEXT TO A SLIDE

The slides you create in this section contain text only. You will edit the layout of the slides so that you can add graphics later in the session. Perform the following steps to create the first two slides in the presentation.

1. Position the mouse pointer over the Title placeholder (appearing as "Click to add title" on the slide) and click the left mouse button once.
2. TYPE: **THE FUTURE OF COMPUTER AND COMMUNICATIONS TECHNOLOGY**
   Notice that the text automatically wraps to the next line in the placeholder box. Do not press ENTER when you are finished typing.
3. CLICK: the Sub-title placeholder (appearing as "Click to add sub-title" on the slide)
   PRESS: ENTER to begin typing on the second line
   TYPE: **by**
   PRESS: ENTER
   TYPE: ***your name***
   Notice that "Slide 1 of 1" appears in the Status bar. Your screen should now appear similar to Figure 2.11.

FIGURE 2.11 SLIDE 1 IN THE "FUTURE TRENDS" PRESENTATION

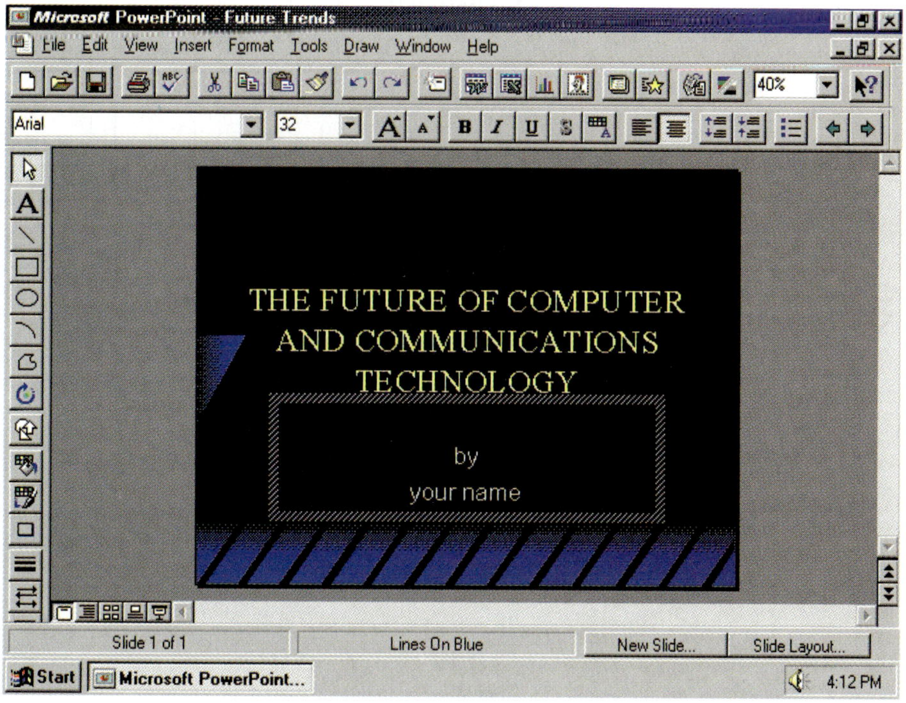

4. Let's add a second slide to the presentation. The easiest way to add a new slide is to use the New Slide hot button, located on the Status bar.
   CLICK: New Slide hot button
   (*Note:* PowerPoint adds the new slide immediately following the currently active slide.)

5. The New Slide dialog box appears, showing you the AutoLayout options for creating a new slide. To pick a layout for the new slide:
   SELECT: Bulleted List
   (*Note:* The Bulleted List may already be selected.) Notice that the name of the AutoLayout appears below the command buttons in the dialog box. Your screen should now appear similar to Figure 2.12.

FIGURE 2.12 THE NEW SLIDE DIALOG BOX

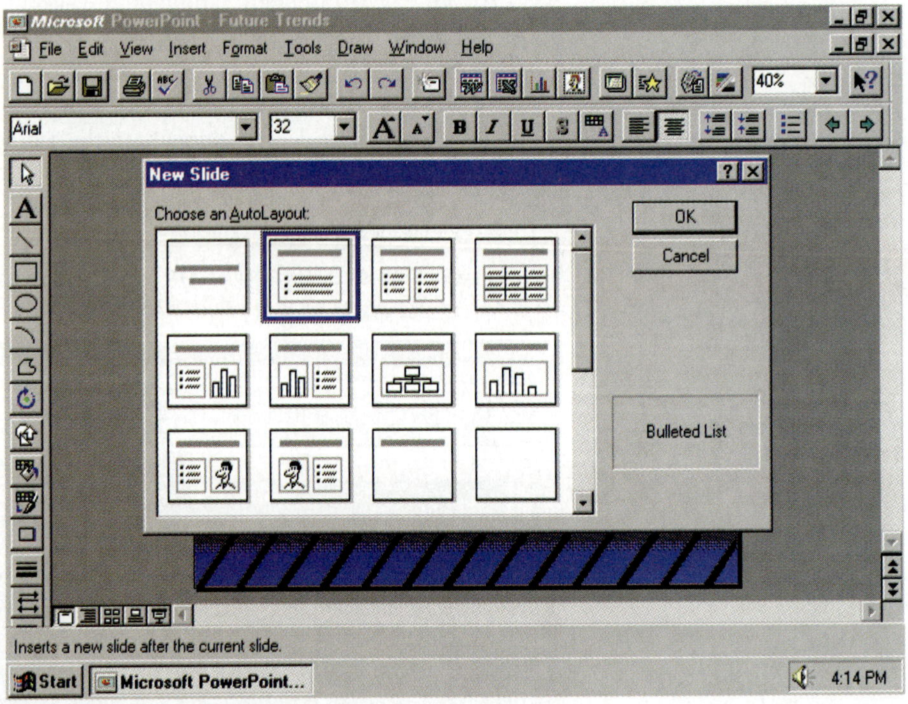

6. PRESS: **ENTER** or CLICK: OK
   A new slide with a Title placeholder and a Text placeholder (appearing as "Click to add text" on the slide) is displayed in the presentation window. These placeholders correspond to the AutoLayout option that you just selected.

7. To add a title to the slide:
   CLICK: Title placeholder
   TYPE: `Coming Trends`

8. To add content to the slide:
   CLICK: Text placeholder
   TYPE: `Connectivity`
   PRESS: ENTER
   TYPE: `Online Information Access`
   PRESS: ENTER
   TYPE: `Interactivity`
   Your screen should now appear similar to Figure 2.13.

FIGURE 2.13 SLIDE 2 IN THE "FUTURE TRENDS" PRESENTATION

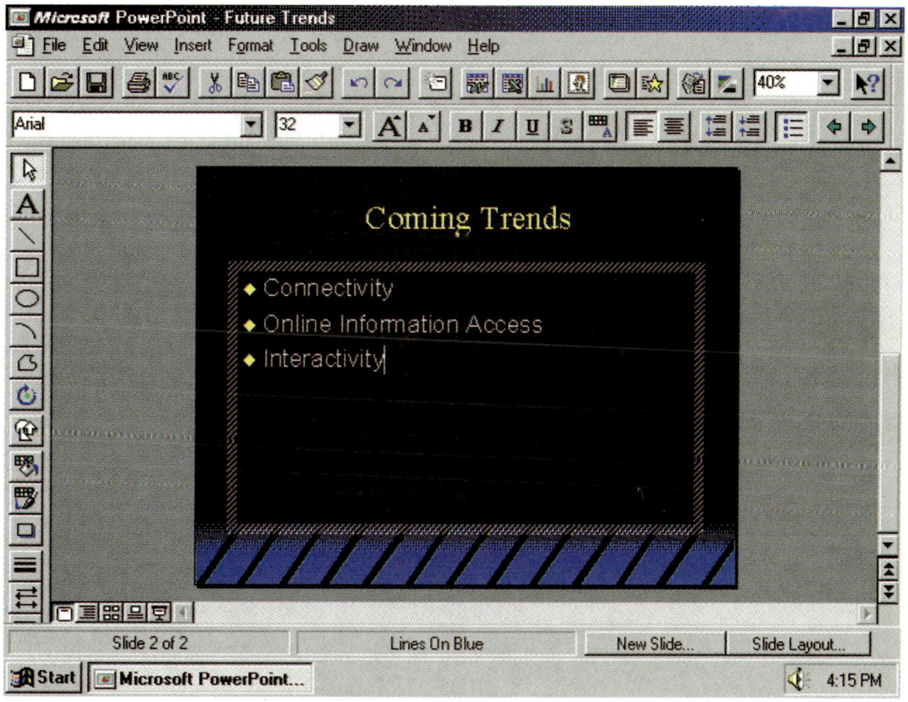

QUICK REFERENCE
Creating a Slide with Text

1. **To create a new slide:**
   CLICK: New Slide hot button, located on the Status bar
   SELECT: an AutoLayout option in the New Slide dialog box
   PRESS: ENTER or CLICK: OK
2. **CLICK: a Title or Text placeholder in the slide**
   TYPE: *the desired text content*

MANIPULATING BULLETS

In the last section, PowerPoint automatically inserted bullets in the Text placeholder when you pressed the ENTER key. In this section, you learn how to manipulate bullets on a slide to group information. People remember information better when it is "chunked" together, so try to organize your slide text hierarchically. To illustrate the effect of chunking information, consider phone numbers and how much easier they are to remember in the form 708-555-1212 as opposed to 7085551212. You can apply this same principle to your slides using hierarchical bullets.

To promote a point and move it up one level in importance, you indent it to the left using the Promote (Indent Less) button (). To demote a point and move it down one level in importance, you indent it to the right using the Demote (Indent More) button (). The Promote () and Demote () buttons appear on the Formatting toolbar. You can also use the mouse to promote and demote bullets by dragging them to the left and right. When you position the mouse pointer over the bullet (not the text), it changes into a black, four-headed arrow (✥). This informs you that you can now drag the bullet back and forth to indent it more or less.

Perform the following steps.

1. To practice promoting and demoting bullets, position the insertion point in the text area of "Online Information Access."
2. To demote this point:
   CLICK: Demote (Indent More) button () on the Formatting toolbar
   Notice that the characteristics of the text change. Not only is the text indented, but the font size has changed.
3. To return this point to its original position:
   CLICK: Promote (Indent Less) button ()
4. Let's now use the mouse to demote this point. Position the mouse pointer over the bullet for "Online Information Access" until the pointer changes to a four-headed arrow (✥).
5. DRAG: the bullet to the right until the vertical line that appears is indented one position
6. Release the mouse button.
7. Practice dragging the other bullets on the screen using the ✥ mouse pointer.
8. Before proceeding to the next section, return all bullets to their original positions.

QUICK REFERENCE
Changing the Indent Level of Bulleted Items

- **CLICK: Promote (Indent Less) button (⬅) to indent text to the left**
- **CLICK: Demote (Indent More) button (➡) to indent text to the right**
- **Use the four-headed arrow (✥) mouse pointer to promote and demote text by dragging.**

FORMATTING TEXT

In this section, you will add the remaining slides for the presentation. You will also apply some formatting to the Title placeholders that is different from the standard template formatting. Perform the following steps.

1. To add a third slide to the presentation:
   CLICK: New Slide hot button
2. Pick a layout for the new slide from the New Slide dialog box:
   SELECT: Bulleted List
   PRESS: ENTER or CLICK: OK
3. CLICK: Title placeholder
   TYPE: **CONNECTIVITY: The ability to connect computers and telephones by telecommunications lines to other devices and sources of information.**
   Notice that the text has scrolled out of view. If you look at the Formatting toolbar, you can see that the current point size is 44. (*Note:* Font sizes are measured in *points,* where a 1-inch-high letter is equal to 72 points.) In the next step, you will change the point size of the selected text from 44 to 28.
4. To select all the text in the Title placeholder:
   CHOOSE: Edit, Select All from the menu
5. CLICK: down arrow beside the *Font Size* box in the Formatting toolbar
   SELECT: 28
   The formatting is applied immediately and the text now fits in the Title placeholder box.
6. CLICK: Text placeholder
   TYPE: **Future Trends:**
   PRESS: ENTER
7. To type text at a new indent level:
   CLICK: Demote (Indent More) button (➡)
   TYPE: **Telecommuting**
   PRESS: ENTER
   TYPE: **Electronic Mail (E-Mail)**
   PRESS: ENTER
   TYPE: **Voice Mail**
   Your screen should now appear similar to Figure 2.14.

FIGURE 2.14 SLIDE 3 IN THE "FUTURE TRENDS" PRESENTATION

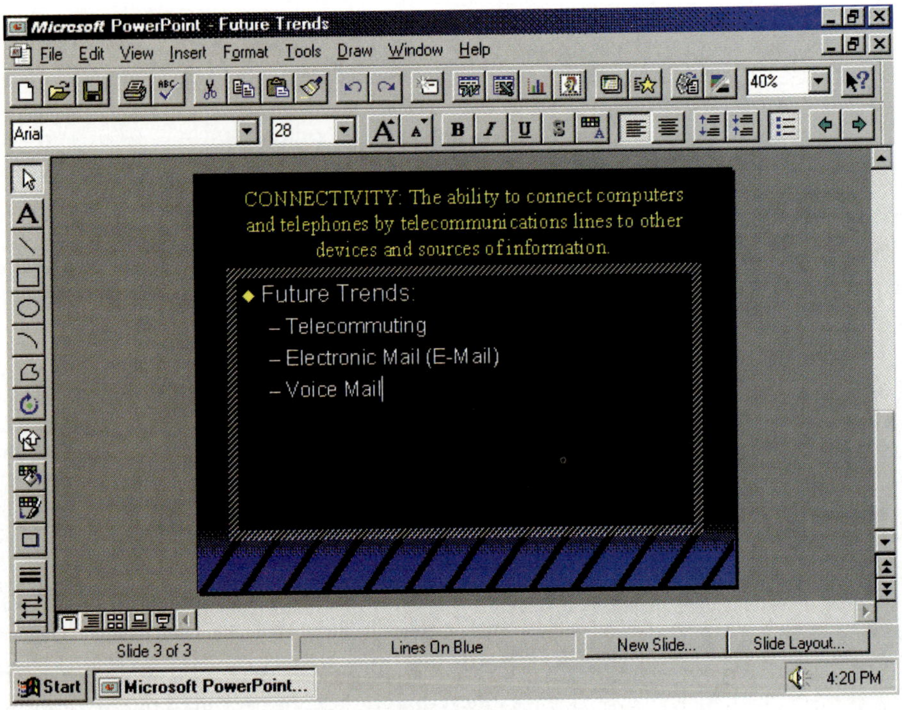

8. To add a fourth slide to the presentation:
   CLICK: New Slide hot button
9. Pick a layout for the new slide from the New Slide dialog box:
   SELECT: Bulleted List
   PRESS: ENTER or CLICK: OK
10. To select a point size of 28 for the Title placeholder prior to typing:
    CLICK: Title placeholder
    CLICK: down arrow beside the *Font Size* box
    SELECT: 28
11. TYPE: **ONLINE INFORMATION ACCESS: The ability to connect to services beyond your desktop via modem or network to other computers.**
12. CLICK: Text placeholder
    TYPE: **Future Trends:**
    PRESS: ENTER

13. To type text at a new indent level:
    CLICK: Demote (Indent More) button (➡)
    TYPE: **Database Access**
    PRESS: ENTER
    TYPE: **Computer Online Services and Networks**
    PRESS: ENTER
    TYPE: **Electronic Bulletin Board Systems (BBS)**
    Your screen should now appear similar to Figure 2.15.

FIGURE 2.15 SLIDE 4 IN THE "FUTURE TRENDS" PRESENTATION

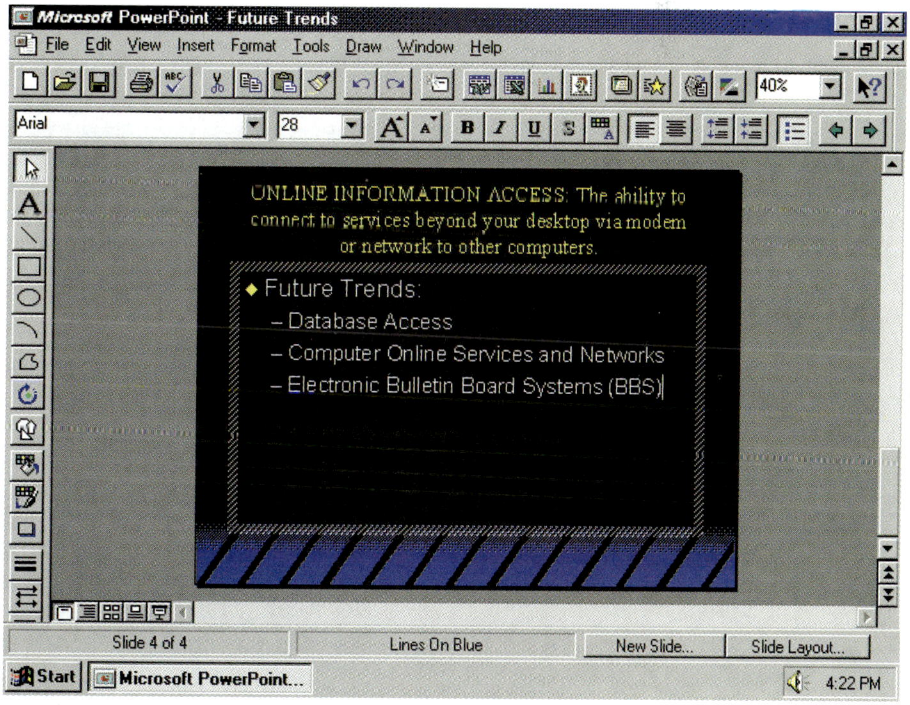

14. To add a fifth slide to the presentation:
    CLICK: New Slide hot button
15. Pick a layout for the new slide from the New Slide dialog box:
    SELECT: Bulleted List
    PRESS: ENTER or CLICK: OK
16. CLICK: Title placeholder
    CLICK: down arrow beside the *Font Size* box
    SELECT: 28
17. TYPE: **INTERACTIVITY: A dialog exists between the user and the computer or communications device.**

18. CLICK: Text placeholder
    TYPE: **Future Trends:**
    PRESS: ENTER

19. To type text at a new indent level:
    CLICK: Demote (Indent More) button (➡)
    TYPE: **Multimedia Computers**
    PRESS: ENTER
    TYPE: **TV/PC "Smart Boxes" and Set-Top Boxes**
    PRESS: ENTER
    TYPE: **Personal Digital Assistants (PDAs)**
    Your screen should now appear similar to Figure 2.16.

FIGURE 2.16 SLIDE 5 IN THE "FUTURE TRENDS" PRESENTATION

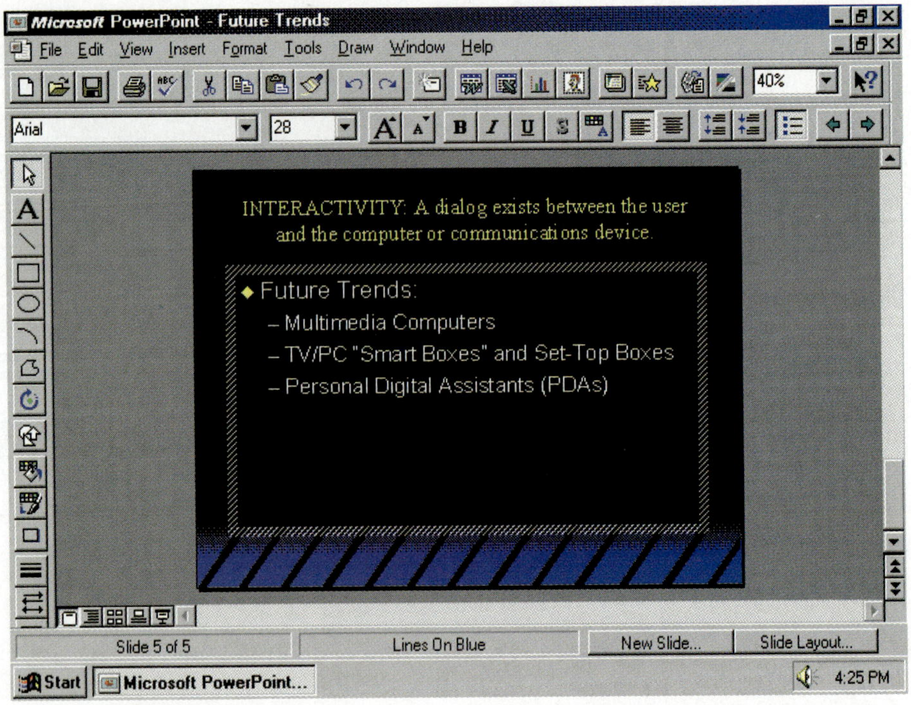

20. To save the presentation:
    CLICK: Save button (💾)

To modify the content of slides you've already created, use the elevator scroll box on the vertical scroll bar (or the double arrows, ⯯ and ⯭, appearing at the bottom of the scroll bar) to move through the presentation. You will practice using the elevator scroll box and arrows later in this session.

REVIEWING YOUR PRESENTATION

To view a presentation as it will appear in its completed form, you use the Slide Show view. To access the Slide Show view, choose View, Slide Show from the Menu bar or click the Slide Show view button (▣). The presentation fills the entire screen with the current slide, that is, the slide that appears in the presentation window. To view a slide show from the beginning, you must remember to first drag the elevator scroll box to the top of the vertical scroll bar. After you view the last slide in your presentation, the presentation window reappears.

Perform the following steps to view the "Future Trends" presentation.

1. DRAG: the elevator scroll box to the top of the vertical scroll bar
   Notice that, as you drag the scroll box, the current slide number and title appear in the presentation window.
2. CLICK: Slide Show view button (▣)
   The first slide fills the entire screen.
3. To display the next slide:
   CLICK: left mouse button
4. To display the previous slide:
   PRESS: ↑
5. Continue by clicking the left mouse button to view the entire presentation. When finished, you are returned to the presentation window where you left off.

Now, let's add some pizzazz to this presentation by inserting some graphics to the slides!

EDITING A PRESENTATION

When installing PowerPoint, you have the option of installing the **ClipArt Gallery,** a collection of hundreds of images from which you can select to include in your presentations. If you choose AutoClipArt from the Tools menu, PowerPoint will analyze the words in your presentation and provide suggestions on which ClipArt images to use. In this section, you will edit slide 3 of the "Future Trends" presentation to include a picture from the ClipArt Gallery (Figure 2.17). You will then resize and move the inserted picture so that it is proportional to the text on the slide.

FIGURE 2.17. SLIDE 3 WITH THE INSERTED CLIP ART

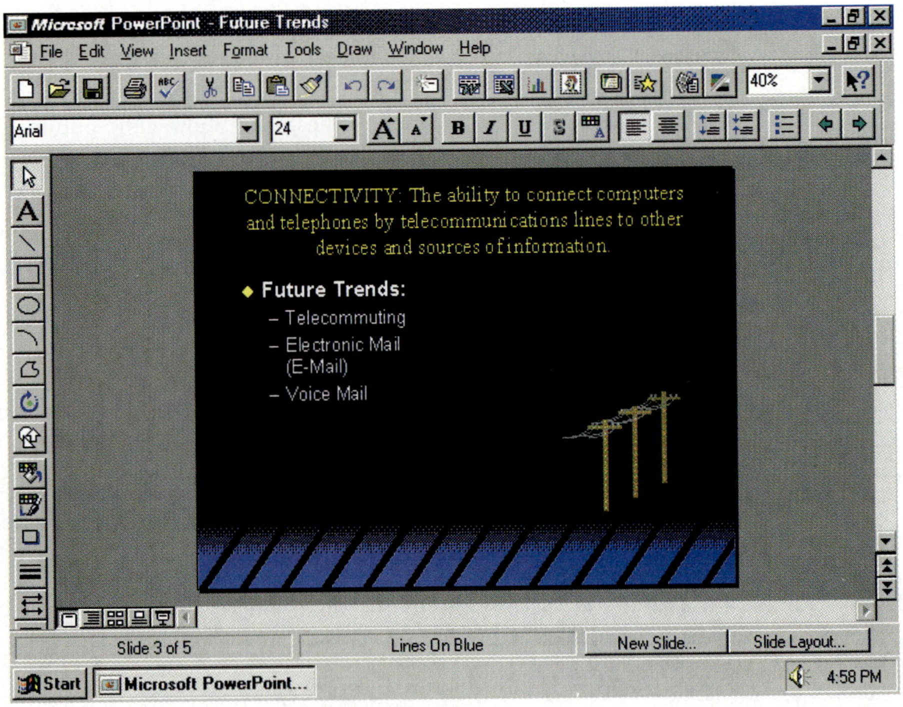

CHANGING THE LAYOUT OF A SLIDE

The easiest way to add clip art or a graphic to an existing slide is to select a new AutoLayout for the slide. First, you make the desired slide active by displaying it in the presentation window. Second, you choose the Format, Slide Layout command or click the Slide Layout hot button on the Status bar. When the Slide Layout dialog box appears, you select a new AutoLayout with a clip art or graphic Object placeholder and then press **ENTER** or click the Apply command button.

Perform the following steps.

1. Ensure that the "Future Trends" presentation appears in the presentation window.
2. To move to slide 3 in the "Future Trends" presentation:
   DRAG: the elevator scroll box to display slide 3
   Remember that you can also click the Next Slide (⏬) and Previous Slide (⏫) buttons on the vertical scroll bar to move through a presentation one slide at a time.

3. To modify the slide's layout to accommodate a ClipArt image:
   CLICK: Slide Layout hot button on the Status bar
   SELECT: Text & Clip Art as the AutoLayout option
   PRESS: ENTER or CLICK: Apply
   Your screen should appear similar to Figure 2.18.

FIGURE 2.18 APPLYING THE TEXT & CLIP ART AUTOLAYOUT TO SLIDE 3 OF THE "FUTURE TRENDS" PRESENTATION

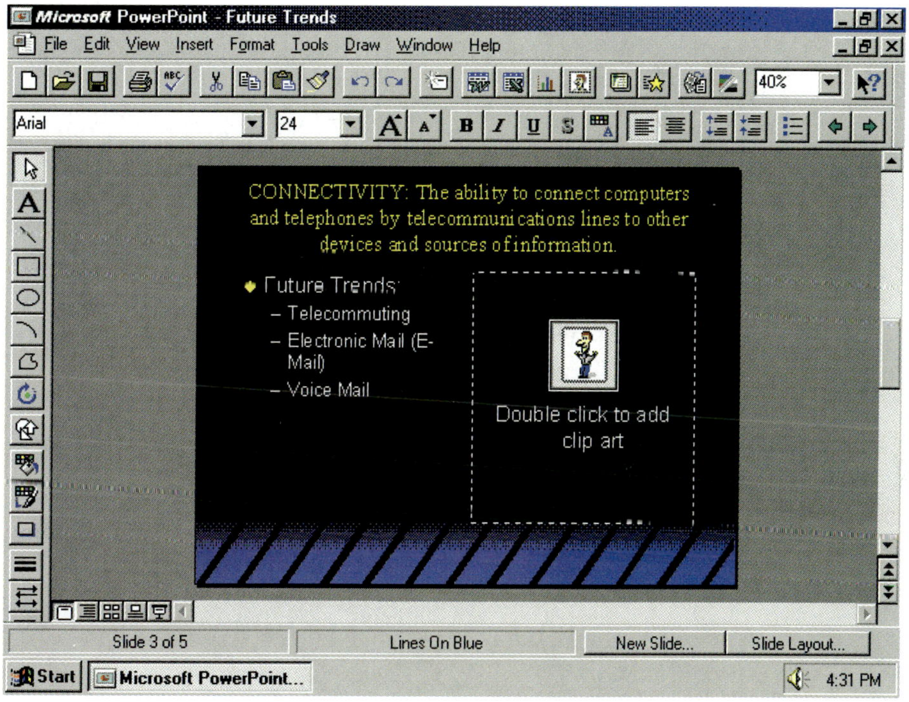

4. Notice that the "Mail" portion of "E-Mail" has wrapped down to the next line. It would look much cleaner if "E-Mail" appeared in its entirety on the next line. Position the insertion point to the left of the open parenthesis for "E-Mail" and then do the following:
   PRESS: SHIFT + ENTER
   Notice that SHIFT + ENTER moves the "(E-Mail)" text to the next line, while keeping it part of the Electronic Mail bullet. If you pressed ENTER instead, PowerPoint would assume that you wanted to make the text "E-Mail" into a new bullet point on the slide.

5. To apply boldface to the text "Future Trends:," first select the text by positioning the I-beam mouse pointer to the left of the text and dragging the mouse to the right.

6. To bold the selected text:
   CLICK: Bold button (B) in the Formatting toolbar

QUICK REFERENCE
Changing the Layout of an Existing Slide

1. **Make the slide that you want to modify active by displaying it in the presentation window.**
2. **CLICK: Slide Layout hot button on the Status bar**
3. **SELECT: a new layout from the Slide Layout dialog box**
4. **PRESS: ENTER or CLICK: Apply**

INSERTING CLIP ART

In this section, you add a picture from the ClipArt Gallery to slide 3 of the "Future Trends" presentation. You will then resize and reposition the art to fit nicely on the slide. Perform the following steps.

1. To add clip art to the slide:
   DOUBLE-CLICK: ClipArt placeholder
   (*Remember:* You double-click Object placeholders to modify their content.) The ClipArt Gallery window appears (Figure 2.19). If this is the first time that you've used the ClipArt Gallery, it must first gather and categorize the images before you see the dialog box appearing in Figure 2.19. This is a one-time process only. (*Note:* If you do not have the ClipArt Gallery installed on your computer, contact your instructor or refer to the Microsoft PowerPoint User's Guide for further assistance.)

FIGURE 2.19 THE CLIPART GALLERY

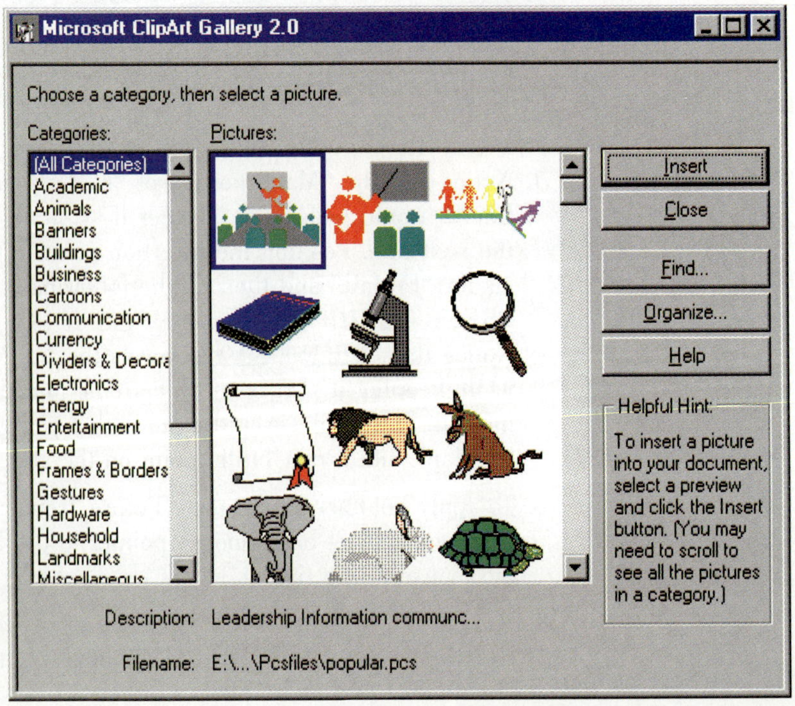

2. Let's select a picture from the Communication category:
   SELECT: Communication from the *Categories* list box
   SELECT: Telephone Lines picture from the *Pictures* list box (also called the "Information Communication" picture)
   PRESS: **ENTER** or CLICK: Insert to add the picture to the slide
   Your screen should now appear similar to Figure 2.20.

FIGURE 2.20 ADDING THE TELEPHONE LINES CLIP ART PICTURE TO SLIDE 3

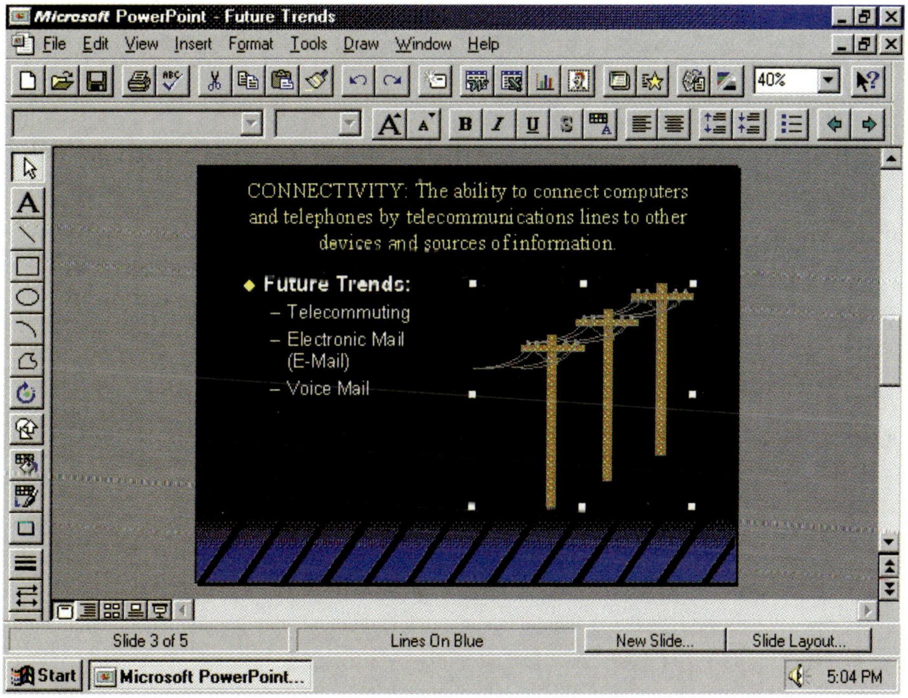

3. Compared to the text, the Telephone Lines picture is disproportionately large. To resize the picture, you select it by clicking once on the object and then you drag its handles (small boxes that appear around the object). You use the corner handles to size an object larger or smaller, but maintain its relative proportions. To move the picture, you position the mouse pointer in the center of the object and drag it on the slide.

   Let's try sizing and moving the Telephone Lines picture.
   DRAG: the handle in the bottom right-hand corner towards the center of the box to make the picture smaller
   DRAG: the center of the object to move the picture on the slide

4. Practice sizing and moving the picture to make it appear as similar to Figure 2.17 as possible.

5. To save your editing changes:
   CLICK: Save button ()

QUICK REFERENCE
Inserting ClipArt

1. **SELECT: an AutoLayout option with a ClipArt placeholder**
2. **DOUBLE-CLICK: ClipArt placeholder**
3. **SELECT: any picture from the ClipArt Gallery**
4. **PRESS: ENTER or CLICK: OK**

QUICK REFERENCE
Resizing and Moving ClipArt

1. **SELECT: ClipArt object by clicking the mouse pointer once over the object (handles appear around the picture when properly selected)**
2. **DRAG: a handle on the object to size the picture, or**
   DRAG: the center of the object to move the picture

USING THE STYLE CHECKER

Before you print a presentation, get an impartial review of it using PowerPoint's **Style Checker.** The Style Checker studies your presentation for spelling errors, visual clarity, and the proper use of punctuation. You respond to the Style Checker's suggestions by clicking the Change or Ignore buttons. Figure 2.21 shows the Style Checker dialog box. The Options command button enables you to further customize what the Style Checker checks for in order to match your company's particular style. For example, let's say that you always want your presentations to use a 32 point size for the text on a Title slide, no more than two fonts or five bullets on any given slide, and all bulleted text to end without a period. You can establish each of these style rules, as well as many others, using the Options button.

FIGURE 2.21 THE STYLE CHECKER DIALOG BOX

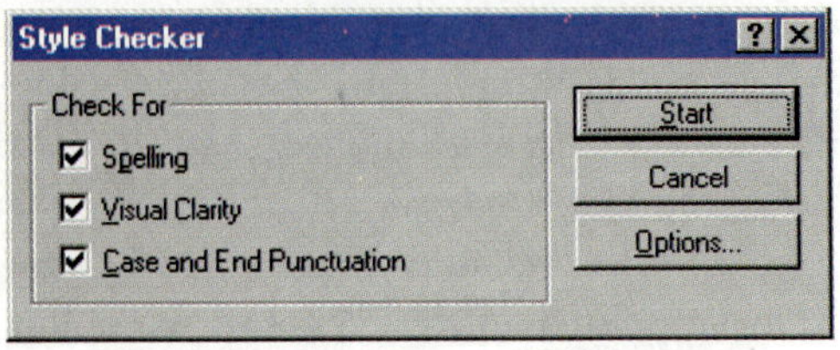

In the following section, you use the Style Checker to review the "Future Trends" presentation. Perform the following steps.

1. Ensure that slide 1 of the "Future Trends" presentation appears in the presentation window.
2. To activate the Style Checker:
   CHOOSE: Tools, Style Checker

3. Before starting the Style Checker, let's look at some of the options that are available to you. Do the following:
   CLICK: Options command button
   SELECT: Case and End Punctuation tab and review the options
   SELECT: Visual Clarity tab and review the options
   Figure 2.22 shows the contents of the two tabs.

FIGURE 2.22 STYLE CHECKER DIALOG BOX: OPTIONS

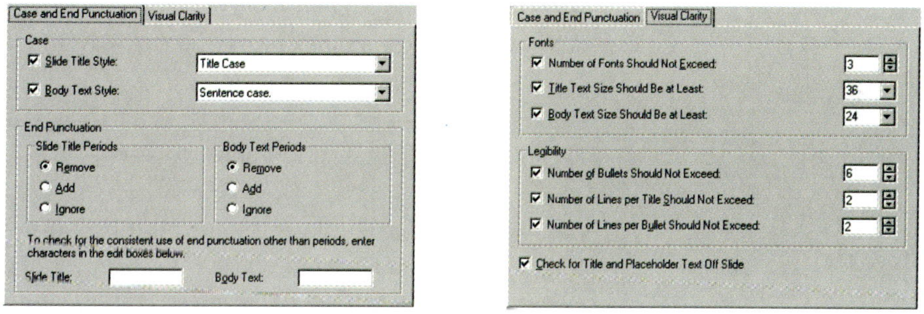

4. To return to the Style Checker dialog box and start the process:
   CLICK: Cancel button
   CLICK: Start button
5. Proceed by clicking the Ignore button to bypass all spelling suggestions and style inconsistency remarks.
6. The Style Checker concludes by displaying the Style Checker Summary dialog box (Figure 2.23). After reviewing its comments:
   PRESS: **ENTER** or CLICK: OK

FIGURE 2.23 STYLE CHECKER SUMMARY DIALOG BOX

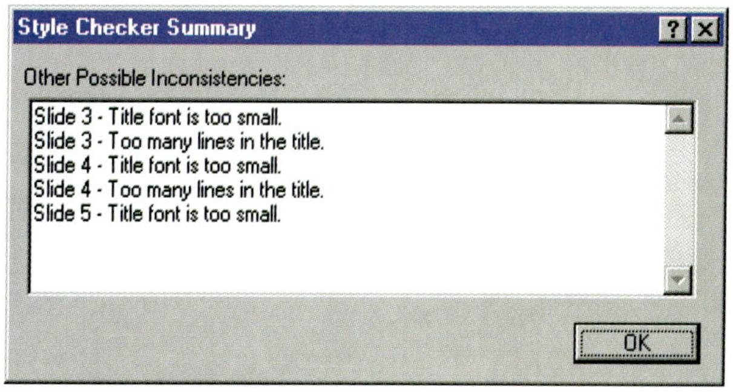

QUICK REFERENCE
Using the Style Checker

1. **CHOOSE: Tools, Style Checker**
2. **Use the Options button to customize style settings, as desired.**
3. **Respond to the Style Checker's suggestions by clicking the Ignore or Change buttons.**

PRINTING A PRESENTATION

Now that you've created a presentation, this section explains how to send it to the printer. This section provides only a brief glimpse at the tools available.

The quickest method for sending a presentation to the printer is to click the Print button ( ) on the Standard toolbar. When you click this button, no dialog boxes appear asking you to confirm your choice, so ensure that the printer is online and has sufficient paper. You can also use the File, Print command to print a document, which causes the Print dialog box to display (Figure 2.24). After making selections, you press ENTER or click OK to proceed.

FIGURE 2.24 PRINT DIALOG BOX

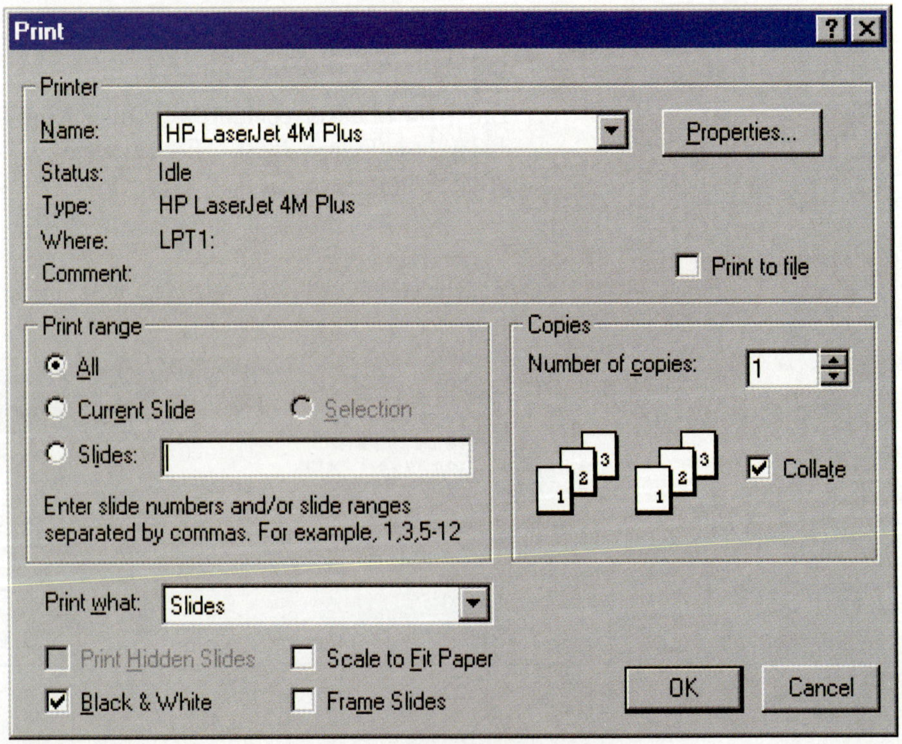

Perform the following steps.

1. To print the "Future Trends" presentation:
   CHOOSE: File, Print
   The Print dialog box appears. (*Note:* You can also press the CTRL+p shortcut key to display the Print dialog box.)
2. At this point, PowerPoint assumes that you want to print the slides in the current presentation window. To see the other options:
   CLICK: down arrow beside the *Print what* drop-down list box
3. To print all of the slides in the presentation:
   SELECT: Slides (the default selection)
   PRESS: ENTER or CLICK: OK
4. Close the presentation window and exit PowerPoint. (*Note:* Do not save the changes to the presentation file.)

QUICK REFERENCE
Printing a Presentation

1. **CHOOSE: File, Print from the menu**
2. **SELECT: what you want to print in the *Print what* drop-down list box**
3. **PRESS: ENTER or CLICK: OK**

SUMMARY

This session introduced you to the fundamentals of creating a presentation. You used one of PowerPoint's intelligent helpers, the AutoContent Wizard, to assist you in structuring and designing your presentation. You then created another presentation by picking a design template and added slides to the presentation by clicking the New Slide button on the Status bar. This session also introduced you to saving, viewing, and editing a slide presentation. You manipulated text, bullets, and formatting options on a slide, in addition to changing its layout and adding clip art. Finally, you performed a style check on a presentation and learned how to print a slide presentation.

COMMAND SUMMARY

Many of the commands and procedures appearing in this session are provided in Table 2.1 below.

TABLE 2.1

Command Summary

Task Description	*Menu Command*	*Alternative Methods*
Create a new presentation	File, New	[New button]
Save a presentation to the disk	File, Save	[Save button]
Save a presentation to a new location or to a different name	File, Save As	
Select all the text in a placeholder	Edit, Select All	CTRL + a
Change the layout of a slide	Format, Slide Layout	New Slide hot button
Use the Style Checker	Tools, Style Checker	
Print a presentation	File, Print	[Print button]

KEY TERMS

AutoContent Wizard
A PowerPoint tool that leads you through creating the structure for your presentation.

AutoLayout
In PowerPoint, a slide format with text and graphic placeholders. You select an AutoLayout for a head start when adding a new slide to a presentation.

build slides
In PowerPoint, a slide in which the bullet points are displayed one at a time.

ClipArt Gallery
A collection of hundreds of professionally designed images that you can include in your presentations.

default presentation format
The design template that is in effect when you start by choosing the Blank Presentation option.

design template
A design template is a presentation whose background, color scheme, typefaces, and other formatting options can be applied to another presentation.

masters

The slide, outline, and notes page templates that determine how the standard slides, outlines, and notes pages are formatted and will appear in a presentation. Any visuals that you include on a master will print on every page in the presentation.

placeholders

In PowerPoint, slide locations where you enter titles, sub-titles, main text, clip art, graphs, and organizational charts.

presentation template

A presentation template is a presentation whose subject outline can be applied to another presentation.

Style Checker

Using this PowerPoint tool, you can review your presentation for spelling errors, clarity of visual style, and use of punctuation.

transition

In PowerPoint, an effect used in computer-based presentations to dissolve or wipe one slide from the screen before the next appears.

EXERCISES

SHORT ANSWER

1. What are the basic steps for creating a presentation?
2. What is the AutoContent Wizard?
3. What is the purpose of the Style Checker?
4. How do you insert a new slide in a presentation?
5. What is the ClipArt Gallery?
6. What is the procedure for printing a presentation using the menu?
7. How do you change a slide's AutoLayout?
8. How do you manipulate bullet levels on a slide?
9. When creating slides, what is the significance of a placeholder?
10. When would you want to use the File, Save As command rather than the File, Save command?

HANDS-ON

(*Note:* Before working through the following exercises, make sure the Advantage Diskette is in drive A: or drive B:.)

1. Perform the following steps to create a three-slide presentation named "Using Color." The objective of your presentation is to describe some guidelines for using color in on-screen presentations.

   a. Load Microsoft PowerPoint.

   b. Create a new on-screen presentation using a design template.
   CHOOSE: File, New
   SELECT: Presentation Designs tab

   c. Select the International template design.

   d. Select the Title Slide AutoLayout from the New Slide dialog box.

   e. The title of your presentation is:
   Using Color Wisely

   f. The sub-title of your presentation is:
   by
   your name

   g. Add a second slide to the presentation, based on the Bulleted List layout, with the following information.

   Title: **Keep It Simple**
   Bullet 1: **Choose colors properly to make powerful statements**
   Bullet 2: **Too many colors or unnecessary colors can dilute the effect**

   h. Add a third slide to the presentation, based on the Bulleted List layout, with the following information.

   Title: **Know the Form of Output**
   Bullet 1: **For 35mm slides, pick dark backgrounds**
   Bullet 2: **For overhead transparencies, pick light backgrounds**

   i. Display the presentation using Slide Show view.

   j. Return to the Slide view.

   k. Save the presentation as "Using Color" onto the Advantage Diskette.

2. In this exercise, you edit slide 3 of the "Using Color" presentation that you created in the last exercise to look like Figure 2.25. Make sure to do the following:

   a. Change the layout of slide 3 to the Text & ClipArt layout.

   b. Add the picture appearing in Figure 2.25 (located in the Academic category of the Microsoft ClipArt Gallery).

FIGURE 2.25 SLIDE 3 OF THE "USING COLOR" PRESENTATION

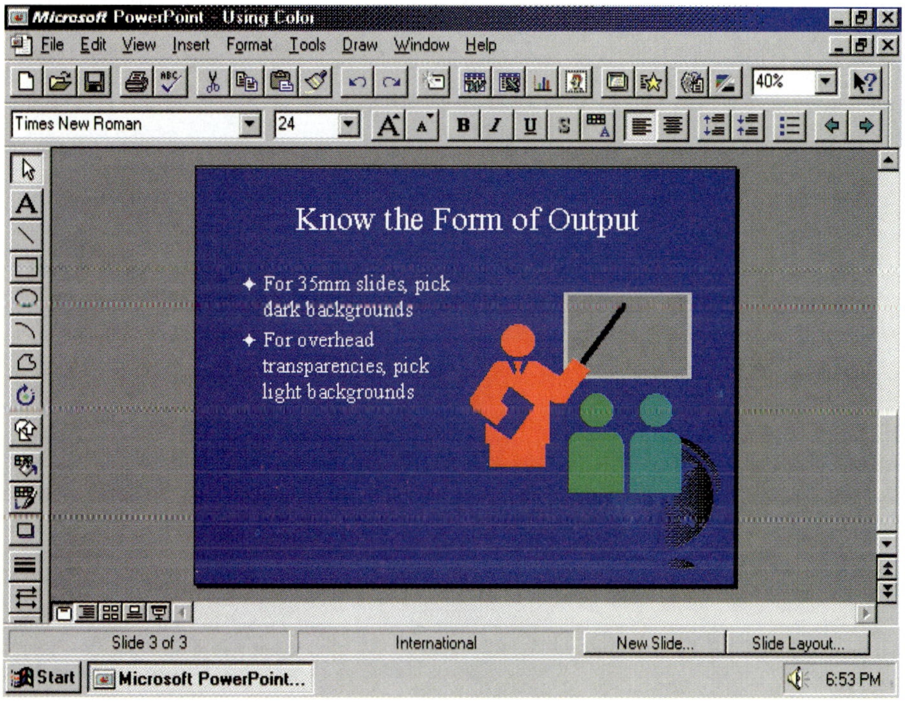

   c. Display the presentation using Slide Show view.

   d. Return to Slide view.

   e. Print the entire presentation.

   f. Save the "Using Color" presentation back to the Advantage Diskette.

   g. Close the presentation.

3. Create a presentation for the five slides shown in Figure 2.26. Save the presentation to the Advantage Diskette as "Advertising."

FIGURE 2.26 SLIDES 1, 2, 3, 4, 5

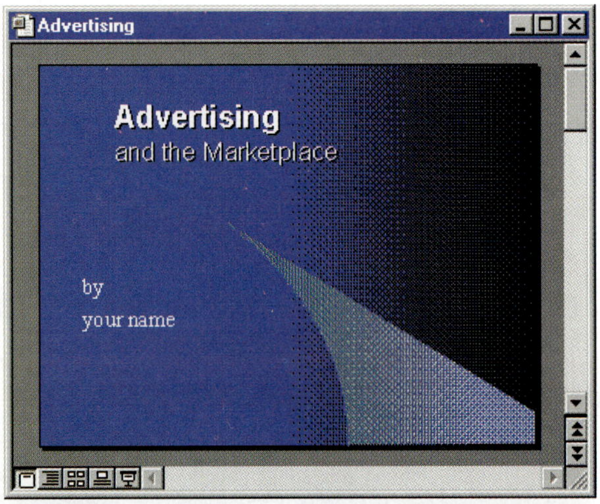

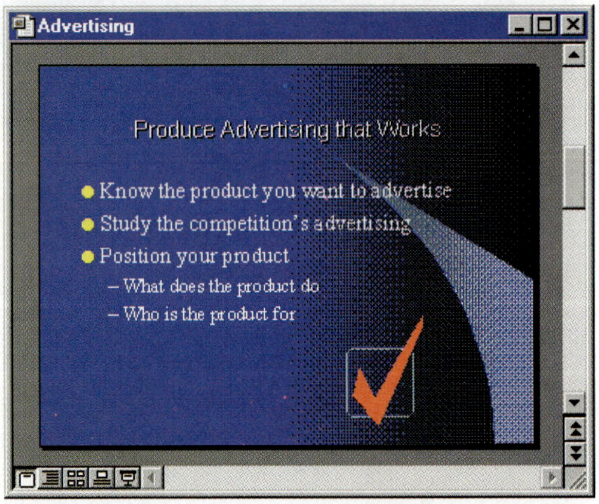

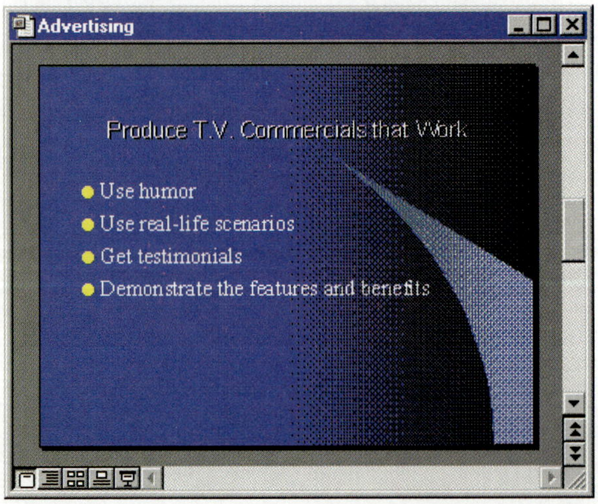

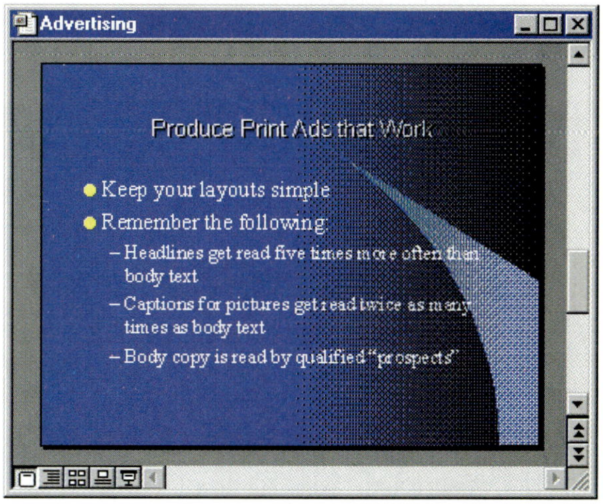

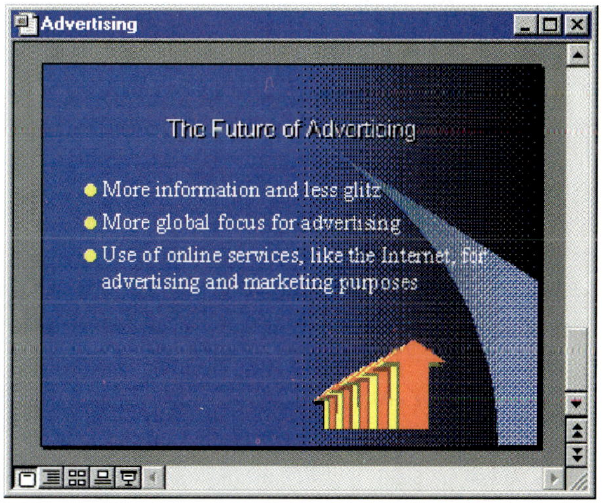

4. Create a presentation on a topic you're interested in (e.g., hiking, traveling, or reading). Include between five and eight slides and at least one clip art picture. Save the presentation as "Session 2 Exercise" on the Advantage Diskette.

CASE PROBLEMS

BERKFORD COLLEGE, PENNSYLVANIA

(*Note:* In the following case problems, assume the role of the primary character or characters and perform the same steps that they identify.)

1. Sharon Rheingold is on a mission. After several evenings of study at the campus computer lab, she is now comfortable using Microsoft PowerPoint to create simple presentations. Fortunately, her roommate Walt had time to show her the AutoContent Wizard and how to use design templates. With the start of classes only a few days away, Sharon is ready to put her first lecture together using PowerPoint.

   Her schedule being quite tight this past week, Sharon was only able to jot down rough notes for her outline:

   Course Title: Public Speaking 101
   Instructor: Sharon Rheingold

   Lecture 1: An Introduction to Public Speaking

   Five Cs for Excellence in Public Speaking
   - *Confident*
   - *Competent*
   - *Credible*
   - *Convincing*
   - *Comfortable*

   Reasons for Experiencing Stage Fright
   - *Fear of failure*
   - *Lack of confidence*
   - *Lack of preparation*
   - *Lack of knowledge about topic*
   - *Lack of knowledge about audience*

   Methods for Overcoming Stage Fright
   - *Be positive*
   - *Practice often*
   - *Prepare thoroughly*
   - *Research your topic*
   - *Research your audience*

   Now Sharon has to enter these notes into PowerPoint in order to create color overhead transparencies. Since her content is fairly well organized, she decides to use one of PowerPoint's presentation design templates. In addition to an opening slide introducing the course and herself, Sharon calculates that the presentation only requires one outline slide for the lecture and three content slides for each of her main discussion topics. At the last minute, she decides to add a closing slide that thanks the students for attending the presentation and wishes them luck for the coming semester. Sharon saves the presentation as "Public Speaking 101" and prints the six slides for review.

2. An experienced public speaker herself, Sharon knows the importance of practicing her presentation before she has to deliver it in front of an audience. She uses PowerPoint's Slide Show view to go through the "Public Speaking 101" presentation and then reviews it again in the Slide Sorter view. "Almost there!" she thinks to herself.

   Although she feels comfortable with the presentation, Sharon notices that the lecture may be too short and decides to add one more slide to the presentation. Using Slide view, she displays the last content slide entitled "Methods for Overcoming Stage Fright" and then clicks the New Slide button on the Status bar. She adds a slide with the following content and then revises her outline slide at the beginning of the presentation.

   Types of Presentations
   - *Technical (for technical specifications)*
   - *Instructional (for communicating a process)*
   - *Illustrative (with anecdotal stories)*
   - *Demonstrative (with live demonstration)*
   - *Discussion (for informal group meetings)*

   Again, Sharon practices the presentation using the Slide view and then saves it and prints it out on the laser printer for Walt to review.

3. Walt returned late from his part-time job after three hours of overtime and was not in the best of moods to review Sharon's presentation. "Why is there so much text here?" exclaimed Walt, rubbing his eyes and trying to focus on the pages Sharon had handed to him. "Can't you put a couple of pictures in this thing to liven it up a little?" Walt walked slowly across the living room and then looked up, "You should have used the ClipArt Gallery to add some pictures. I know—there's one picture in there of a person standing at a podium. You can use that one for this 'Five Cs' slide. And for the last slide, don't just say 'Thank You'—insert a fun graphic to let them know that they're in the best public speaking section on campus!"

   Sharon thought about Walt's comments and took each to heart. She would add some pictures to her presentation using the ClipArt Gallery, perform one more practice run, and then print out the final presentation for her students.

   Save Sharon's presentation as "Public Speaking 101" onto the Advantage Diskette.

4. During morning coffee, Dr. Tomas Ritchie, the law faculty's premier authority on Canadian business law, listened intently to Dr. Antoski's enthusiastic recount of Sharon Rheingold's first class. Since Tomas had known Sharon for two years now, he was not surprised at Kirsten's glowing report of his star pupil. However, he was quite surprised that Sharon was a skilled computer user and could prepare such high-quality materials. He would definitely keep this fact in mind for future projects!

Two weeks later, Dr. Ritchie approached Sharon to ask her help in preparing a lecture he was conducting for the American Business Association. The presentation, "Understanding Canadian Business Law," was to be delivered the next day at the association's annual general meeting. The original speaker had canceled at the last moment due to a family emergency, and Dr. Ritchie was contacted as her replacement. Fortunately, the original speaker had already arranged the equipment and room for a computer-based presentation. The only item Dr. Ritchie was missing was the presentation!

Dr. Ritchie showed Sharon a quick outline and asked her to prepare a "computerized slide show." He didn't have any details for content and would most likely have to "wing it" at the podium. However, he wanted her to produce an introductory slide with his name and the name of the presentation, along with a separate slide for each topic he was going to discuss. The topics included:

The Law of Torts in Canada
- *The tort concept*
- *Elements of a tort*
- *Burden of proof*
- *Professional liability*

Types of Contracts
- *Contract of sale*
- *Contract of employment*

Formation of a Contract
- *Offer and acceptance*
- *Consideration*
- *Intention to enter into a contract*
- *Capacity to contract*
- *Requirement of writing*

Effects of and Remedies for a Breach of Contract
- *What is a breach?*
- *Express repudiation*
- *Damages*
- *Quantum meruit*

Forms of Business Organization
- *Sole proprietorship*
- *Partnership*
- *Corporation*

Knowing that Dr. Ritchie would be a great ally in coming years, Sharon wanted to do everything she could to impress her advisor. She created and printed the presentation in less than an hour, handing it to him just as he was about to leave for home. Sharon would have to remember to thank Walt for introducing her to Microsoft PowerPoint!

Save this presentation as "Canadian Law" onto the Advantage Diskette.

Microsoft PowerPoint 7.0 for Windows 95

Designing a Presentation

SESSION OUTLINE

Applying Templates
Using the Slide Master
The Importance of Color
Viewing Slides in Black and White
Working More with Text
Summary
Key Terms
Exercises

INTRODUCTION

In this session, you learn to use some of PowerPoint's more productive features, including methods that help you take control of your presentations. You soon discover that when it comes to designing a presentation in PowerPoint, you have endless options at your fingertips. Rather than show you every design and productivity feature, this session concentrates on the most commonly used tools.

CASE STUDY H2 UNDERSCAPING LTD.

In 1989 Chip Yee started H2 UnderScaping Ltd. (H2U), a landscaping operation that sells and installs underground sprinkler systems. Since that time, H2U has grown from annual sales of $30,000 to its current year's projection of over $700,000. Now that his employees perform most of the administrative duties and manual labor, Chip has more time on his hands to get involved in the community.

Chip is an active member in both the local Chamber of Commerce and the Downtown Business Association. The Chamber's president, Mrs. Vi Krieg, recently approached Chip to act as spokesperson at this year's Business Show. Specifically, Vi asked Chip to prepare an electronic presentation for the evening banquet and emphasized that there would be representatives from neighboring Chambers in the audience. Obviously the president wanted to impress her peers with their group's professionalism and technical proficiency!

Fortunately, Chip is familiar with Microsoft Office and has become quite good at using Microsoft Word. Although he has created only one or two simple presentations in PowerPoint, Chip finds the programs in Microsoft Office work alike in many ways, making them easy to learn and use. But this presentation would be challenging. In addition to creating a content-rich presentation, Chip will have to pull off an Oscar-winning performance to satisfy Mrs. Krieg.

In this session, you and Chip learn some features for making your PowerPoint presentations stand out from the crowd. Rather than relying on PowerPoint's stock designs, you learn to enhance the design templates, edit the Slide Master, and utilize color. In addition, you customize bullets, manipulate text in Outline view, and learn to position text anywhere on a slide. Good luck to you both!

APPLYING TEMPLATES

Using templates is like having the fastest graphics design specialist as part of your staff. Fortunately for you, PowerPoint's graphic design specialist knows over 100 different designs and lets you apply any one of them to your presentations. Just think of the time savings—after typing the content for a presentation in Outline view, you simply pick and choose from multiple design templates to finalize the look and feel of your presentation for a particular audience. You could even deliver the same presentation to two different groups using two different design templates.

If you can remember back to Session 2, you chose a design template named "Lines on Blue." This template displayed diagonal blue bars along the bottom border and all slide titles appeared in yellow. All of PowerPoint's templates, including the Lines on Blue template, are stored in separate files on the hard disk. Actually, a template is defined as any presentation whose design and format specifications you want to apply to another presentation.

Not only can you pick from the templates provided by PowerPoint, any presentation you create can serve as a template for another presentation. The advantage of using PowerPoint's templates is that they were all created by professional artists and presentation designers. To apply a template, choose Format, Apply Design Template from the menu. In the Presentation Template dialog box that appears, you select the desired template and then click the Apply command button.

Perform the following steps to apply a different template to the "Future Trends" presentation you created in Session 2.

1. Make sure that you've loaded Microsoft PowerPoint and that the Advantage Diskette is inserted into drive A: or drive B:.
2. Open the "Future Trends" presentation stored on the Advantage Diskette. (*CAUTION:* You will not be able to perform the exercises in this session if you have not completed Session 2!)
3. The first slide of the "Future Trends" presentation should appear in the presentation window. To select a new template for the presentation:
   CHOOSE: Format, Apply Design Template
   The Apply Design Template dialog box appears, as shown in Figure 3.1.

FIGURE 3.1 APPLY DESIGN TEMPLATE DIALOG BOX

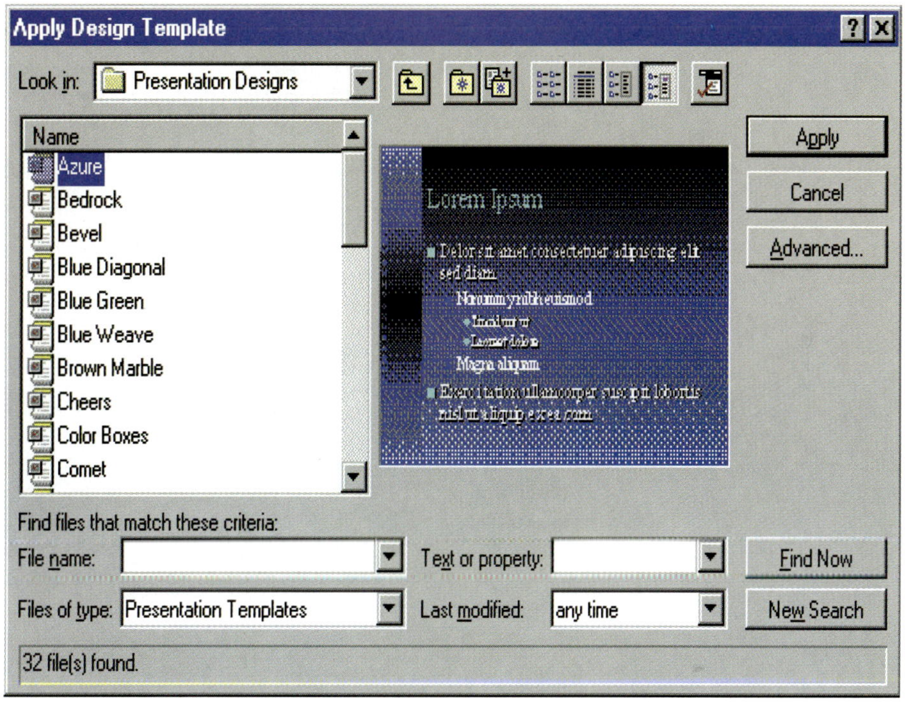

4. The templates are listed in alphabetical order. Using the mouse, click on several templates in the *Name* list box. You will notice that a representation of the selected template appears in the Preview area. Before proceeding to the next step:
   SELECT: Sparkle from the *Name* list box
   PRESS: **ENTER** or CLICK: Apply
   After a few seconds, the new template will be applied to every slide in your presentation. When finished, your screen should appear similar to Figure 3.2. (*CAUTION:* Once you've applied a template to a presentation, it can't be undone! To change the template design, you must apply a different template.)

FIGURE 3.2 THE "FUTURE TRENDS" PRESENTATION USING THE SPARKLE TEMPLATE

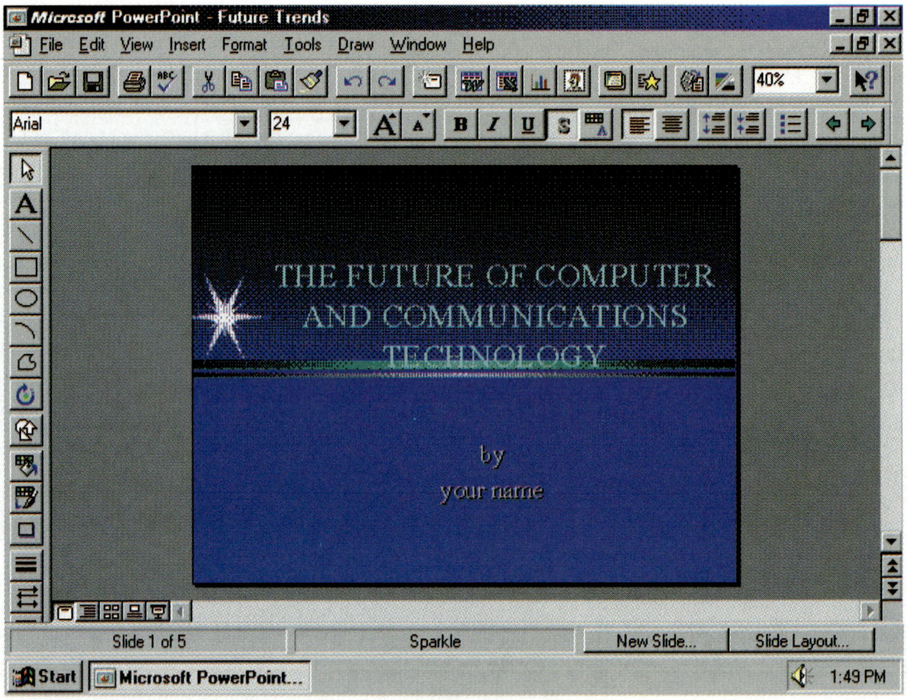

5. To get a better feel for how the template actually looks:
   CLICK: Slide Show view button ()
   CLICK: left mouse button repeatedly, until you've run through the entire presentation
6. After being returned from Slide Show view to Slide view in the presentation window, save the presentation with the new template:
   CLICK: Save button ()

QUICK REFERENCE
Applying a New Template to an Existing Presentation

1. **Open the desired presentation and switch to Slide view.**
2. **CHOOSE: Format, Apply Design Template**
3. **SELECT: a template from the Apply Design Template dialog box**
4. **PRESS: ENTER or CLICK: Apply**

USING THE SLIDE MASTER

PowerPoint provides a master page for each element of your presentation: slides, handouts, and notes pages. Any text, graphic, or other object that you place on a master page appears on every page of that type in the presentation. For example, you can place your company's logo on the Audience Handout Master so that it prints out on every handout page automatically. In this section, you edit the **Title Master** and **Slide Master** to customize your presentation.

As with all masters, the Title and Slide Masters are part of every presentation you create. Any text or background objects appearing on the Title Master will appear on any Title slides that you've included in your presentation. Any text or objects appearing on the Slide Master will appear on all slides except Title slides. These two masters hold the formatting specifications for the Title and Text placeholders and color schemes of your presentation. If, for example, you italicize the title of the Slide Master, all titles in your presentation, except for those on Title slides, will be italicized. Used properly, masters can provide you with a huge productivity boost when creating or modifying presentations.

EDITING THE SLIDE MASTER

To help you imagine the contents of an actual slide, PowerPoint inserts Title and Text placeholders on the Title and Slide Masters. However, you do not type text into the placeholders—they are there only to show you the formatting specifications. If you want text to appear on every slide in your presentation, you must use the Text tool on the Drawing toolbar, described later in this session.

You will now change the appearance of all the titles in your presentation by editing the Title Master and Slide Master. Perform the following steps.

1. Assuming that you just completed the last section, slide 1 of the "Future Trends" presentation should appear in the presentation window. Ensure that you are viewing slide 1 in Slide view before proceeding.
2. To practice changing the Slide Master:
   CHOOSE: View, Master, Slide Master
   Your screen should now appear similar to Figure 3.3.

FIGURE 3.3 THE SLIDE MASTER FOR THE "FUTURE TRENDS" PRESENTATION

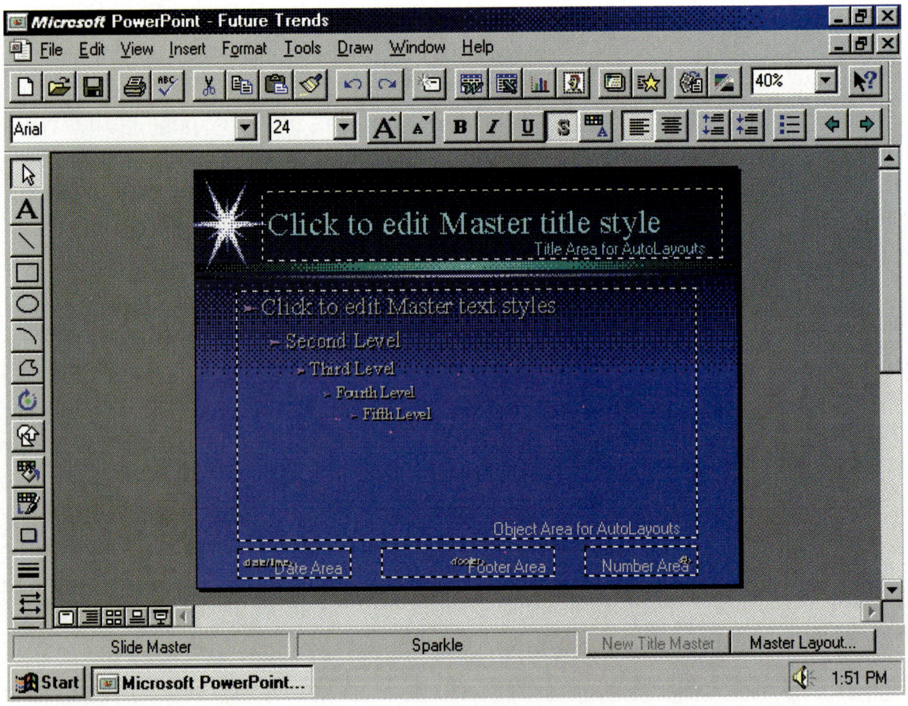

3. Currently, the titles in the "Future Trends" presentation are displayed using Times New Roman. To include italic formatting in the title:
   CLICK: Master title placeholder (which appears as "Click to edit Master title style")
   CLICK: Italic button ( ) on the Formatting toolbar
   Notice that you do not need to select the text in the placeholder to change its formatting characteristics. You simply position the insertion point in the placeholder.

4. To preview the slides using the new format:
   CHOOSE: View, Slides
   Notice that the title on the first slide isn't italicized. To change the characteristics of the Title slide you must use the Title Master.

5. To view the next slide:
   CLICK: Next Slide button ( ) on the vertical scroll bar
   Notice that the title of slide 2 is italicized.

6. To italicize the title of the Title slide:
   CHOOSE: View, Master, Title Master
   CLICK: Master title placeholder (which appears as "Click to edit Master title style")
   CLICK: Italic button ( ) on the Formatting toolbar

7. To preview the slides using the new format:
   CHOOSE: View, Slides
   CLICK: Previous Slide button (▲) on the vertical scroll bar
   Notice that the Title slide is now italicized.

You should now understand the fundamentals of working with masters. In this and subsequent sessions, as you learn more about designing a presentation and adding visuals, you will periodically make changes to the Slide Master. In general, however, you should edit the Slide Master only when you want to change the format of the entire presentation.

QUICK REFERENCE
Editing the Slide Master

1. **Open the desired presentation and switch to Slide View.**
2. **CHOOSE: View, Master, Title Master to edit all Title slides**
   CHOOSE: View, Master, Slide Master to edit all other slides
3. **Edit the Title and Text placeholders on the Title and Slide Masters, add text boxes, insert graphics and charts, and add other objects as desired.**
4. **CHOOSE: View, Slides to return to Slide view**

EDITING AN INDIVIDUAL SLIDE

If you want to format more than one slide at once, change the Title or Slide Master. Otherwise, modify individual slides. It is important to note that any changes you make to individual slides are considered *exceptions* to the Slide Master. If you later change the Slide Master or apply a design template, PowerPoint applies the new format but retains your exceptions. In this section, you learn to edit an individual slide in the "Future Trends" presentation.

Perform the following steps to remove the italic attribute from the first slide and add the bold attribute.

1. Ensure that you are viewing slide 2 in Slide view before proceeding.
2. Unlike formatting the Master title placeholder in the last section, formatting a single title requires that you first select all the text in the Title placeholder. To do so, position the I-beam mouse pointer in the Text placeholder by clicking the left mouse button once and then:
   CHOOSE: Edit, Select All
   (*Hint:* You can also drag the I-beam mouse pointer across the text or press CTRL+a to quickly select all the text in a placeholder.)
3. To remove the italic attribute and apply boldface to the selection:
   CLICK: Italic button (*I*) to turn off the italic attribute
   CLICK: Bold button (**B**) to turn on the bold attribute

4. To remove the active selection from the placeholder:
   CLICK: anywhere outside the placeholder area (e.g., click near the top right-hand corner of the slide)
   Slide 2 should now look similar to Figure 3.4.

FIGURE 3.4 SLIDE 2 AFTER FORMATTING CHANGES

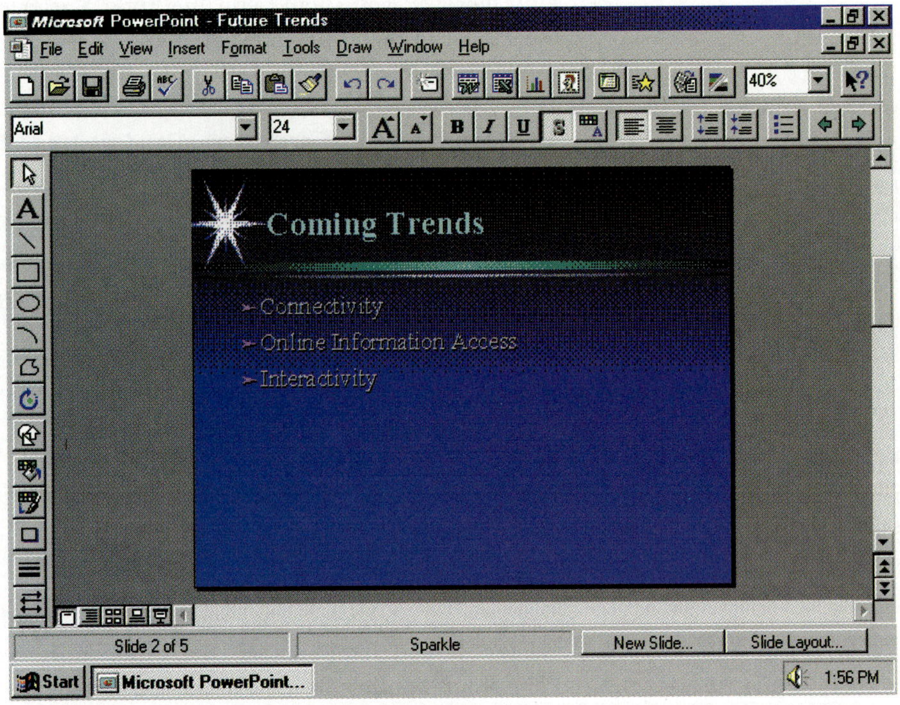

5. Slide 2 no longer conforms to the Slide Master. If you make a formatting change in the Slide Master, for example, all the slides in your presentation will change *except* for slide 2. But what if you want slide 2 to reinherit the Slide Master attributes so that it will change along with the other slides? To do so, perform the following:
   CLICK: Slide Layout hot button on the Status bar
   CLICK: Reapply button
   The text now conforms to the Slide Master once again.

QUICK REFERENCE
Reapplying the Slide Master Format to a Slide

1. **Make the desired slide active in the presentation window.**
2. **CLICK: Slide Layout hot button on the Status bar, or CHOOSE: Format, Slide Layout**
3. **CLICK: Reapply command button**

THE IMPORTANCE OF COLOR

The colors used in a presentation can influence how an audience responds to your message. Colors not only bring emotion to a presentation, they communicate its formality. For example, a presentation that uses deep blues and grays better suits IBM's serious image than Apple's flamboyant image. Used improperly, colors can also undermine your presentation's theme and distract the audience. You would not want to use red, the internationally recognized color for "stop," as the background color for a presentation on entrepreneurship. You should also be aware that a significant portion of your audience—especially adult males—may be color-blind and not perceive the differences between two or more colors. Keeping all these points in mind, you are best advised to keep your color selection simple and restrained.

Fortunately for us, Microsoft hired professional artists to compile PowerPoint's numerous color schemes. A **color scheme** is a set of eight colors that you can apply to individual slides, notes pages, and audience handouts. The eight main colors include a background color, title text color, text and line color, fill color, shadows color, and three colors for accents. By using color schemes, you ensure that all the colors in your presentation are balanced and will work well together. Also, color schemes make it easy to apply a new set of colors to your presentation, just as using templates makes it easy to change its overall design.

To experiment with the colors that are available, you can choose Format, Slide Color Scheme from the menu to display the Slide Color Scheme dialog box (shown in Figure 3.5). Using the Standard tab, you can choose one of three preset color schemes that change the way colors are used for all the objects on your slides. (*Note:* You can also add your own color schemes to the Color Scheme dialog box.) These schemes range from dark to light. As a general rule of thumb, you should pick darker backgrounds for 35 mm slides and on-screen presentations, and light background colors for overhead transparencies. The Custom tab gives you control over individual slide objects. When you are satisfied with your color selections, you select the Apply command button to apply the new color scheme to the current slide or the Apply to All command button to change the entire presentation. It is important to note that the Apply to All option changes the color scheme for the Slide Master as well.

EDITING THE CURRENT COLOR SCHEME

In the following steps, you will change the colors used in the "Future Trends" presentation.

1. Ensure that you are viewing slide 1 in Slide view before proceeding.
2. CHOOSE: Format, Slide Color Scheme
   The dialog box in Figure 3.5 should appear.

FIGURE 3.5 SLIDE COLOR SCHEME DIALOG BOX: STANDARD TAB

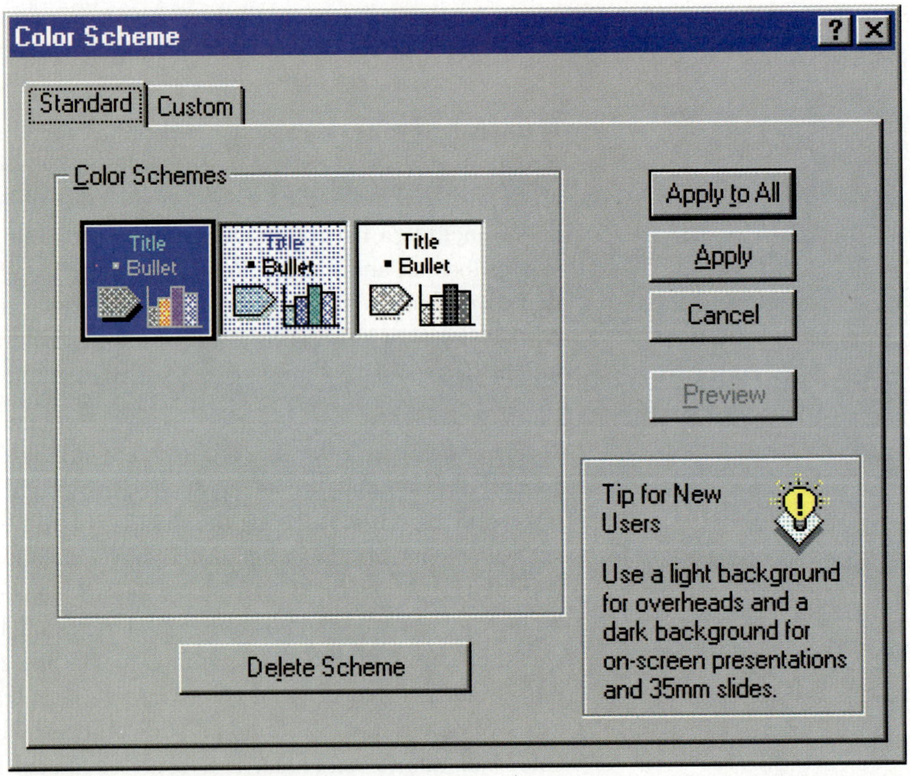

3. To pick one of the standard color schemes and then preview it:
   SELECT: any color scheme
   CLICK: Preview button
   DRAG: Color Scheme dialog box to reveal more of the preview image
4. DRAG: Color Scheme dialog box back to its original position
5. To pick the original color scheme:
   SELECT: the color scheme in the upper left-hand corner
   You may find that a standard color scheme works well for you. If not, you will want to create a color scheme that is customized to your needs.

6. To change the color for individual slide objects, do the following:
   SELECT: Custom tab
   Your screen should now appear similar to Figure 3.6.

FIGURE 3.6 SLIDE COLOR SCHEME DIALOG BOX: CUSTOM TAB

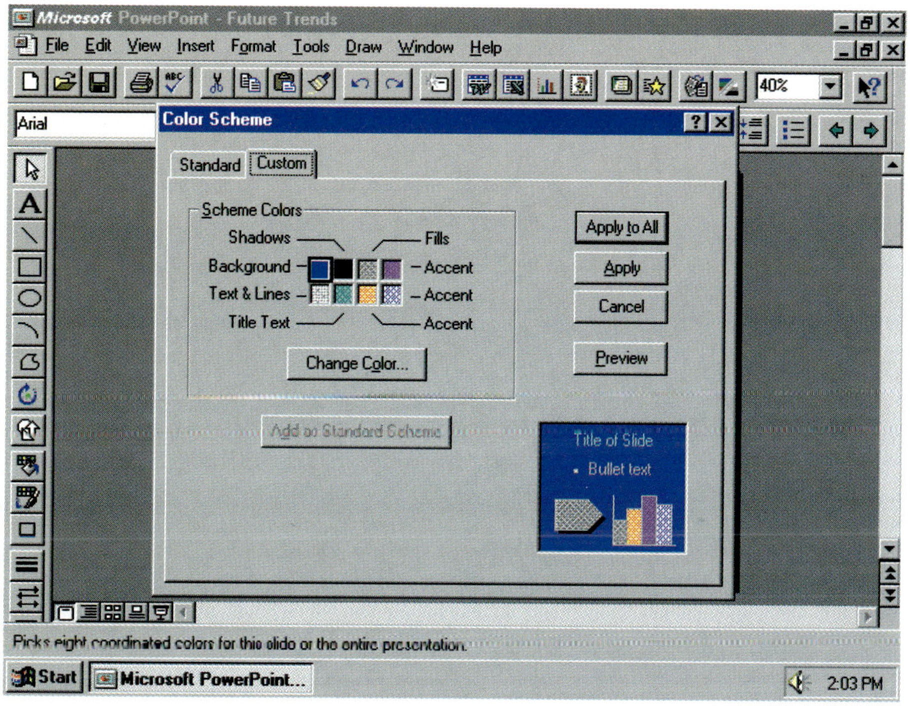

7. To modify the foreground or text color for the Title placeholder:
   CLICK: *Title Text* color box (in the *Scheme Colors* area)
   CLICK: Change Color command button
   SELECT: a light green color
   CLICK: OK command button
8. To apply the new color to the current slide only:
   CLICK: Apply command button
   Notice that the title is now displayed in a light green color.
9. On your own, display the other slides in the "Future Trends" presentation. You'll notice that they still conform to the Slide Master's color scheme. When you are done, return to viewing slide 1 in Slide view.
10. To reapply the original color scheme to slide 1:
    CHOOSE: Format, Slide Color Scheme
    SELECT: Standard tab
    SELECT: the original color scheme
    CLICK: Apply command button
    Slide 1 should now conform to the original color scheme.

QUICK REFERENCE
Changing an Individual Color

1. **CHOOSE: Format, Slide Color Scheme**
2. **SELECT: Custom tab**
3. **SELECT: a slide object (in the Scheme Colors area)**
4. **CLICK: Change Color command button**
5. **SELECT: a new color to appear in the color box**
6. **CLICK: Apply to change the color on the current slide, or**
   CLICK: Apply to All to change the color for all slides

QUICK REFERENCE
Reapplying the Slide Master Colors

1. **Make the desired slide active in the presentation window.**
2. **CHOOSE: Format, Slide Color Scheme**
3. **SELECT: Standard tab**
4. **SELECT: the master color scheme (in the Color Schemes area)**
5. **CLICK: Apply command button**

VIEWING SLIDES IN BLACK AND WHITE

Depending on how you plan to output your presentation, you may at some point want to see how your presentation looks in black and white. This feature is especially relevant if you plan to print slides, handouts, or notes pages on a black and white laser printer. To view your presentation in black and white, click the B&W View button ( ) on the Standard toolbar or choose View, Black and White from the Menu bar. PowerPoint will automatically convert your on-screen colors to black, white, and shades of gray. In this view mode, you can also change how selected objects appear by choosing Black and White from the shortcut menu and then choosing a display option.

In the following steps, you view the "Future Trends" presentation in Black and White View.

1. Ensure that you are viewing slide 3 of the "Future Trends" presentation before continuing.
2. To display the presentation in black and white:
   CLICK: B&W View button ( )
   Notice that PowerPoint displays a color miniature of the current slide in the presentation window.
3. Point to the clip art object in the bottom right-hand corner and then right-click to display the shortcut menu.

4. CHOOSE: Black and White
Your screen should appear similar to Figure 3.7. Using the options on the shortcut menu, you can change the appearance of the selected object or choose "Don't Show" to remove the object from view.

FIGURE 3.7 BLACK AND WHITE SHORTCUT MENU

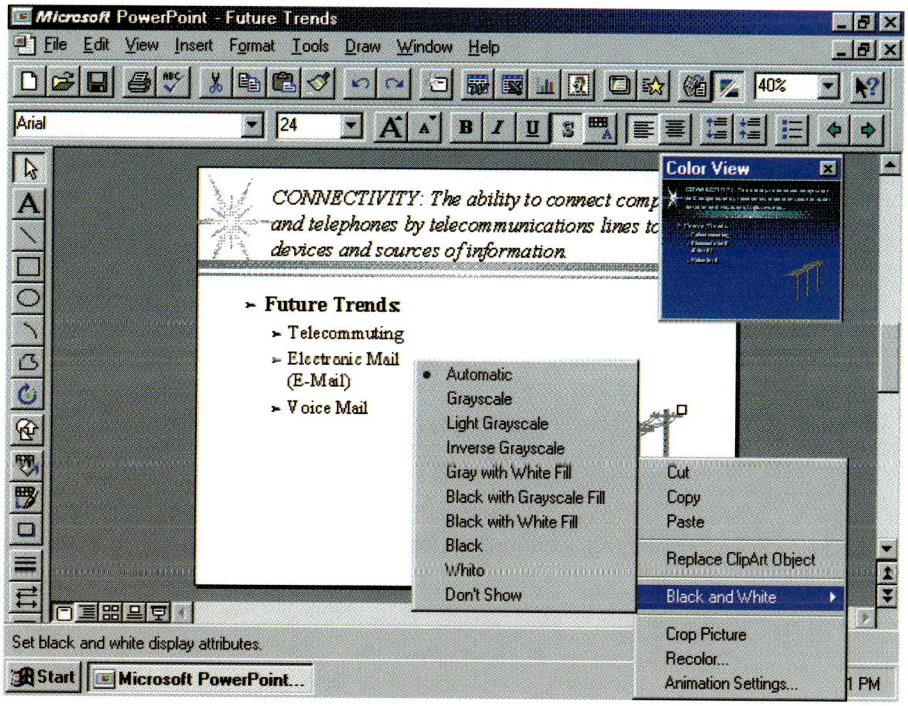

5. To remove the shortcut menu, click anywhere in the presentation window.
6. To switch back to color mode:
CLICK: B&W View button ( )

QUICK REFERENCE
Viewing a Presentation in Black and White

1. **CLICK: B&W View button ( ), or**
CHOOSE: View, Black and White
2. **Change the way objects appear by choosing Black and White from the shortcut menu and then choosing an available option.**

WORKING MORE WITH TEXT

After completing the following sections, you will be able to take full control over the display of text in your presentations. Specifically, you learn how to customize the use of bullets, edit and organize textual content using the Outline view, and position text on the slide using the Text tool. In terms of formatting guidelines for text, keep in mind the following points as you work through this section:

- Strive for visible and readable text
- Strive for consistency in formatting
- Strive for simplicity and less as more
- Do not mix case (e.g., This Is Difficult To Read On A Slide)
- Do not use too many typefaces
- Avoid writing sentences on your slide; use phrases and summaries
- Ensure parallelism (e.g., consistent use of passive or active voice)

TEXT BULLETS

A bulleted list, as a format, is one technique for controlling and organizing the amount of text displayed on a slide. Bulleted lists are also used to emphasize certain points on a slide. A **bullet** is the graphic (usually a circle) that precedes an item in a list. As you've seen in this learning guide, PowerPoint adds bullets to some placeholders; that is, when you press ENTER after typing a line of text, a bullet is inserted automatically on the next line.

PowerPoint lets you control the display of bullets and also lets you select custom bullet symbols. You can remove or add bullets to a Text placeholder using the Bullet On/Off tool (☰) on the Formatting toolbar. You can also insert custom bullets using the Format, Bullet command. For review, you may want to refer back to Manipulating Bullets in the Adding Slides section of Session 2 before proceeding.

In the following steps, you change the way bullets are displayed in the "Future Trends" presentation.

1. Display slide 3 of "Future Trends" in Slide view before proceeding.
2. Notice that the text "Future Trends" appears fairly close to the Title text above. To insert a blank line and move "Future Trends" down, position the insertion point to the left of "Future Trends" and do the following:
   PRESS: ENTER
   Although the text "Future Trends" moves down, you will now notice that a bullet appears on the first line without any text.

3. To remove the new bullet, position the insertion point to the right of the bullet and do the following:
   CLICK: Bullet On/Off button ( )
   The bullet disappears.

4. To use a custom bullet symbol for all slides in your presentation, let's edit the Slide Master. Specifically, let's change the main-level bullets from ➤ to ➔. Do the following:
   CHOOSE: View, Master, Slide Master

5. CLICK: Master text placeholder (it appears as "Click to edit Master text styles" on the slide)

6. To change the ➤ bullet symbol, ensure that the insertion point is on the "Click to edit Master text styles" line of the Master text placeholder. Then, do the following:
   CHOOSE: Format, Bullet
   CLICK: down arrow beside the *Bullets From* drop-down list box
   SELECT: Wingdings
   (*Note:* You may have to scroll through to find Wingdings near the bottom of the list.) Your screen should now appear similar to Figure 3.8.

FIGURE 3.8 BULLET DIALOG BOX, SHOWING THE WINGDING SYMBOLS

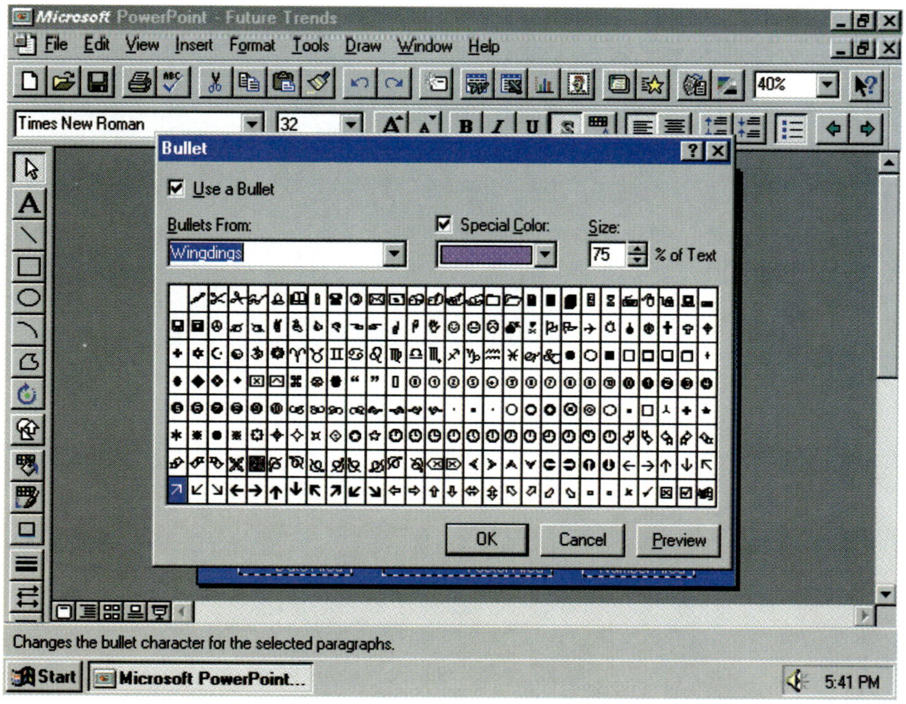

7. To specify a new symbol for the bullet:
   SELECT: ➔
   PRESS: ENTER or CLICK: OK
8. To view the slides:
   CHOOSE: View, Slides
9. Display the presentation using Slide Show view. Notice that arrows are now used for the major bullet points. As an example, slide 3 (which was also edited previously in this section) should look like Figure 3.9.

FIGURE 3.9 SLIDE 3 OF THE "FUTURE TRENDS" PRESENTATION

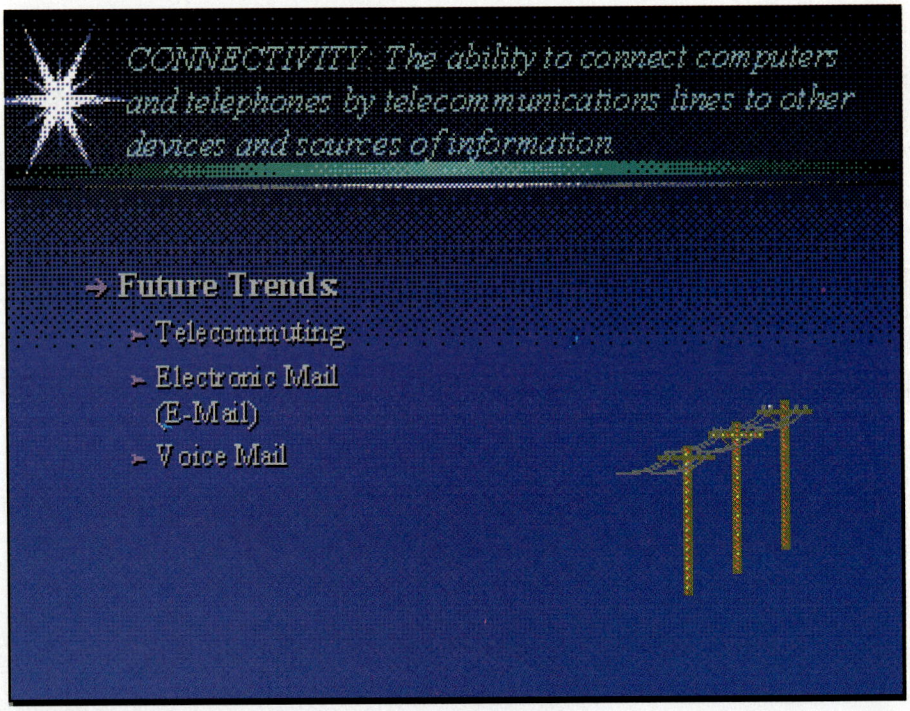

10. To save your changes:
    CLICK: Save button (💾)

QUICK REFERENCE
Changing a Bullet Symbol

1. **Display the Slide Master, or an individual slide.**
2. **Position the insertion point in the line that contains the bullet you want to change.**
3. **CHOOSE: Format, Bullet**
4. **SELECT: a symbol font from the *Bullets From* drop-down list box**
5. **SELECT: a symbol from the Bullet dialog box**
6. **PRESS: ENTER or CLICK: OK**

MANIPULATING TEXT IN OUTLINE VIEW

The majority of our time so far has been spent in Slide view and Slide Show view. Many of the tasks you have performed, including changing indent levels and bullets, can also be accomplished using the Outline view. In Outline view, you can apply formatting and reorder your slides. Many people prefer working in Outline view because it lets you see the textual content from more than one slide at a time. Graphics do not display in this mode; there is, however, an icon beside each slide number that indicates whether graphics appear on that slide.

Perform the following steps to practice using the Outlining toolbar, moving a paragraph, and moving a slide so that it displays at a different point in the presentation.

1. Display slide 1 of "Future Trends" in Slide view before proceeding. To change the view mode to Outline view:
   CLICK: Outline view button (▤)
2. If the viewing area isn't maximized, maximize the presentation window by clicking its Maximize button (□).
3. To ensure that you are at the beginning of the outline:
   PRESS: CTRL + HOME
   (*Note:* The above instruction means to hold down CTRL and then press HOME.) Your screen should now appear similar to Figure 3.10.

FIGURE 3.10 OUTLINE VIEW

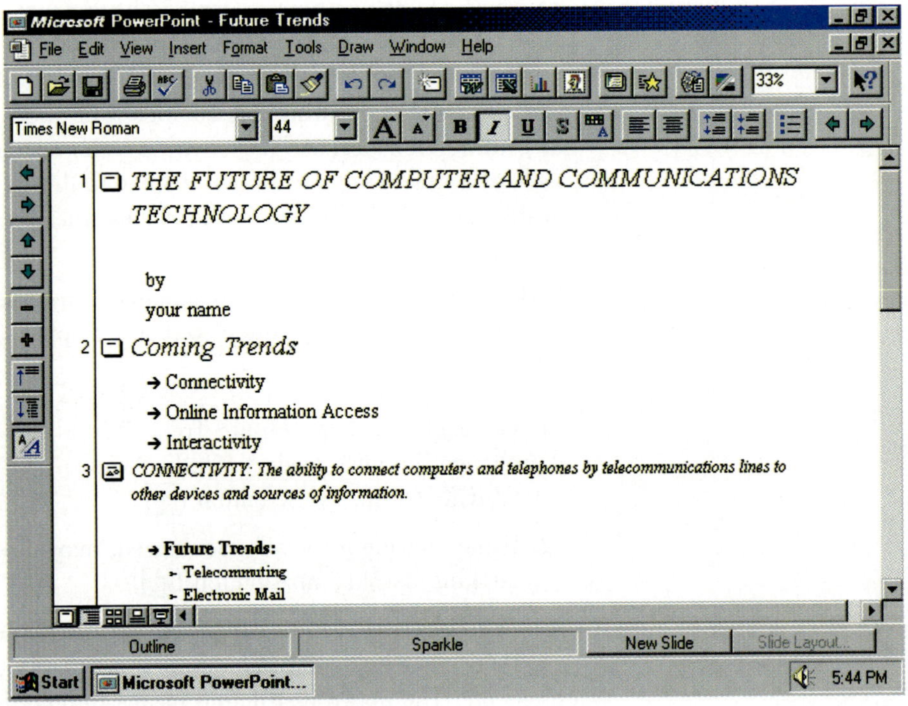

4. To get an overview of the presentation, display the slide titles only:
   CLICK: Show Titles button () on the Outlining toolbar
5. To redisplay all of the text:
   CLICK: Show All button () on the Outlining toolbar
6. If you find the text format distracting in the Outline, you can easily remove it. Do the following:
   CLICK: Show Formatting button () on the Outlining toolbar
   Your screen should now appear similar to Figure 3.11.

FIGURE 3.11 OUTLINE VIEW WITHOUT FORMATTING

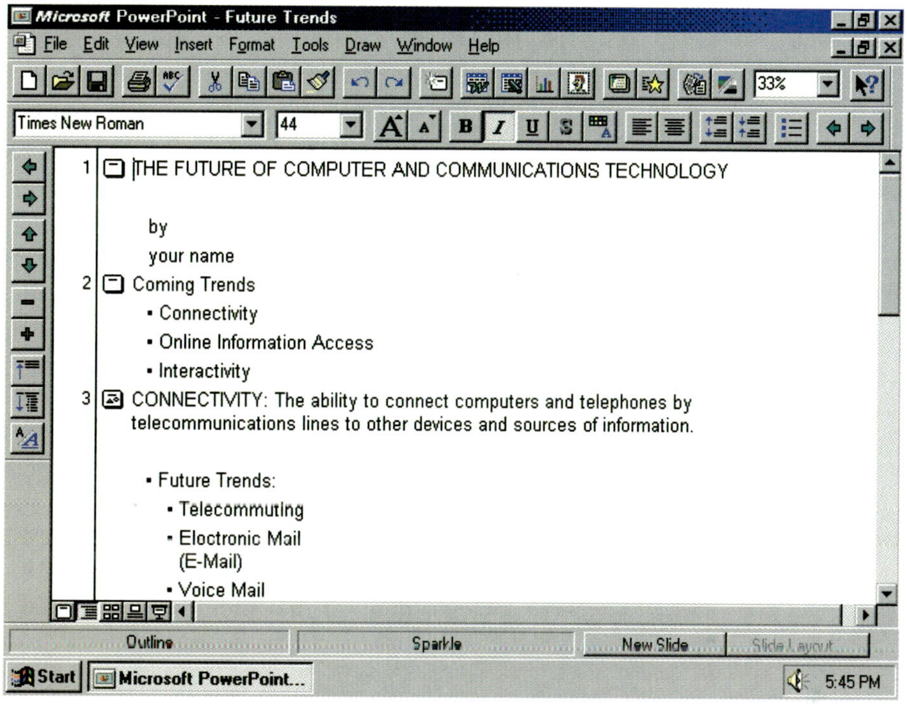

7. To redisplay the formatting:
   CLICK: Show Formatting button (A) again

8. To select all the text on the first slide so that you can apply additional formatting, do the following:
   CLICK: slide icon for slide 1
   When you move the mouse pointer over the icon, it changes to a four-headed arrow (✥).

9. To display the text in bold letters:
   CLICK: Bold button (B)

10. To select an individual line or bullet of text on a slide, you position the four-headed arrow (✥) mouse pointer over the associated bullet and click the left mouse button once. To practice moving a paragraph:
    SELECT: "Electronic Mail (E-Mail)" on slide 3

11. To move this item so that it displays first in the list:
    CLICK: Move Up button (⇧) on the Outlining toolbar
    (*Note:* You can also drag the bullet up or down in the list using the mouse.)

12. Using the mouse:
    DRAG: "Voice Mail" bullet above "Telecommuting" on slide 3

13. To move slide 2 so that it displays at the end of the presentation (after slide 5), you must first select the slide by clicking its slide icon:
    SELECT: slide 2
14. DRAG: slide 2 icon to the bottom of the presentation, below slide 5 (*Note:* A horizontal line marks where the slide will be positioned. Ensure that this line is below slide 5 before you release the mouse button. If you make a mistake, choose Edit, Undo and then retry.)
15. DRAG: slide 5, entitled "Coming Trends," back to its original position immediately following slide 1
16. Return to Slide view before proceeding to the next section.

USING THE TEXT TOOL

The Title and Text placeholders are great for entering textual content that flows in a consistent and regular fashion. For those other times when you need more flexibility in positioning text on a slide, you use the **Text tool** (A) on the Drawing toolbar. Also, you must use the Text tool if you want to place text on the Slide Master so that it appears on every slide. You cannot use the Title and Text placeholders on the Slide Master to hold text; they are visible only for changing formatting characteristics.

In this section, you insert free-form text in the bottom right-hand corner of a slide. When you finish, slide 2 of the "Future Trends" presentation will look like Figure 3.12. (*Note:* You must display the presentation using Slide view in order to use the Text tool. Also, text entered using the Text tool doesn't display in the Outline view.)

FIGURE 3.12

FREE-FORM TEXT PLACED ON SLIDE 2 OF THE "FUTURE TRENDS" PRESENTATION

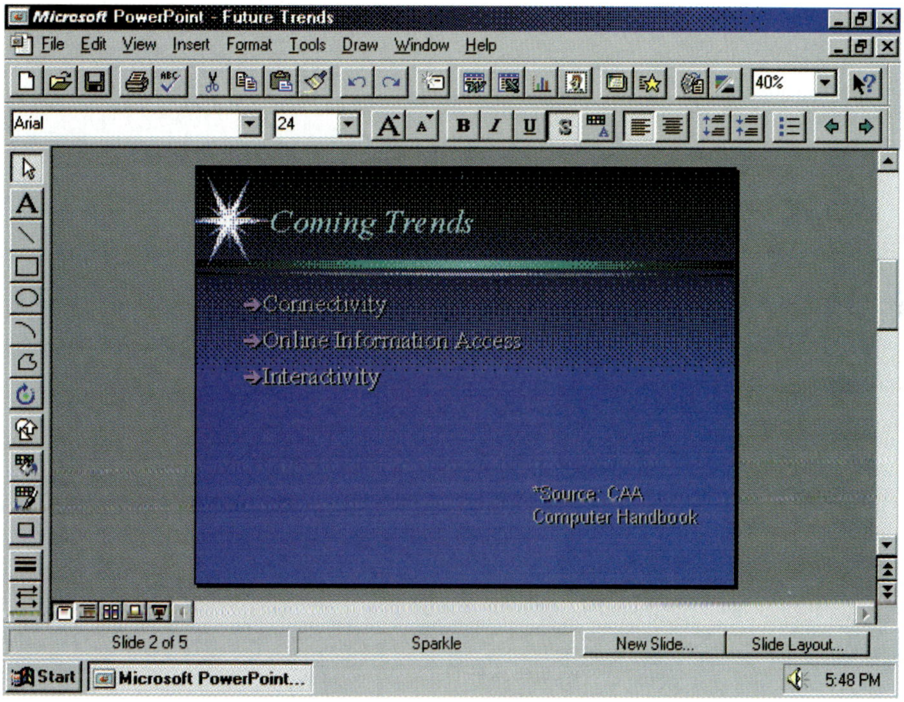

Perform the following steps.

1. In Slide view, display slide 2 of the "Future Trends" presentation.
2. To enter free-form text using the Text tool:
   CLICK: Text tool (A) on the Drawing toolbar
3. Position the mouse pointer over the location where you want to begin typing text (see Figure 3.12) and click the left mouse button once.
4. An insertion point appears and starts blinking inside a small box. The box will expand as you begin to type. Do the following:
   TYPE: ***Source: CAA**
   PRESS: ENTER
   TYPE: **Computer Handbook**
   Your screen should now appear similar to Figure 3.12.
5. By default, the text that you type using the Text tool doesn't automatically wrap. In Step 4, you forced some text onto the second line by pressing ENTER. If you want text to wrap automatically, you must first draw a text box and then type in its contents. To create the text box appearing in Figure 3.13, do the following:
   CLICK: Text tool (A) on the Drawing toolbar

FIGURE 3.13 A TEXT BOX PLACED ON SLIDE 2 OF THE "FUTURE TRENDS" PRESENTATION

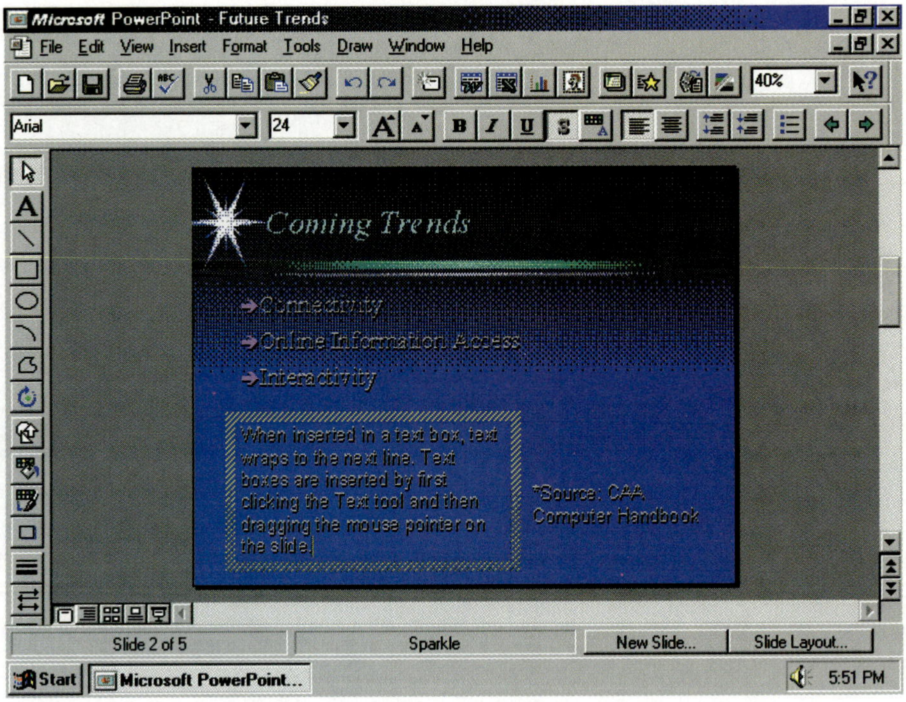

6. Position the mouse pointer at the upper left-hand corner of where you want the box to begin (see Figure 3.13) and then drag down and to the right. When you are satisfied with its shape, release the mouse button. Notice that the text box retains its width but retreats vertically to show only one line. The box will expand downward as you enter text.
7. An insertion point appears and starts blinking inside the box. Do the following to enter text:
   TYPE: **When inserted in a text box, text wraps to the next line. Text boxes are inserted by first clicking the Text tool and then dragging the mouse pointer on the slide.**
   Notice that the text automatically wraps to the next line. Slide 2 should now appear similar to Figure 3.13.
8. To delete the text box from your slide, you must first select it. Position the mouse pointer over one of the edges of the text box and click the left mouse button once. You should see handles (small boxes) appear around the text box.
9. To delete the text box:
   PRESS: DELETE
10. Close the "Future Trends" presentation without saving its changes.

> **QUICK REFERENCE**
> Inserting Text Using the Text Tool
>
> 1. **Make the desired slide active in the presentation window.**
> 2. **CLICK: Text tool button () located on the Drawing toolbar**
> 3. **CLICK: the left mouse button once to position the insertion point, or**
>   **DRAG: the mouse pointer on the slide to create a text box**

SUMMARY

In this session, you learned how to add your own design flair to a presentation. The session began by describing PowerPoint's templates, which you can use to define how text will appear on a slide, where objects will be positioned, and which colors will be used. You also learned to edit the Title Master and Slide Master, which hold the formatting specifications for the Title and Text placeholders and the background for the entire presentation. In the second half of the session, you learned the importance of selecting colors for a presentation and how to choose and apply a color scheme. The session concluded by leading you through selecting a custom bullet, manipulating text in the Outline view, and inserting free-form text on a slide using the Text tool.

COMMAND SUMMARY

Many of the commands and procedures appearing in this session are provided in Table 3.1 below.

TABLE 3.1
Command Summary

Task Description	*Menu Command*	*Alternative Methods*
Apply a new design template	Format, Apply Design Template	
Edit the Title Master	View, Master, Title Master	
Edit the Slide Master	View, Master, Slide Master	
Reapply the Slide Master attributes	Format, Slide Layout	Slide Layout hot button
Change the color scheme	Format, Slide Color Scheme	
Select a custom bullet symbol	Format, Bullet	
Reverse the last command executed	Edit, Undo	

KEY TERMS

bullet
A graphic that precedes an item in a list.

color scheme
In PowerPoint, a set of eight colors that are used as the main colors in your presentation.

Slide Master
In PowerPoint, this slide holds the formatting specifications for the placeholders and background of all slides except Title slides.

Text tool
This tool is available on the Drawing toolbar and lets you enter text on a slide without using the placeholders.

Title Master
In PowerPoint, this slide holds the formatting specifications for the placeholders and background of all Title slides.

EXERCISES

SHORT ANSWER

1. What is the Slide Master?
2. What is a color scheme?
3. What are the advantages of working in Outline view?
4. List the seven formatting guidelines discussed in this session.
5. Why is it significant that changes you make to individual slides are considered *exceptions* to the Slide Master?
6. In Outline View, how do you select all the text on a slide?
7. In Outline View, how do you move a slide?
8. When would you use the Bullet On/Off button?
9. When would you use the Text tool?
10. When would you want to draw a text box using the Text tool?

HANDS-ON

(*Note:* The following exercises assume that you've completed the hands-on exercises for Session 2 and saved the results on the Advantage Diskette, as instructed. Before continuing, make sure the Advantage Diskette is inserted into the diskette drive.)

1. In this exercise, you edit the "Using Color" presentation that you created in Session 2. The presentation is stored on the Advantage Diskette.
   a. Using the Slide Master, modify the presentation so that the title and main text display in italic.
   b. Using the Slide Master, select a new custom bullet symbol (☛) to replace the main bullet symbol (♦).
   c. Edit the current color scheme to change the background color to black. Apply the new background color to the entire presentation.
   d. Display the presentation using Slide Show view.
   e. Return to Slide view.
   f. Save the "Using Color" presentation back to the Advantage Diskette.
   g. Close the presentation.
2. In this exercise, you edit the "Advertising" presentation that you created in Session 2.
   a. Increase the size of the clip art picture that appears on slide 2.
   b. Using the Text tool (A), insert the following text in the bottom left-hand corner of slide 1:
   Prepared on:
   today's date
   c. Change the size of the newly inserted text to 18 points.
   d. Display the presentation in Outline view.
   e. Move slide 4 (Print Ads) above slide 3 (T.V. Commercials).
   f. Except for the title slide, apply bold to the Title placeholder only on each remaining slide.
   g. Display the presentation using Slide Show view.
   h. Return to Slide view.
   i. Save the presentation back to the Advantage Diskette.
   j. Close the presentation.

3. In Session 2, you created a presentation named "Session 2 Exercise" in one of the hands-on exercises. Edit the presentation to include the following:
    - *a.* Select a different symbol for main-level bullets.
    - *b.* Edit the current color scheme and then apply the new color scheme to the entire presentation.
    - *c.* Use the Text tool to insert descriptive text on at least one slide.
    - *d.* Edit the Slide Master to change the formatting for all of the Titles in the presentation.
    - *e.* Display the presentation using Slide Show view.
    - *f.* Return to Slide view.
    - *g.* Save the revised presentation as "Session 3 Exercise" onto the Advantage Diskette. (*Hint:* Remember to use the File, Save As command.)

CASE PROBLEMS

H2 UNDERSCAPING LTD.

(*Note:* In the following case problems, assume the role of the primary character or characters and perform the same steps that they identify.)

1. By his next lunch meeting with Vi Krieg, Chip had already developed a storyboard for his presentation. "A storyboard," he explained to Vi, "reduces the amount of wasted time typically spent brainstorming around the computer. I simply jot down everything that I want to show on each slide in these little boxes. It's a great way to organize my thoughts for a presentation." Vi was very impressed with the page Chip handed to her (an example of which appears on the next page.)

Title: Business Show, 1996 **#1** **Sub-title:** Presented by Chip Yee H2 UnderScaping Ltd.	**Title:** Evening's Agenda **#2** **Bullets:** • Chamber's mission • Benefits of membership • Community affairs • Member profile • Summary
Title: Chamber's Mission **#3** **Bullets:** • To lobby for changes in law to promote economic prosperity for all • To work for opportunity and education for small businesses nationwide • To promote the policies and initiatives of the National Chambers of Commerce	**Title:** Benefits of Membership **#4** **Bullets:** • Business-to-business directory • Monthly luncheon meetings • Monthly newsletter • Corporate library • Special events and guest speakers
Title: Community Affairs **#5** **Bullets:** • High-school career prep program • Organizer of celebrity auction for children's charities • Organizer of downtown Easter parade • Fund-raiser for local women's center	**Title:** Member Profile **#6** **Bullets:** Donna Osaki, M.D., is off to Saudi Arabia to set up the country's first community health center. Donna accepted this position immediately when approached by the Surgeon General. We wish Donna the very best overseas!
Title: Summary **#7** **Bullets:** • Our Chamber is true to its ideals • Our Chamber works for its members • Our Chamber works for its community • Our Chamber has the best people!	**Title:** Closing **#8** **Sub-title:** Thank you for attending this evening!

"Are you sure we can pull this off using a computer-based presentation?" asked Vi, wondering if Chip realized the actual time and effort it would involve. Chip nodded confidently. "You see, Vi, I've already planned out how this will work on the computer. First, I'll take my storyboard and create an on-screen presentation using the Embossed template since it communicates a dignified and professional image for the Chamber. Next,

I'll position your name as our Chamber president in the bottom right-hand corner of each slide using the Text tool on the Slide Master. Everything will look just stunning!"

Vi was getting excited about Chip's plans for the presentation. She couldn't wait to see the final product and begged Chip to send her a printed copy of his work as soon as he was finished. Chip agreed, and they departed from their lunch feeling well-nourished and anticipating a wonderful Business Show!

Save this presentation as "Business Show" onto the Advantage Diskette.

2. Two weeks before he was to make his Chamber presentation, Chip received a letter from Ms. Paula Deviq, a business administration teacher at the local high school. The letter read, "*Dear Mr. Yee, I understand that you are preparing a presentation for the Chamber at this year's Business Show banquet. I have a proposition for you. I would like you to deliver your presentation to my senior class in business administration early next week. In return, you would enjoy an opportunity to practice your speech and receive constructive criticism from my class. Please consider this invitation and reply to me as soon as possible. Sincerely, Paula Deviq.*" Chip called Paula immediately after reading the letter and accepted her polite, and timely, invitation.

   Thinking about the presentation for Paula's class that evening, Chip decided that he should change the look and feel of the presentation to better suit high school students. Instead of using the look of the Embossed template, he decided to pick something much livelier and more colorful to keep their attention. Also, he would look through the ClipArt Gallery to find some relevant pictures. Specifically, he wanted to add three different pictures—on each of slides 4, 5, and 6. Another change he would make would be to select custom bullet symbols, perhaps ♣ or ➲. Lastly, Chip would remove Vi Krieg's name from the Slide Master and replace it with his favorite quote, "Do what you love and the money will follow!" All of these changes would take some time, but he knew the payoff would be worth the effort.

   Once finished, Chip proceeded through a dry run of his presentation using the Slide Show view. Happy with the results, he saved the presentation to his Advantage Diskette as "School Presentation 1."

3. Chip arrived at the high school 30 minutes early for his presentation. He was just opening the front door to the school when he was greeted by a well-dressed woman in her mid-thirties. "Mr. Yee, I presume?" Chip smiled and extended his hand to the teacher. "Yes, I hope I'm not too early for your class, Ms. Deviq?" "Oh, no, no . . . but we've experienced a small technical problem this morning with our A.V. system. I'm afraid we won't be able to connect your laptop computer to an LCD projection panel. I was hoping that you could print out your presentation onto black-and-white overheads using my laser printer. I'm sorry to make you deliver your presentation the old-fashioned way, but I'm sure my students would enjoy it all the same."

   Chip immediately began rehearsing the procedure in his mind. He would have to change his template from an on-screen presentation to a black and white overhead presentation. He would display the presentation in black and white and then review it on-screen to see how the objects looked. Realizing that he had been staring at Paula and saying nothing for the past ten seconds, Chip apologized and assured her that it was not a problem to convert his presentation to overheads. He then asked to be shown to her office to begin the process.

   Save this presentation as "School Presentation 2" onto the Advantage Diskette.

4. Back at his office, Chip received an official "Invitation to Quote" from the federal government. The government is nearing completion on a million-dollar expansion of their administration wing and requires landscaping services to be completed for their opening next month. Each vendor is being asked to prepare a 15-minute presentation on their company's strengths and present it to the selection committee this coming Monday.

   Using the storyboards shown on the next page, Chip completed the handwritten version of the presentation. Unfortunately, he had to fly to Denver on family business and could not finish converting the presentation to PowerPoint. As his office assistant, you must now take Chip's storyboards and create a presentation appropriate for the federal government's selection committee, complete with introduction and closing slides. Chip also mentioned that you should choose templates, color schemes, typefaces, and clip art for the presentation. Good luck!

Introduction **#1**	Company Background **#2**
(Remember to put the title of the presentation, my name, and the company's name on this slide!)	Started in 1992 by Mr. Chip Yee, H2U has become an innovator in the business of underground sprinkler systems.
Why We Are the Best **#3**	Partial Client List **#4**
The Most Talented Designers The Most Dedicated Staff The Most Current Technology The Most Satified Clients!	Mount Rushmore Society New Jersey Turnpike Assoc. Yasgusa's Farm, Inc. Willy's Motor Inn, Route 66
Summary **#5**	Closing Slide **#6**
(Remember to put a summary of the presentation here.)	(Remember to thank them for attending the presentation and provide time for questions.

Save the presentation as "Federal Government" to the Advantage Diskette.

Adding Visual Effects

SESSION OUTLINE

Working with Objects
Inserting Clip Art
Inserting Pictures
Creating Graphs
Creating Organizational Charts
Running Slide Shows
Summary
Key Terms
Exercises

INTRODUCTION

PowerPoint provides you with powerful graphic and visual support, which makes it relatively easy to add professional touches to your presentations. In this session, we show you how to work with many kinds of visual objects including clip art objects, graphs, and organizational charts. In addition, we lead you through adding special effects to your electronic presentations.

CASE STUDY IMMACULATE PERCEPTIONS, INC.

"Creating a memorable corporate identity for all of our clients!" screamed the black letters on a bright yellow sign. This sign did not appear on a billboard, or even on a bus stop bench; it was placed dead center over the reception desk for Immaculate Perceptions, Inc. (IPI), a young and striving advertising agency in Brandon, Oregon. Started in 1991 as a partnership between Connie Appleton and Bobbie Brukowski, IPI now specializes in providing customers with marketing and advertising materials for trade shows and point-of-purchase (POP) displays.

Last week, Bobbie introduced the company's creative staff to Microsoft PowerPoint as a vehicle for communicating their clients' images and as a possible source of revenue. "It's great!" exclaimed Bobbie, pacing around the boardroom table. "You can add pictures and clip art, create graphs of financial and statistical information, and even match the presentation to their corporate colors. And the best part is that you can create a self-running slide show for use at a trade show booth— they don't even have to be present!" The staff was very receptive to Bobbie's pitch. Connie, who had listened to every word but had not spoken until this point, summarized the meeting with "Let's find out as much as we can about PowerPoint's visual tools and then meet again on Monday to discuss its uses for the upcoming Computer and Communications Show at the Shoreline Center. Remember, learn as much as you can about PowerPoint in the next week!"

WORKING WITH OBJECTS

Microsoft provides several **mini-apps** that can be used by PowerPoint. These mini-apps enable you to create objects that may be embedded into a presentation. To find out which mini-apps are available to you, choose the Insert, Object command from the menu and then browse through the list of objects that appears in the dialog box (Figure 4.1). You may also see the names of other software applications such as CorelDRAW!, depending on which applications you have installed on your computer. The Insert Object dialog box lists all the programs on your computer for which you may insert output, such as a drawing object from CorelDRAW!, into your PowerPoint presentation.

FIGURE 4.1 INSERT OBJECT DIALOG BOX

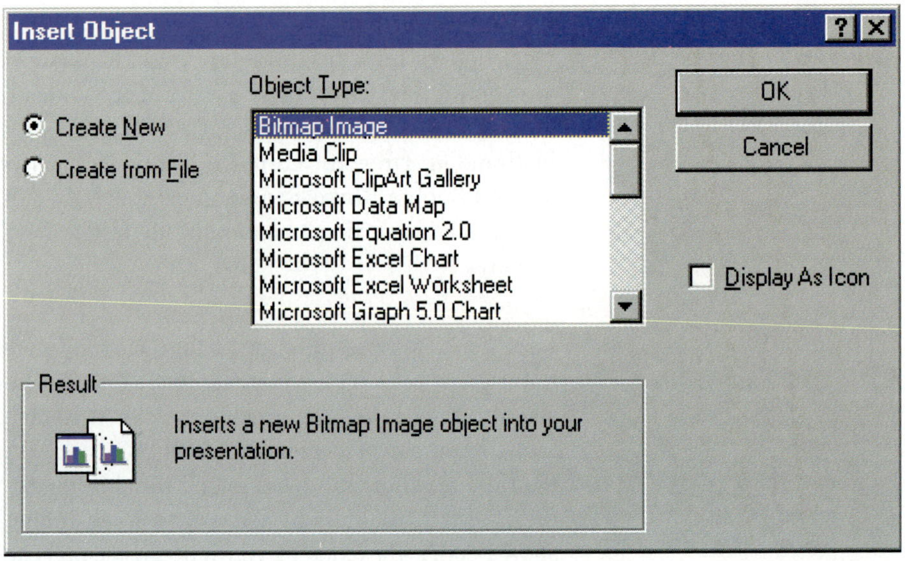

Although not all of these may be installed on your computer, Microsoft's mini-apps include the following:

ClipArt Gallery Enables you to select and insert clip art from a library of cataloged images. For example:

Equation Editor Enables you to create complex equations using special math symbols and typesetting standards. For example:

$$\sigma^2 = \frac{\sum_{i=1}^{N}(X_i - \mu)^2}{N}$$

Graph Enables you to easily insert a graph into your document without having to launch Excel. For example:

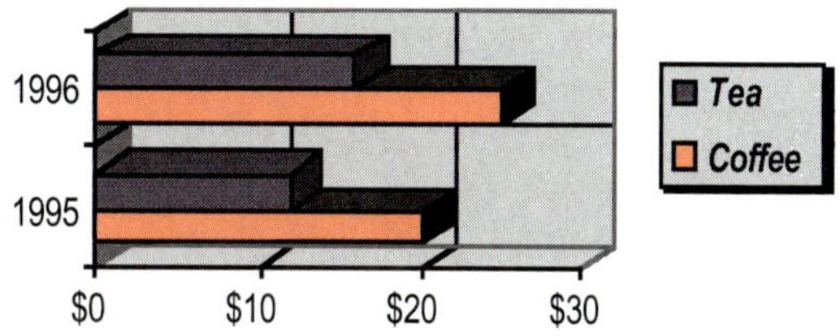

Organization Chart Enables you to design, build, and insert an organization chart into your document. For example:

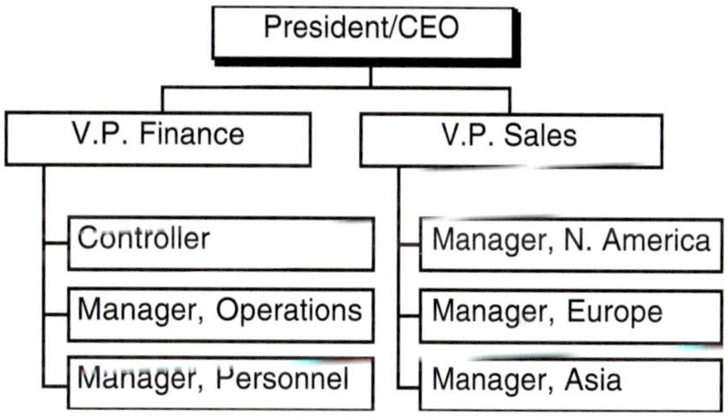

WordArt Allows you to apply special effects to textual information in your document.

For further information on inserting and manipulating objects, refer to the *Integrating Microsoft Office 95* Student Learning Guide in the Advantage Series for Computer Education.

INSERTING CLIP ART

A picture is worth a thousand words! Although this phrase is overused, its truth is undeniable. Graphics add personality to your presentation and convey information more efficiently than text alone. Unfortunately, many new computer users struggle with the tendency to place too many graphics on a single screen. To assist your planning of how and when to use graphics, apply these basic principles: strive for simplicity, use emphasis sparingly, and ensure a visual balance between graphics and text. Fortunately, PowerPoint's AutoLayouts already encourage a balanced and visually appealing use of graphics.

The Microsoft ClipArt Gallery mini-app provides a one-stop shopping mall for all your clip art images. A clip art image is a computer graphic or picture that you can insert into your documents, usually without having to pay royalties or licensing fees to the artist or designer. Microsoft's ClipArt Gallery provides hundreds of images organized into over 25 categories. You can also use the Gallery to add your own images, delete existing images, and move images. Here are three examples of images stored in the ClipArt Gallery:

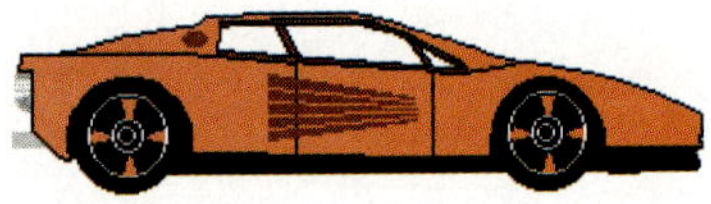

Although you've already inserted a clip art image in Session 2, you will now learn skills for moving and resizing an image. Also in this session, you learn to search through the thousand images for that one picture that conveys the "right" information, attitude, and emotion.

PowerPoint provides you with a variety of methods for inserting a clip art image on a slide (concentrate on using the first two, when possible):

- CLICK: Insert Clip Art button ( ) on the Standard toolbar
- DOUBLE-CLICK: art placeholder on an AutoLayout slide
- CHOOSE: Insert, Clip Art from the menu
- CHOOSE: Insert, Object from the menu and select Microsoft ClipArt Gallery from the dialog box

FINDING THE ART YOU WANT

In this section, we will use an example to describe how to find and insert clip art. The "Applications Software" presentation, stored on the Advantage Diskette, describes different categories for applications software. Your task will be to find an appropriate picture to insert on slide 1 of the "Applications Software" presentation. With a thousand pictures in the ClipArt Gallery, this could take some time. Unless, of course, you know how to search for that perfect picture.

Perform the following steps.

1. Make sure that you've loaded Microsoft PowerPoint and that the Advantage Diskette is inserted into drive A: or drive B:.
2. Open the "Applications Software" presentation stored on the Advantage Diskette.
3. The first slide of the "Applications Software" presentation should appear in the presentation window. To insert a clip art image onto the slide, you could change the slide's AutoLayout or you could do the following:
   CLICK: Insert Clip Art button ( )
   The ClipArt Gallery dialog box appears.
4. To search the Gallery for a picture:
   CLICK: Find command button
   Your screen should now appear similar to Figure 4.2.

FIGURE 4.2 FIND PICTURE DIALOG BOX

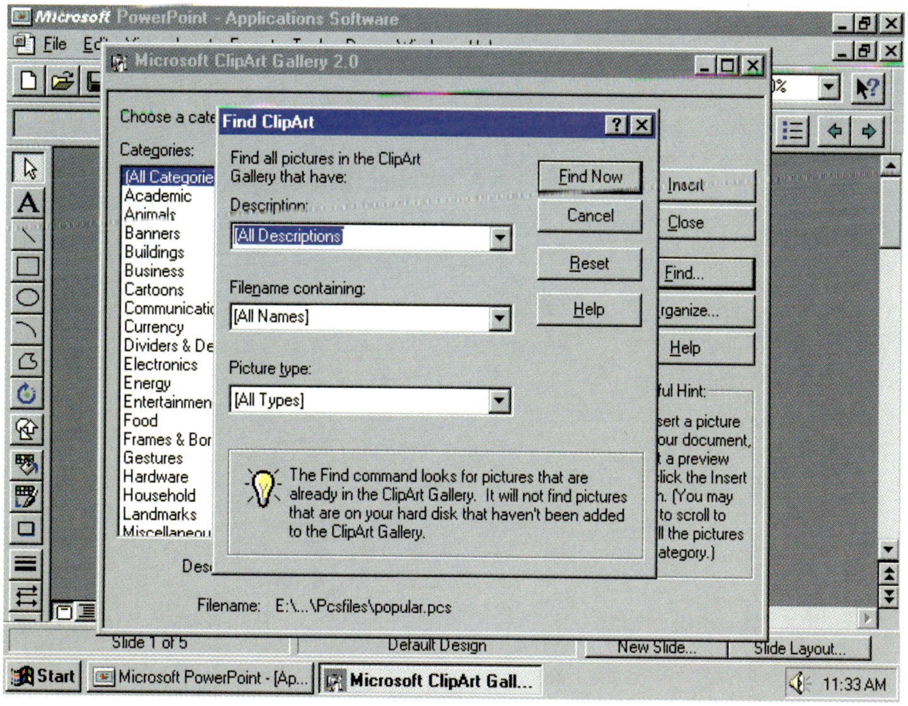

5. To find a picture that has the word "disk" in the description:
   TYPE: **disk** in the *Description* text box
   PRESS: ENTER or CLICK: Find Now
   Your screen should now look similar to Figure 4.3.

FIGURE 4.3 A PICTURE NAMED "FLOPPY DISK" APPEARS IN THE CLIPART GALLERY

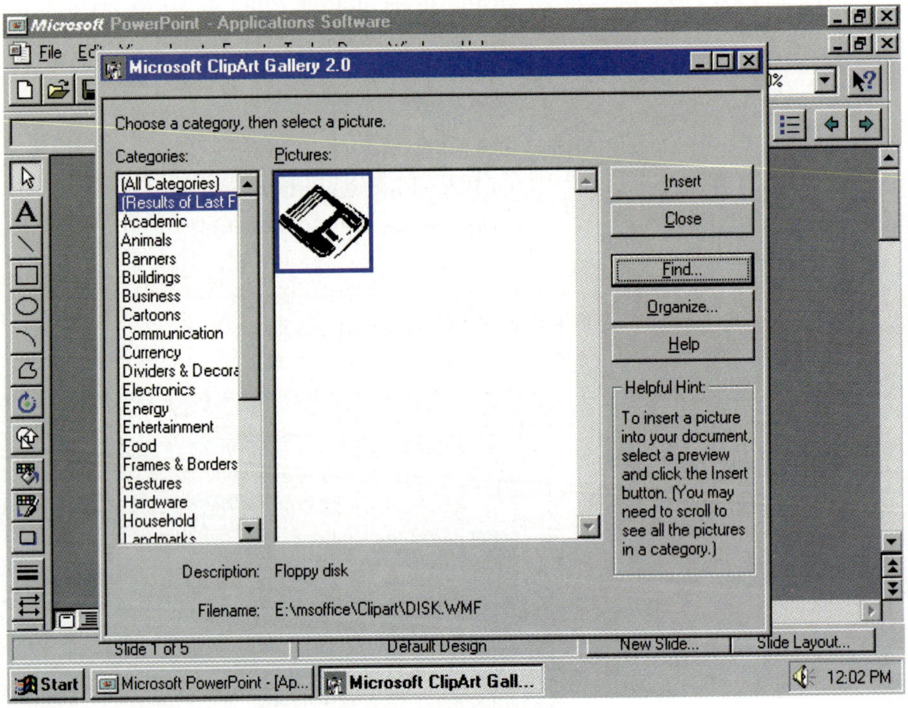

6. To insert the picture onto slide 1 of the "Applications Software" presentation:
   DOUBLE-CLICK: "Floppy disk" image
   Your screen should now appear similar to Figure 4.4. In the next section you will learn how to move and resize the picture.

FIGURE 4.4 SLIDE 1 AFTER INSERTING CLIP ART

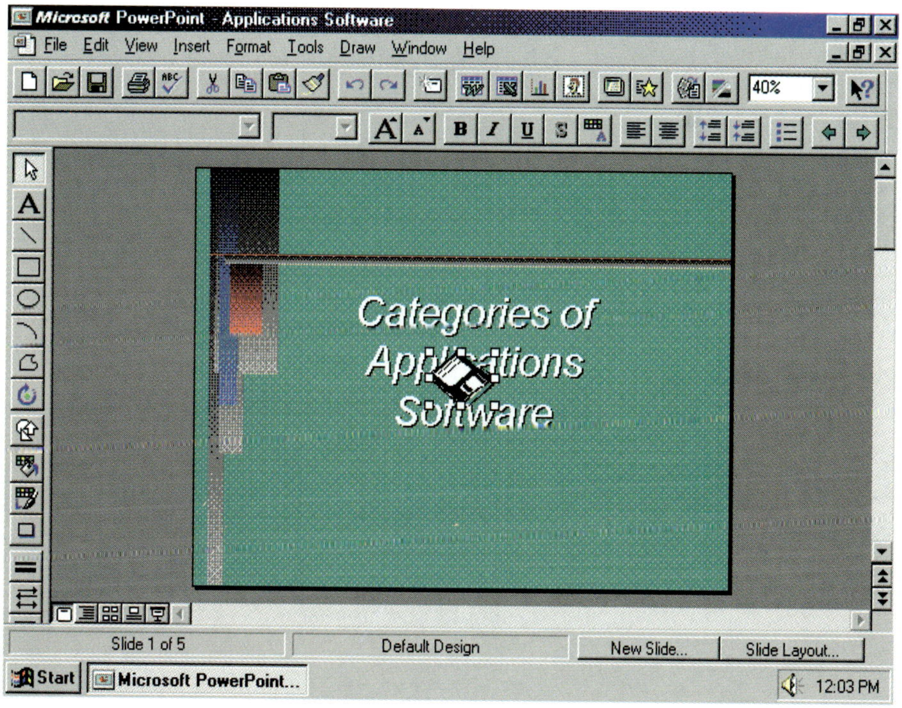

QUICK REFERENCE
Finding and Inserting an Image from the ClipArt Gallery

1. **SELECT: the slide to which you want to add clip art**
2. **CLICK: Insert Clip Art button ( ) on the Standard toolbar**
3. **SELECT: Find command button**
4. **TYPE:** *any description* **into the Description text box**
5. **PRESS: ENTER or CLICK: Find Now**

MOVING AND RESIZING CLIP ART

To move a clip art image, you point to it using the mouse pointer and then click and hold down the mouse button as you move the mouse pointer across the screen. To resize a clip art image, you select the image and then point to one of the selection handles that surrounds the image. You drag the handle inward to make the picture smaller and outward to make it larger. To size the image proportionally, ensure that you drag a corner handle and not one that appears on a horizontal or vertical edge.

Perform the following steps.

1. Ensure that slide 1 of the "Applications Software" presentation appears in the presentation window.
2. If you just completed the last section, the "Floppy disk" image should already appear selected. Handles that look like small boxes should appear around the image. If the image isn't selected:
   SELECT: "Floppy disk" image by pointing to it and then clicking the mouse button once
3. To move the selected clip art image to the bottom of the slide:
   DRAG: the image to the bottom of the window
   (*Note:* Make sure that you position the mouse pointer in the middle of the clip art image to move it by dragging. Otherwise, you may accidentally select a border and resize the image. As you move the mouse, you should see an empty frame appear to help you position the picture.) Your screen should now appear similar to Figure 4.5.

FIGURE 4.5 MOVING THE CLIP ART IMAGE DOWNWARD

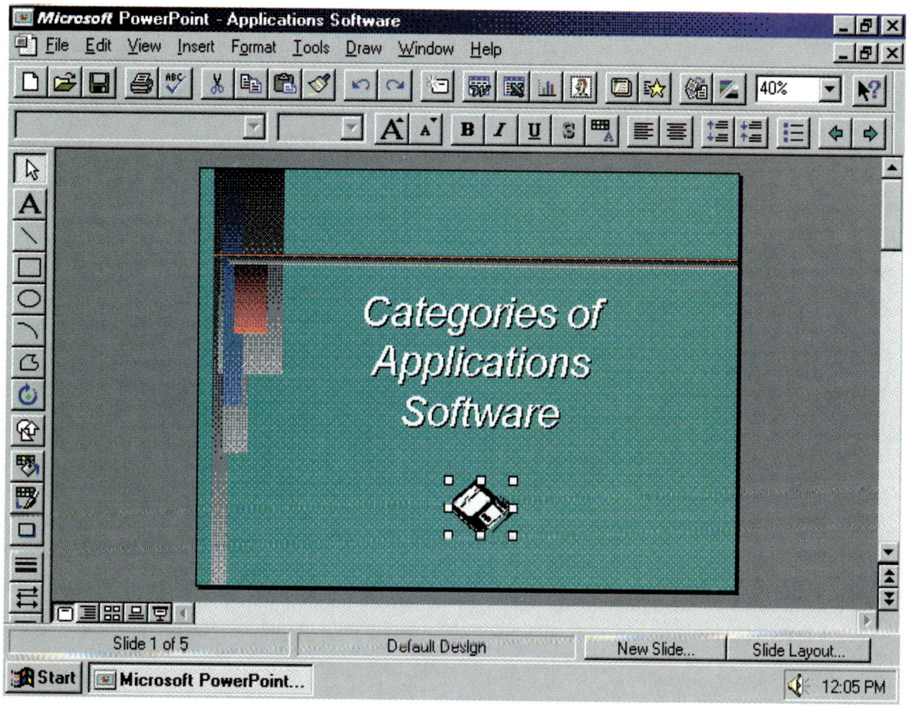

QUICK REFERENCE
Moving Clip Art

1. **SELECT: the desired clip art image**
2. **DRAG: the selected image to its new location**

4. To resize the picture so that it is larger:
   DRAG: one of the corner handles outward by ½ inch
   The picture should now appear larger.
5. To return the picture to its original size:
   CHOOSE: Edit, Undo
6. To save the "Applications Software" presentation:
   CLICK: Save button (💾)

QUICK REFERENCE
Resizing Clip Art

1. **SELECT: the desired clip art image**
2. **DRAG: one of the selection handles inward or outward**

INSERTING PICTURES

In addition to clip art images, you can insert graphic files into your presentation. A computer **graphic file** is usually created by an artist, designer, or desktop publisher. However, you can easily create your own graphic files if you have access to a **scanner.** A scanner is a hardware device that converts photographs and other paper-based material into computer images. Just as a photocopier makes a representation from paper to paper, a scanner makes a copy from paper to computer. Once it is saved to the disk, you can insert a computer graphic file into PowerPoint using the Insert, Picture command.

QUICK REFERENCE
Inserting Graphics

1. **Position the insertion point where you want to insert the object.**
2. **CHOOSE: Insert, Picture**
3. **SELECT: the desired disk drive, file type, and file name**
4. **PRESS: ENTER or CLICK: OK**

IN ADDITION

INSERTING MOVIES AND AUDIO TRACKS

You can insert movies and audio tracks for playback from within your presentation using the Insert, Movies command and the Insert, Sound command. To play back the video clip, display the presentation in Slide Show view and then click on the object. (*Note:* You computer must be multimedia-capable with Video for Windows to play back movies.)

CREATING GRAPHS

Most people recognize the benefit of using graphics to improve their effectiveness in communicating information. Clearly, a chart or graph is easier to decipher than rows and columns of tiny numbers. Fortunately, PowerPoint makes it relatively easy for you to include graphs in your presentations. It comes with a powerful supplementary program called **Microsoft Graph.** The Microsoft Graph 5.0 mini-app helps you produce great-looking charts and graphs—right from within PowerPoint! Graph does not replace a full-featured spreadsheet application like Microsoft Excel, but it does provide a more convenient tool for embedding simple charts into presentations.

A variety of methods exists for adding a graph to a slide (again, concentrate on using the first two).

- CLICK: Insert Graph button (📊) on the Standard toolbar
- DOUBLE-CLICK: graph placeholder on an AutoLayout slide
- CHOOSE: Insert, Microsoft Graph from the menu
- CHOOSE: Insert, Object from the menu and select Microsoft Graph from the dialog box

To add a graph to a slide, perform the following steps.

1. Ensure that the "Applications Software" presentation appears in the presentation window.
2. Display the last slide in the presentation (slide 5) by dragging the elevator scroll box to the bottom of the vertical scroll bar.
3. To insert a new slide:
   CLICK: New Slide hot button
4. To select the Graph AutoLayout slide:
   SELECT: Graph AutoLayout option
5. To display the slide:
   PRESS: ENTER or CLICK: OK
   Your screen should now appear similar to Figure 4.6.

FIGURE 4.6 SLIDE 6 WITH THE PLACEHOLDERS VISIBLE

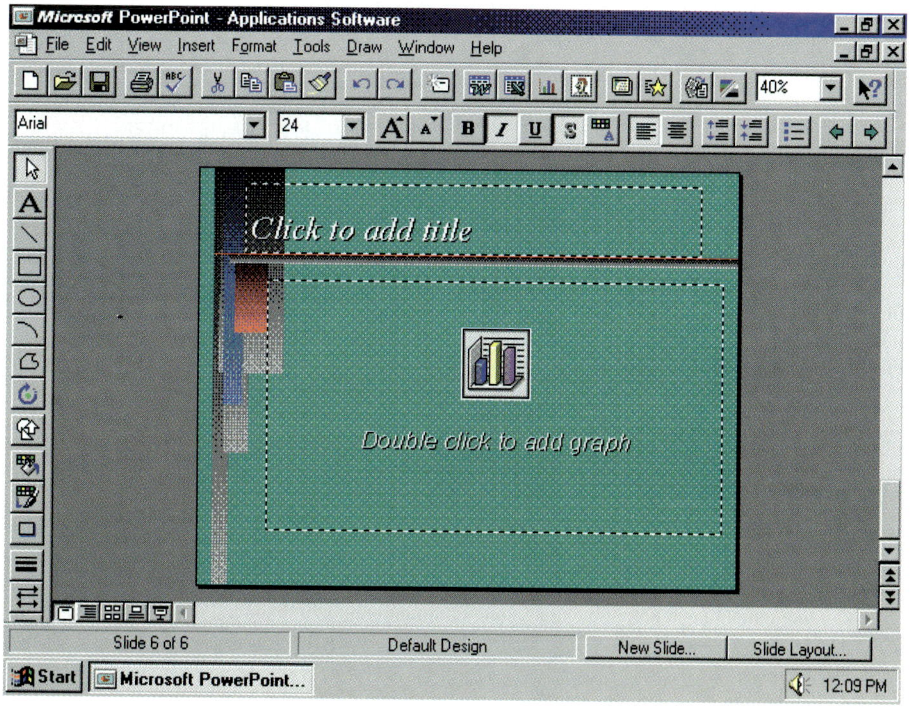

6. CLICK: Title placeholder
   TYPE: **APPLICATIONS SOFTWARE**
   PRESS: ENTER
   TYPE: **Sales Comparison**
7. To center the text in the placeholder:
   CLICK: Center button ( )
8. To insert a graph:
   DOUBLE-CLICK: the graph placeholder
   The Graph datasheet appears in a separate window with sample information. As in using an electronic spreadsheet, you add and edit data in the datasheet that you want to plot on a graph.
9. To edit the title information, you click the cross-hair mouse pointer on the *cell* (the intersection of a row and a column):
   SELECT: the cell with "1st Qtr" text
   TYPE: **WP** (which stands for Word Processing)
   SELECT: the cell with "2nd Qtr" text
   TYPE: **SS** (which stands for Spreadsheet)
   SELECT: the cell with "3rd Qtr" text
   TYPE: **DBMS** (which stands for Database Management System)
   SELECT: the cell with "4th Qtr" text
   TYPE: **PR** (which stands for Presentation)
   Your screen should now appear similar to Figure 4.7.

FIGURE 4.7 GRAPH DATASHEET AFTER MODIFYING THE COLUMN HEADINGS

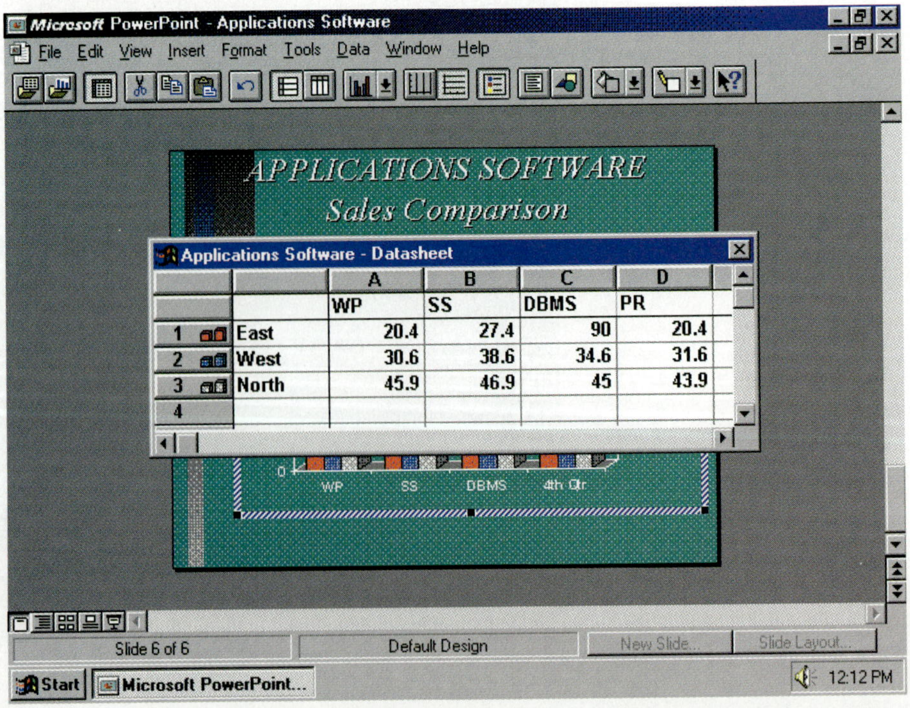

10. Rather than editing the remaining information, let's assume that it is correct and display the graph on the slide:
    CLICK: anywhere on the slide
    The graph is inserted automatically into your presentation.
11. To manipulate the graph, you must first click outside the graph area to end the editing mode. You can then move, resize, and change the colors on the image, just as you did using clip art. On your own, manipulate the graph to appear similar to slide 6 in Figure 4.8.

FIGURE 4.8 SLIDE 6 WITH A GRAPH INSERTED

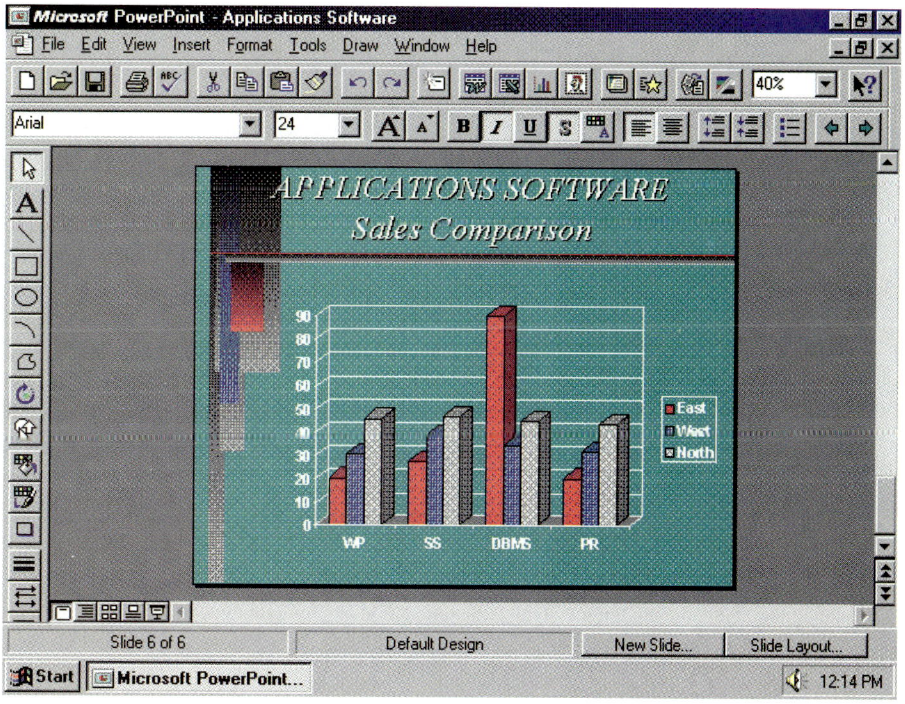

12. To save the "Applications Software" presentation:
    CLICK: Save button ( )

(*Note:* To learn more about working with graphs, access Microsoft Graph's Help facility or refer to the *Integrating Microsoft Office 95* Student Learning Guide in the Advantage Series for Computer Education.)

QUICK REFERENCE
Inserting a Graph

1. **CLICK: Insert Graph button ( ) on the Standard toolbar**
2. **DOUBLE-CLICK: graph placeholder on an AutoLayout slide**
3. **CHOOSE: Insert, Microsoft Graph from the menu**
4. **CHOOSE: Insert, Object and then select Microsoft Graph**

CREATING ORGANIZATIONAL CHARTS

Microsoft Organization Chart allows you to create organization charts and other hierarchical diagrams. As in working with graphics, you apply the principles of simplicity, emphasis, and balance to creating **organization charts.** In the following steps, you will insert a simple organizational chart into the "Applications Software" presentation.

There are a few methods for inserting an organization chart on a slide.

- DOUBLE-CLICK: organization chart placeholder on an AutoLayout slide
- CHOOSE: Insert, Object and select Microsoft Organization Chart

To add an organization chart, perform the following steps.

1. Ensure that the "Applications Software" presentation appears in the presentation window.
2. Display the first slide in the presentation (slide 1) by dragging the elevator scroll box to the top of the vertical scroll bar.
3. To insert a new slide:
   CLICK: New Slide hot button
4. To select the Organization Chart AutoLayout slide:
   SELECT: Organization Chart AutoLayout option
   PRESS: ENTER or CLICK: OK
   Your screen should now appear similar to Figure 4.9.

FIGURE 4.9 ORGANIZATION CHART PLACEHOLDER ON A NEW SLIDE

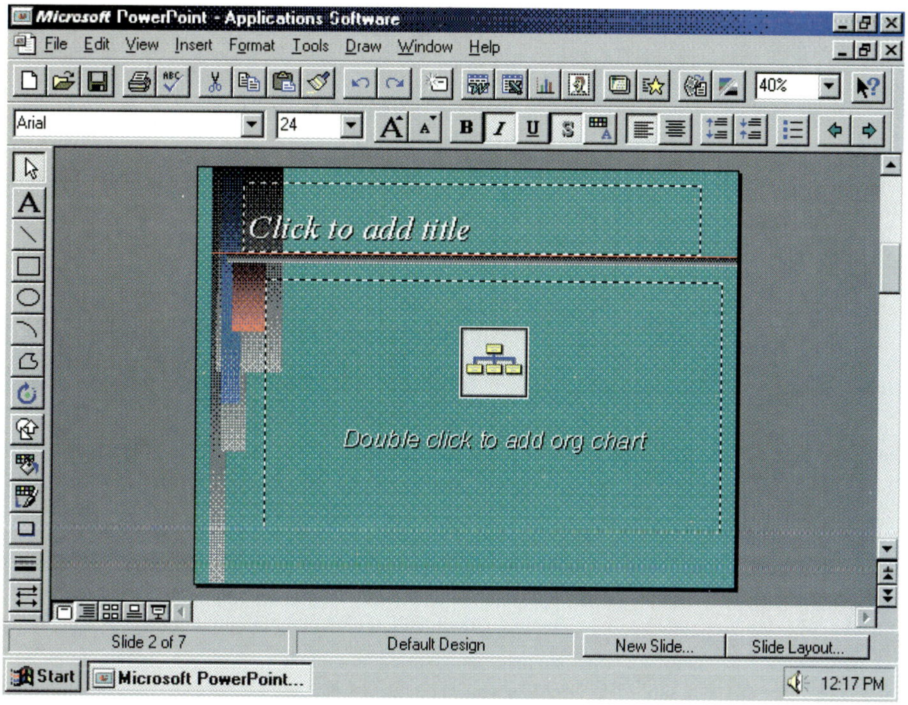

5. CLICK: Title placeholder
   TYPE: **SOFTWARE APPLICATIONS**
6. To center the text in the placeholder:
   CLICK: Center button ()
7. To insert an organization chart:
   DOUBLE-CLICK: the organization chart placeholder
   You should see four boxes on the screen; the topmost box should already be selected.
8. To edit the content of the organization chart boxes:
   TYPE: **CATEGORIES**
   PRESS: ENTER
   PRESS: DELETE to remove the "Type title here" text
   Notice that the text is replaced by <Title>. This is a placeholder for text and will not appear in the final organizational chart. The <Content> placeholders won't print either.
9. CLICK: the far left box, under the CATEGORIES box
   TYPE: **Word**
   PRESS: ENTER
   TYPE: **Processing**

10. CLICK: the center box, under the CATEGORIES box
    TYPE: **Electronic**
    PRESS: ENTER
    TYPE: **Spreadsheets**
11. CLICK: the far right box, under the CATEGORIES box
    TYPE: **Database**
    PRESS: ENTER
    PRESS: DELETE to remove the "Type title here" text
12. To add a new box to the chart:
    CLICK: Subordinate button (Subordinate:) in the toolbar
    CLICK: CATEGORIES box once
    A new box appears under the CATEGORIES box.
13. Because the new box is already selected, do the following:
    TYPE: **Presentation**
    CLICK: anywhere outside of the chart to remove the active selection
    The Microsoft Organization Chart window should now appear similar to Figure 4.10.

FIGURE 4.10 THE COMPLETED ORGANIZATION CHART

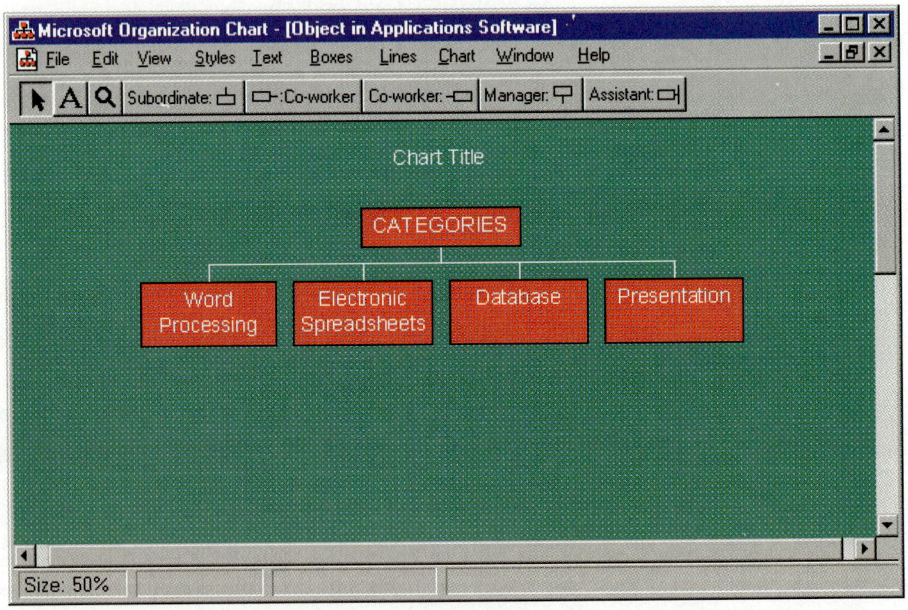

14. To return to PowerPoint and update the slide:
    CHOOSE: File, Exit and Return to Applications Software
    (*CAUTION:* Choose the command from the Microsoft Organization Chart Menu bar and not the PowerPoint Menu bar.)
15. CLICK: Yes command button to update the presentation

16. To save the "Applications Software" presentation:
    CLICK: Save button (🖫)

Once you've inserted an organization chart on a slide, you can edit it at any time by double-clicking the image on the slide to load Microsoft Organization Chart. You may, for example, decide to change the box colors, border color, border style, and so on. While displaying a presentation in Slide view, you use the same techniques for sizing and moving an organization chart image as you used for manipulating clip art images.

(*Note:* To learn more about working with organization charts, access Microsoft Organization Chart's Help facility or refer to the *Integrating Microsoft Office 95* Student Learning Guide in the Advantage Series.)

QUICK REFERENCE
Inserting an Organization Chart

- **DOUBLE-CLICK: organization chart placeholder on an AutoLayout slide**
- **CHOOSE: Insert, Object and then select Microsoft Organization Chart**

RUNNING SLIDE SHOWS

So far in this learning guide, you've viewed a slide show using PowerPoint's default settings. No transitions between slides or timed pauses have been added to Slide Show view. In the following sections, you learn how to take control of your electronic presentations by setting timings, adding transitions, and creating build slides.

SETTING TIMINGS

Timing refers to the amount of time a slide stays on the screen during Slide Show view. Timing is especially useful for those occasions when you want to let a presentation run unattended in a continuous loop. You specify timings for your presentation by choosing View, Slide Show command or by clicking the Rehearse New Timings button (⏱) in Slide Sorter view.

Perform the following steps.

1. Ensure that slide 1 of the "Applications Software" presentation appears in the presentation window.
2. To display the presentation in Slide Show view:
   CLICK: Slide Show view button (▭)
3. View the entire presentation by clicking the left mouse button to proceed from slide to slide. When you finish, slide 1 should appear in Slide view in the presentation window.

4. To build timings into the slide show:
   CHOOSE: View, Slide Show
   Your screen should now appear similar to Figure 4.11.

FIGURE 4.11 SLIDE SHOW DIALOG BOX

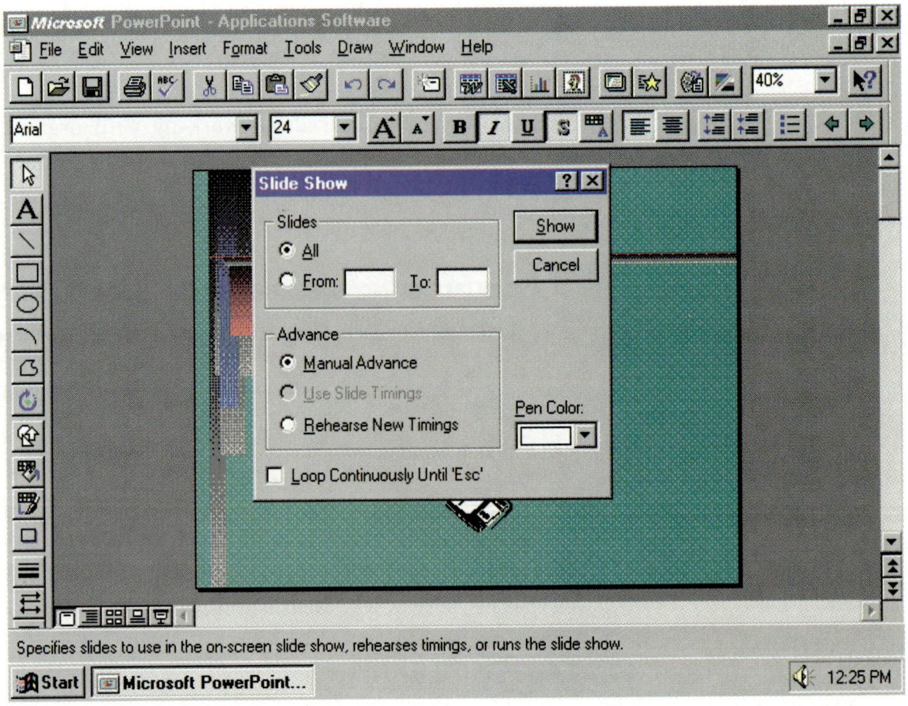

5. You're now going to build timings into the slide show. When you're finished, the slide show will advance automatically to the next slide unattended. In other words, you won't need to click the mouse to display the next slide. To set timings:
   SELECT: *Rehearse New Timings* option button
   CLICK: Show command button
   PowerPoint displays the first slide with the Rehearsal dialog box in the bottom right-hand corner of the screen. A running clock appears in the Rehearsal dialog box.

6. CLICK: ▷ after the clock reaches 10 seconds
   CLICK: ▷ after 5 seconds, for each remaining slide

7. When the slide show is finished, PowerPoint displays a dialog box on the screen showing the total number of seconds that elapsed. To record the timings and view them in Slide Sorter view:
   CLICK: Yes command button

8. To view the presentation with the new timings:
   CHOOSE: View, Slide Show
   SELECT: *Use Slide Timings* option button
   CLICK: Show command button
   Now, sit back and watch the show! (*Hint:* You can also select the *Run Continuously* check box at the bottom of this dialog box for self-running displays at trade shows and other presentations.)

9. When it is finished, save the "Applications Software" presentation back to the Advantage Diskette.

QUICK REFERENCE
Setting Timings

1. **CHOOSE: View, Slide Show**
2. **SELECT: *Rehearse New Timings* option button**
3. **CLICK: Show command button**
4. **CLICK: the mouse button after the desired seconds on each slide**
5. **After viewing the entire presentation:**
   CLICK: Yes command button to record the slide timings
6. **To view the slide show with the new timings:**
   CHOOSE: View, Slide Show
   SELECT: *Use Slide Timings* option button
   CLICK: Show command button

IN ADDITION

PLAYING MULTIPLE PRESENTATIONS CONSECUTIVELY

With PowerPoint, you can run multiple presentations consecutively, even unattended. When the first presentation is finished, the second presentation automatically begins. To do this, you assemble a play list.

For more information on this topic, double-click the Help button () and then select the Index tab. Type `play lists` and then click the Display button to display a list of related topics.

ADDING TRANSITIONS

In this section, you learn to incorporate transitions between slides. Transitions are the special effects you see when you go from one slide to the next. Previously only available in higher-end multimedia authoring programs, transitions can now be easily inserted into any of your PowerPoint presentations.

Perform the following steps.

1. Ensure that the "Applications Software" presentation appears in Slide Sorter view.

2. To add a transition to slide 1:
   SELECT: slide 1 in Slide Sorter view
   CLICK: Transition button ( ) on the Slide Sorter toolbar
   (*Note:* You can also choose the Tools, Slide Transition command from the menu.) Your screen should now appear similar to Figure 4.12.

FIGURE 4.12 TRANSITION DIALOG BOX

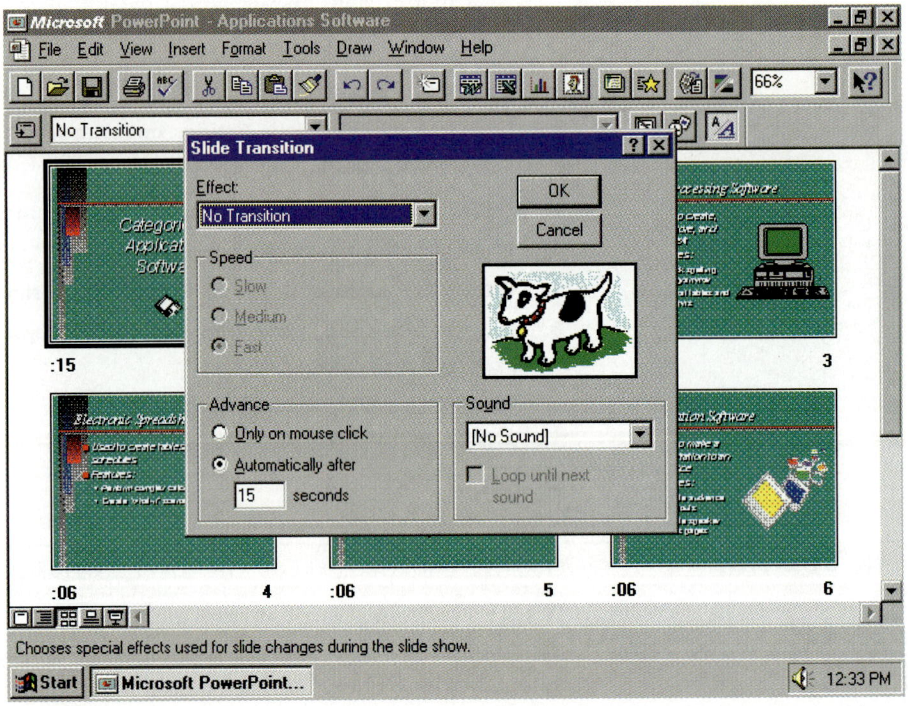

3. CLICK: down arrow beside the *Effect* drop-down list box
   (*Note:* You can also display the same options by selecting the *Transition Effects* drop-down list box in the Slide Sorter toolbar.)
4. CLICK: several transition effects
   Notice that they appear in the preview area of the dialog box.
5. SELECT: Random Transition
   (*Note:* You'll find the Random Transition option at the bottom of the *Effect* drop-down list box.)
6. PRESS: **ENTER** or CLICK: OK
   When you run the slide show, slide 1 will display with a random transition.
7. SELECT: slide 2 in Slide Sorter view
   CLICK: Transition button ( ) on the Slide Sorter toolbar
   SELECT: Blinds Vertical from the *Effect* drop-down list box
   PRESS: **ENTER** or CLICK: OK

8. For each of the remaining slides:
SELECT: a different transition effect from the *Effect* drop-down list
9. To view the slide show:
CHOOSE: View, Slide Show
SELECT: *Use Slide Timings* option button
CLICK: Show command button
10. Again, sit back and watch the show! When the presentation is finished, the presentation will again display in Slide Sorter view. (*Note:* In this view mode, you can see how a particular slide will transition by clicking the transition icon that is located on the bottom left of each slide. Also, the timing for the slide appears below its image.)

QUICK REFERENCE
Applying Transitions

1. **CHOOSE: View, Slide Sorter**
2. **SELECT: any slide in the presentation**
3. **CLICK: Transition button ( ) on the Slide Sorter toolbar**
4. **SELECT: a transition effect**
5. **PRESS: ENTER or CLICK: OK**

CREATING A BUILD SLIDE

Build slides let you reveal one bullet at a time in Slide Show view. You can also specify how the bullet appears (e.g., enters from the right), and whether you want to dim previously displayed items when you display a new bulleted item.

Perform the following steps.

1. Ensure that the "Applications Software" presentation appears in Slide Sorter view.
2. To add a build slide to the presentation:
SELECT: slide 4 in Slide Sorter view
(*Note:* This slide contains bulleted items describing electronic spreadsheet software.)
3. To create a build slide:
CLICK: down arrow beside the *Text Build Effects* drop-down list box on the Slide Sorter toolbar
(*Note:* You can also choose the Tools, Build Slide Text command from the menu.)
4. SELECT: Fly From Top

5. To display the slide show:
   CLICK: Slide Show view button
   (*Note:* After viewing a build slide, you may decide the slide needs more time to display. You can set its timing manually by choosing Tools, Slide Transition and then typing in a new time.)
6. Save the "Applications Software" presentation back to the Advantage Diskette.

QUICK REFERENCE
Creating a Build Slide

1. **CHOOSE: View, Slide Sorter**
2. **SELECT: any slide in the presentation**
3. **CLICK: down arrow beside the *Text Build Effects* drop-down list box on the Slide Sorter toolbar**
4. **SELECT: a build effect**

ADDING ANIMATION

Does your computer have a sound card and speakers? If so, you can play sound effects and add animation to your presentations. For example, you can listen to screeching brakes as text rolls in from the left side of the screen; how about hearing a laser sound as each letter drops into place; or a whoosh sound as text races in from the left. These animated effects combine sound and motion and are only a few of the effects accessible from the Animation Effects toolbar. By adding a bit of drama to your presentation, these effects will not only keep your audience interested, but also entertained. The Animation Effects toolbar appears below.

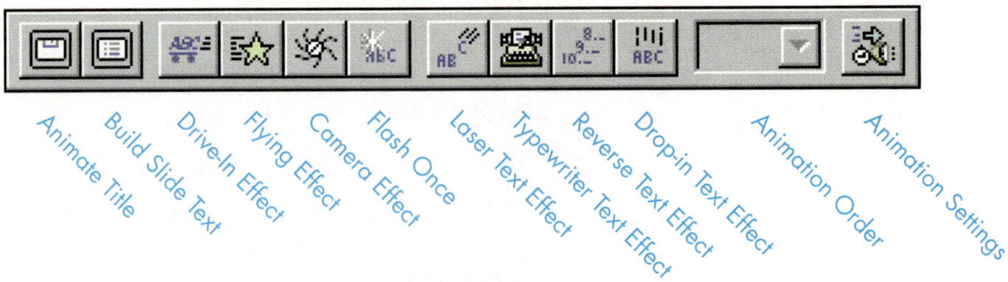

In the following steps, you use the Animation Effects toolbar to animate a slide in the "Applications Software" presentation.

1. Ensure that Slide 4 of the "Applications Software" presentation appears in Slide view.
2. To display the Animation Effects toolbar:
   CLICK: Animation Effects button on the Standard toolbar
   Your screen should now appear similar to Figure 4.13.

FIGURE 4.13 DISPLAYING THE ANIMATION EFFECTS TOOLBAR

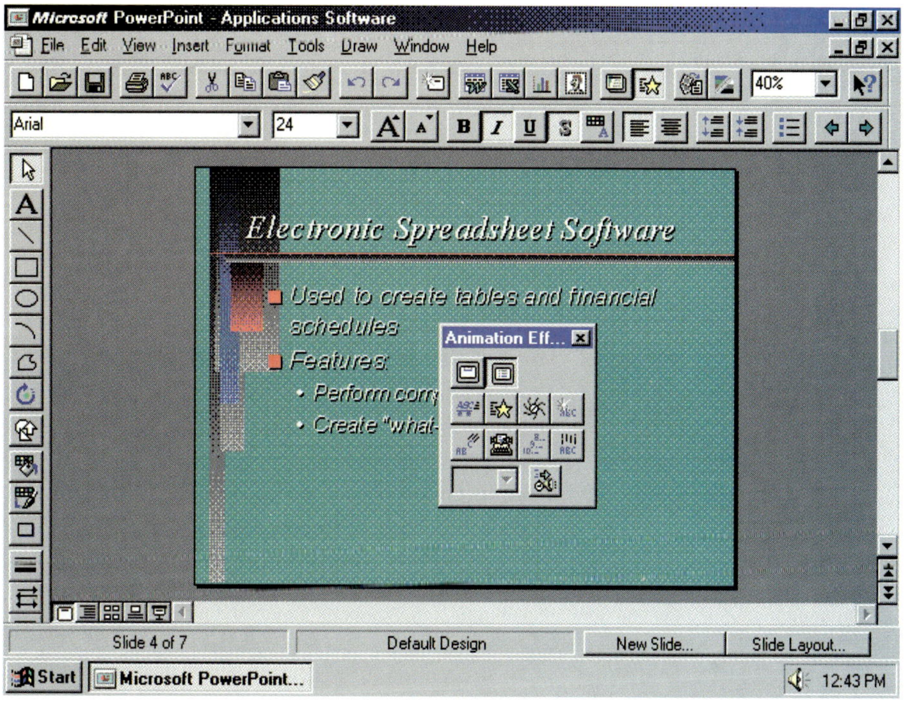

3. If the Animation Effects toolbar is covering part of your slide, as in Figure 4.13, drag it to one of the edges of the presentation window.
4. In this step, you are going to add the Laser Text Effect ( ) to the bulleted text on slide 4. Before adding an animation effect, the cursor must be positioned in the area you want to animate. In this case, you must click in the bulleted text area. Do the following:
   CLICK: anywhere in the bulleted text area
   CLICK: Laser Text Effect button ( )
5. To see the effect of the animation:
   CLICK: Slide Show view button ( )
6. To display the first bulleted text item:
   CLICK: left mouse button once
7. To display the next bulleted item:
   CLICK: left mouse button once
8. PRESS: ESC to display the presentation in Slide View
9. On your own, try out other animation effects.
10. Before proceeding, remove the Animation Effects toolbar from view.
    RIGHT-CLICK: Animation Effects toolbar
    CHOOSE: Animation Effects

11. Close the presentation.
12. Exit Microsoft PowerPoint.

QUICK REFERENCE
Adding Animation Effects

1. **CLICK: Animation Effects button ( ) on the Standard toolbar**
2. **CLICK: the area of the slide you want to animate**
3. **CLICK: the desired effect on the Animation Effects toolbar**

SUMMARY

This session focused on adding visual objects and effects to your presentations. You learned more about working with clip art, including how to find a clip art image and how to move and resize an image. You also learned to insert a graph and an organization chart on a slide using Microsoft Graph and Microsoft Organization Chart. The session concluded by showing you how to add special effects to your electronic presentations. Specifically, you learned to set slide timings, add transitions, create build slides, and add animated effects.

COMMAND SUMMARY

Many of the commands and procedures appearing in this session are provided in Table 4.1 below.

TABLE 4.1
Command Summary

Task Description	*Menu Command*	*Alternative Method*
Insert a clip art image	Insert, Clip Art	
Insert a graph	Insert, Microsoft Graph	
Insert an organization chart	Insert, Object	
Build timings into a slide show	View, Slide Show	
Add transitions to a slide show	Tools, Slide Transition	
Create build slides (from Slide Sorter view)	Tools, Build Slide Text	
Add animated effects		

KEY TERMS

graphic file
A computer graphic, created by an artist or scanned from an existing picture or photograph, that you can insert into your document using the Insert, Picture command.

Microsoft Graph
A supplementary program or *mini-app* that lets you create graphs and insert them onto a PowerPoint slide.

Microsoft Organization Chart
A supplementary program or *mini-app* that lets you create organization charts and insert them onto a PowerPoint slide.

mini-apps
Small application programs that are bundled with Microsoft Windows products to enhance the primary applications; most mini-apps are accessed using the Insert, Object command.

organization charts
A diagram showing the internal management reporting structure of a company, organization, institution, or other such group; also used for flowchart diagrams.

scanner
A hardware device that converts an existing picture or photograph into a computer image that is stored digitally on the disk.

EXERCISES

SHORT ANSWER

1. Why is it necessary to know how to search for an image in the Microsoft ClipArt Gallery?
2. How do you size a clip art image?
3. How do you move a clip art image?
4. Describe some of the effects accessible using the Animation Effects toolbar.
5. What application enables you to create organization charts?
6. Why would you want to build timing into a presentation?
7. Why would you want to build transitions into a presentation?

8. In an electronic slide show, what is a transition? Give some examples.
9. Describe the process of creating and inserting a graph on a slide.
10. What is a build slide? Give some examples of build effects.

HANDS-ON

(*Note:* Before working through the following exercises, make sure you have completed the tasks presented in this session. Also, make sure the Advantage Diskette is in drive A: or drive B:.)

1. Open the "Using Color" presentation that you created in Session 2 and edited in Session 3. Perform the following modifications to the presentation:
   a. Add timing to the presentation, whereby each slide stays on the screen for at least ten seconds before switching to the next slide.
   b. Make slides 2 and 3 build slides.
   c. Specify transitions between all the slides in the presentation.
   d. Display the presentation in Slide Show view using the Loop Continuously option.
   e. Save the presentation onto the Advantage Diskette.
2. Create a presentation that includes the five slides pictured in Figure 4.14. Create build slides and add transitions. Then, save the presentation as "PC Hardware Components."

FIGURE 4.14 SLIDES 1, 2, 3, 4, AND 5

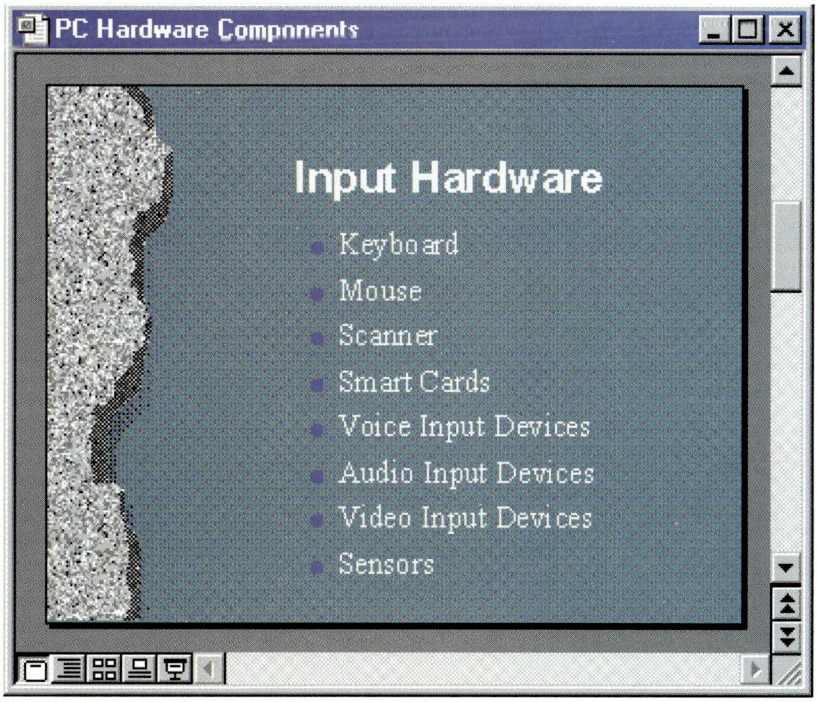

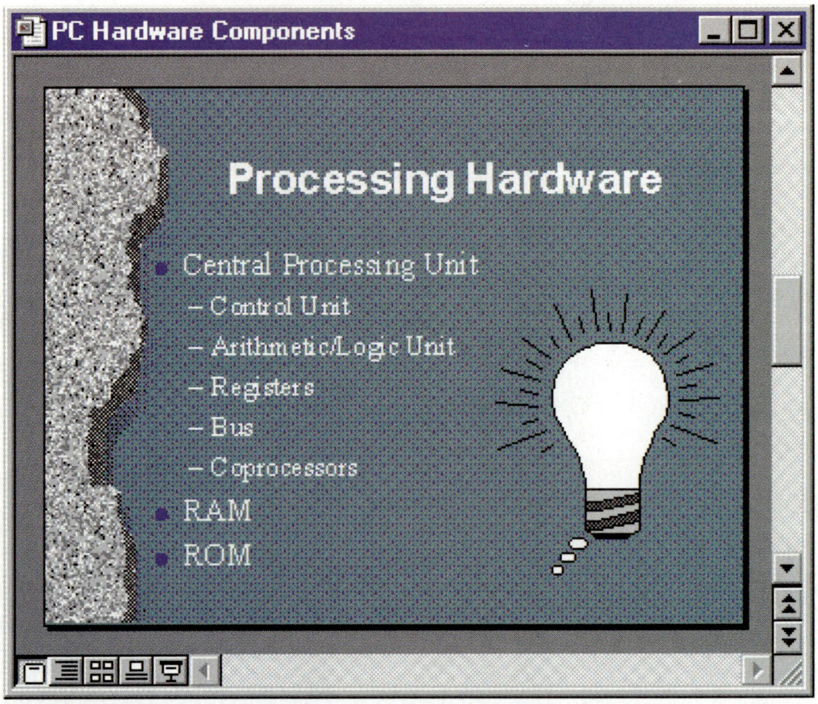
PC Hardware Components
Processing Hardware
Central Processing Unit
– Control Unit
– Arithmetic/Logic Unit
– Registers
– Bus
– Coprocessors
RAM
ROM

PC Hardware Components
Storage Hardware
Hard Disk
Floppy Diskettes
CD ROM Drives
Worm Drives

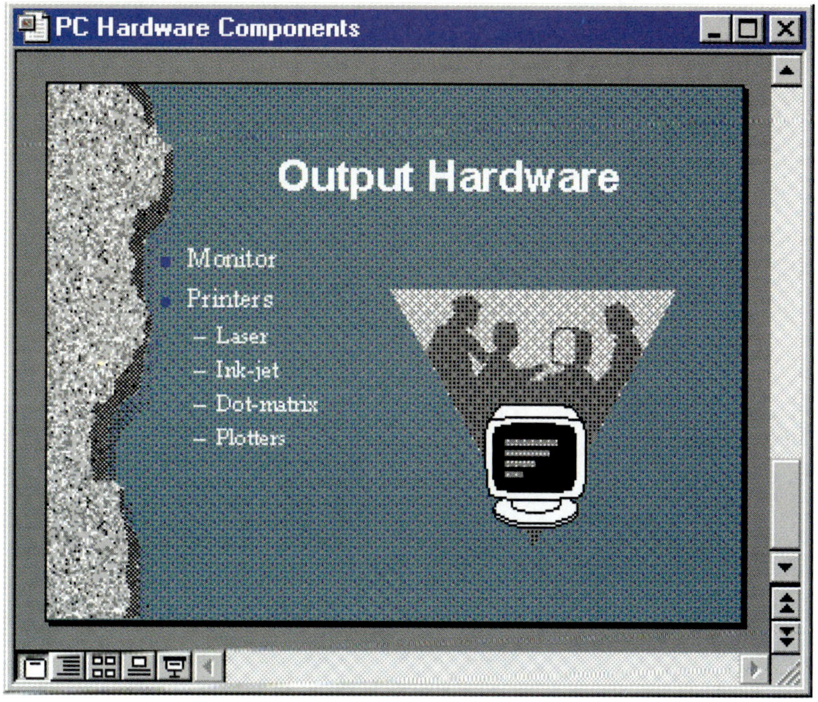

3. Create an electronic presentation on a topic you're interested in. When finished, save the presentation as "Session 4 Exercise." The presentation should contain at least five slides and include the following:

   a. A graph

   b. An organization chart

   c. A clip art image

   d. Text that you've inserted with the Text tool

   e. Customized bullets

   f. Build slides

   g. Transitions between slides

   h. Timed pauses between slides

   i. Animated effects

CASE PROBLEMS

IMMACULATE PERCEPTIONS, INC. (IPI)

(*Note:* In the following case problems, assume the role of the primary character or characters and perform the same steps that they identify.)

1. It was late Friday afternoon and most of the staff had already left the IPI offices for the long weekend. Roy MacGregor, on the other hand, was just arriving at IPI for the first time that day. Roy is the marketing manager for IPI and had taken an early commuter flight to Portland that morning to spend the day with a new client. Both Connie and Bobbie went to their office doors to greet him, but Roy got the first words out. "You're never going to believe this! I just spent an entire day with Gloria Gallego at Windermere's Windshield Wiper Warehouse. We had a $400,000 contract tied up by lunch and then she asked me some ridiculous questions about presentation software." Connie and Bobbie stole a quick glance at each other as Roy proceeded with his story. "Four hundred big ones down the drain because we can't deliver some sort of electronic slide show for their trade show exhibit. I've never even heard of the thing before—something like PowerPress or Point-to-Power, I don't know!"

   Connie and Bobbie led Roy to the boardroom and explained the meeting they had held with the creative staff that morning. Connie added, "We can do this presentation for them, Roy. I want you to call Gloria immediately and tell her that we'll send a sample presentation by Tuesday afternoon. Did you take any notes of what they wanted in an electronic slide show?" After shuffling some papers back and forth, Roy handed Connie one page of notes and left for his office to call Gloria.

   Upon Roy's return, Connie had summarized what the presentation should look like and what information it should contain. Using the following notes, you must now create a presentation for Windermere's Windshield Wiper Warehouse.

   PowerPoint Presentation for Windermere's Windshield Wiper Warehouse

   The presentation must include the following features:

   - *Be continuously self-running for display in trade show booths*
   - *Use their corporate colors of White, Black, and Red*
   - *Use transitions that wipe left and right like windshield wipers*
   - *Contain transportation-related clip art, like the image of a truck*
   - *Contain 8 slides with the following content*

#1: An introduction slide with the company's name and the clip art image of a truck	#2: Why W4 Wipers Work Best • Lifetime rubber compound • Durable steel construction • Tested and guaranteed
#3: Lifetime Rubber Compound • Lasts forever and a day • New coating stops streaking • Good from −30 to over 100 degrees in temperature	#4: Durable Steel Construction • Lasts forever and a day • Maintenance-free parts • Carried by hundreds of mechanics on the West Coast
#5: Tested and Guaranteed • Used on many makes and models of automobiles • Certified by the Windshield Manufacturer's Association	#6: Company name again • Friendly, courteous staff • Toll-free phone number • Terms of credit available (make this a build slide)
#7: A summary slide of the major points. Make it the same as slide #2 to save time.	#8: A conclusion slide with the company name and a message that the presentation will begin again in 15 seconds.

After viewing the presentation in Slide Show view, save the file as "Windermere" onto the Advantage Diskette.

2. Connie and Bobbie have been asked to present a company overview to the board of directors of IPI. This is a very formal presentation to their lawyers, accountants, bankers, and major investors. Create a PowerPoint presentation with an introduction and conclusion slide, and include the following components. Save the presentation as "IPI Board" onto the Advantage Diskette.

   Company Products

   - *Image consulting*
   - *Trade show materials*
   - *Point-of-purchase displays*
   - *PowerPoint presentations*

   Growth History (1991 to 1996)

   - *Staff: 2 to 14*
   - *Clients: 8 to 26*
   - *Sales: $65,000 to $1.6 million*

Staff

- *Two directors*
- *Two managers*
- *Six creative staff*
- *Four administrative personnel*

Organization Chart

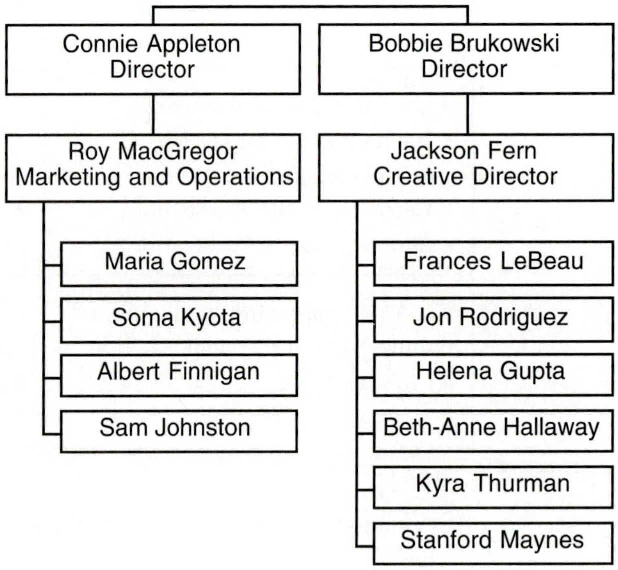

3. Add the following financial projections to the IPI company overview presentation, complete with a table of figures on one slide and a graph on another. Also, incorporate slide transition effects and use build slides in the presentation. Save the presentation to the Advantage Diskette.

(in 000s)	1995	1996
Sales Revenue	$1,450	$1,620
Cost of Sales	580	700
Gross Profit	870	920
Fixed Costs	450	480
Net Profit	$ 420	$ 440

Notes, Handouts, and Printing

SESSION 5

SESSION OUTLINE

- Public Speaking Tips
- Speaker's Notes
- Audience Handouts
- Print Options for Slides
- Packaging Your Presentation
- Summary
- Key Terms
- Exercises

INTRODUCTION

In this session, you learn to create and print speaker notes and audience handouts, two useful components of any presentation. Like slides, notes and handouts have associated masters called the **Notes Master** and the **Handout Master,** respectively. You also learn to print the different elements of your presentation, including how to set up a 35mm slide format for output.

CASE STUDY

SPRINGS COLLEGE, COLORADO

Situated on a hillside of fir trees with a breathtaking view of the valley, the Springs College campus provides a beautiful and convenient retreat for residents of Denver and Colorado Springs. In addition to its surroundings, the school is well known in the state for its progressive business and computer programs. Bradley Neumann was very fortunate to land his first-ever teaching position with Springs College, especially considering his alternative offer from Wolf Bay University in Canada's Northwest Territories!

After two months, Bradley felt comfortable with the marketing courses that he had recently assumed from Gayle Fanning, who was taking a year's sabbatical to conduct marketing research for a large computer manufacturer. He wasn't expecting to hear from Gayle for another ten months when he received an e-mail over the Internet: *Hi Bradley, I trust that you're into the full swing of things now that it's been a couple of months. I've been collecting some very interesting research that I think you should include in your Marketing Research 201 curriculum. I've received authorization from the company I'm working with to send you reports every two weeks with my findings and conclusions. I think this information will greatly benefit your students. I'll be in touch soon, Gayle.*

In this session, you and Bradley will learn to create speaker's notes pages and audience handouts. These two elements of a presentation are extremely valuable when you are presenting someone else's ideas and need the supporting documentation close at hand. You also learn to create 35mm slides for taking your presentations on the road.

PUBLIC SPEAKING TIPS

One of the greatest skills that you can possess is a talent for public speaking. Whatever career choice you've made or will make, the time will come when you must present an opinion, train a co-worker, or give an impromptu speech at your son's or daughter's kindergarten class. In the real world, however, some people would rather streak across the field during the Super Bowl than say a few words in front of their peers.

Here are some techniques to help you combat your platform jitters and pull off a winning presentation:

- Prepare your presentation materials thoroughly.
- Practice your delivery in front of the mirror or use a tape recorder.
- Polish your delivery (e.g., remember to make eye contact).

- Psyche yourself up and project positive thoughts.
- Visualize yourself doing an excellent job!

When preparing to give a presentation, allot yourself approximately two minutes to present each slide. Therefore, a 30-minute presentation will have about 15 slides. You may feel that you need more content than this to "save you" for half an hour, but the actual time that it takes to present a slide to an audience is rarely less than two minutes. You do not want to put all your information into your slide presentation anyway. Otherwise, you might as well just distribute handouts to the audience and send them on their way. Remember, the audience is there to listen to what you will say and how you will say it! Every successful speaker communicates his or her interest in and enthusiasm for a topic and remains courteous to the audience at all times.

SPEAKER'S NOTES

In preparing for a presentation, you should consider creating cheat sheets or crib notes. Many an accomplished speaker has adopted the recipe card format for speaker's notes. These notes help you avoid a common pitfall among novice presenters—putting too much text on the slides. Keep your slides brief and to the point. Use the notes pages in PowerPoint (as a replacement or complement to your recipe cards) to store reminders to yourself, relevant facts, and anecdotes. These notes pages also come in handy for question periods at the end of presentations.

In PowerPoint, a typical **notes page** provides a smaller, printed version of a slide at the top of the page with an area for text and graphics appearing below. Using the Notes Master, you can add designs and logos to all of your notes pages, or you can edit individual pages. To select the Notes Pages view, click the Notes Pages view button () or choose View, Notes Pages from the menu.

CREATING AND PRINTING SPEAKER'S NOTES

In this section, you create a notes page for the "Computer Training" presentation that is stored on the Advantage Diskette.

Perform the following steps.

1. Make sure that you've loaded Microsoft PowerPoint and that the Advantage Diskette is inserted into drive A: or B:.
2. Open the "Computer Training" presentation stored on the Advantage Diskette.
3. The first slide of the "Computer Training" presentation should appear in the presentation window.

4. CLICK: Notes Pages View button ( )
   SELECT: 50% from the *Zoom Control* drop-down list box
   Your screen should now appear similar to Figure 5.1.

FIGURE 5.1 A NOTES PAGE FROM THE "COMPUTER TRAINING" PRESENTATION

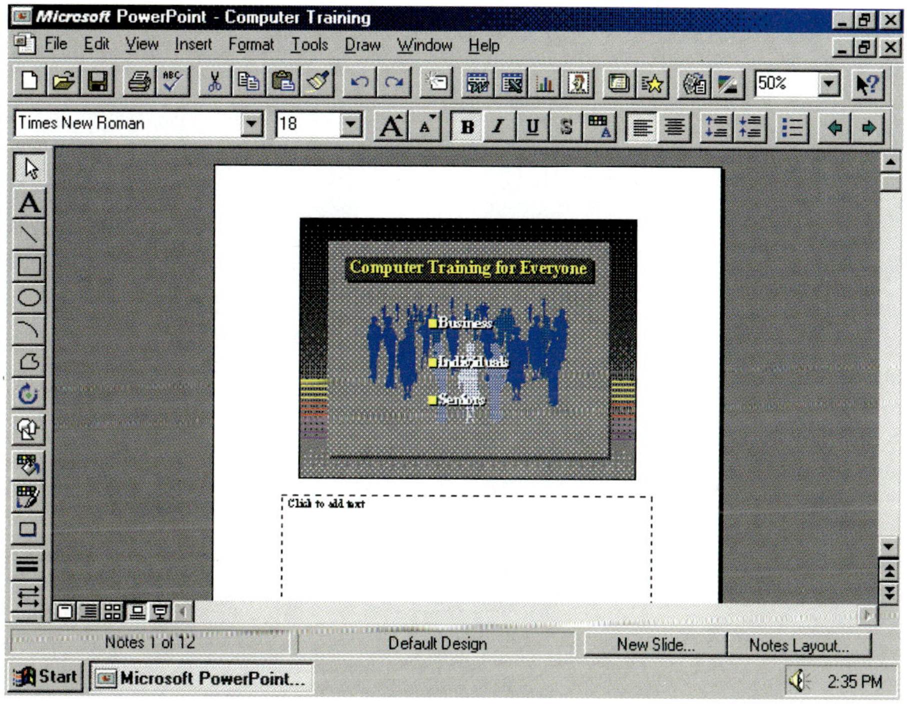

5. To add notes:
   CLICK: anywhere in the notes box to position the insertion point
6. To enlarge your view of the notes box so it's easier to see:
   SELECT: 75% from the *Zoom Control* drop-down list box
   (*Hint:* As needed, you can also resize the page space taken up by the image or notes area by selecting the area's border and dragging its handles.)
7. Ensure that the insertion point or cursor is blinking inside the notes box. Do the following:
   TYPE: **Welcome to MPC College.**
   PRESS: ENTER twice
   TYPE: **And welcome to our first computer training orientation meeting. We are anxious to share with you the elements of our training program and to take you on a tour of MPC's training facilities.**
   PRESS: ENTER twice

TYPE: **Please feel free to ask questions at any point during the presentation.**

Your screen should now appear similar to Figure 5.2.

FIGURE 5.2 ENTERING TEXT INTO A NOTES PAGE

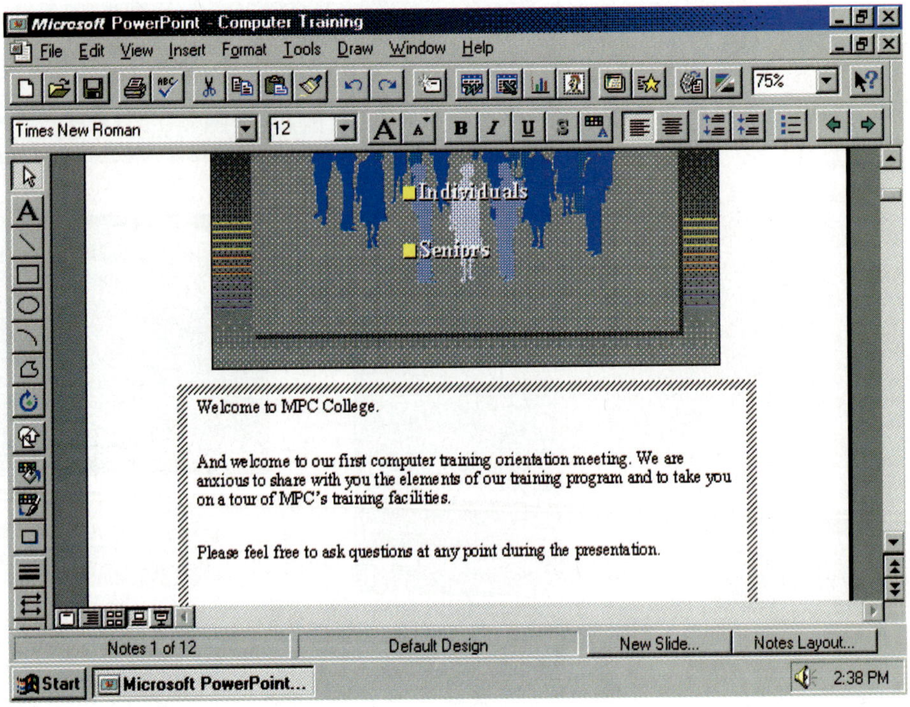

8. To print the notes page:
   CHOOSE: File, Print
   CLICK: down arrow beside the *Print what* drop-down list box
   SELECT: Notes Pages
9. To print just the current slide:
   SELECT: Current Slide option button in the *Print range* area
   PRESS: **ENTER** or CLICK: OK

QUICK REFERENCE
Creating a Notes Page

1. **Make the desired slide active in the presentation window.**
2. **CHOOSE: View, Notes Pages, or**
   CLICK: Notes Pages View button ( )
3. **CLICK: anywhere in the Notes placeholder box**
4. **TYPE:** `desired notes`

MODIFYING THE NOTES MASTER

Let's place your name in the footer of the Notes Master. A *footer* is a word processing term for the area that appears at the bottom of every page. A *header* is a word processing term for the area that appears at the top of every page. This page currently has a footer with the page number and current slide number. You can also insert clip art images and other graphic pictures in the header and footer of a page.

Perform the following steps.

1. To create a footer that appears on every page, you need to modify the Notes Master. Let's display this master page:
   CHOOSE: View, Master, Notes Master
2. DRAG: the elevator scroll box to the bottom of the vertical scroll bar so that you can see the bottom of the page
3. Click the mouse button in the bottom left-hand corner of the page in the Footer Area text box. It doesn't matter whether the cursor is positioned before or after the <footer> placeholder. This code is non-printing and will not appear in your printout.
4. To change the point size of the text:
   CLICK: down arrow beside the *Font Size* drop-down list box
   SELECT: 12
5. TYPE: **Presented by *your name***
   Enter your name where specified in the above instruction. Your screen should now appear similar to Figure 5.3. (*Remember:* The <footer> code won't appear in your printout; it is a non-printing code.)

FIGURE 5.3 THE MODIFIED NOTES MASTER

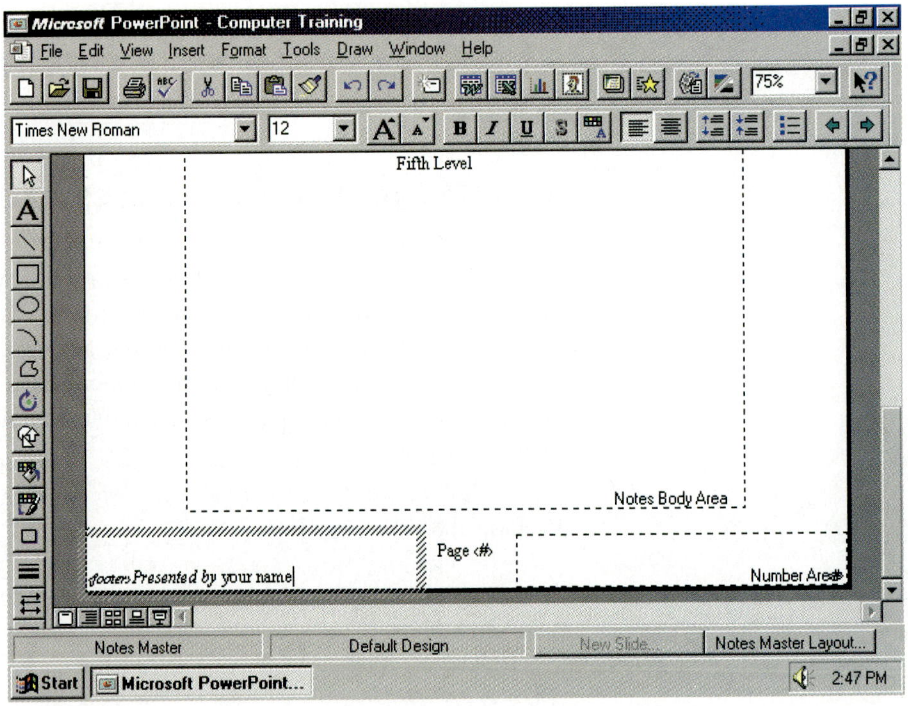

6. To return to the Notes Pages view:
   CLICK: Notes Page view button ( )
   Notice that the text you entered above now appears in the footer of the active page.
7. Save your work to the Advantage Diskette.

QUICK REFERENCE
Modifying the Notes Master

1. **CHOOSE: View, Master, Notes Master**
2. **Modify the formatting specifications of the Text placeholder or add text and graphics to the Notes Master.**

AUDIENCE HANDOUTS

Preparing handouts for your audience is a courtesy. However, you do not want to provide too much information in audience handouts; otherwise, there is no incentive to sit through your presentation. Many presenters create audience handouts in which important information is missing from the slide representations on the page. As the speaker proceeds through each slide, important information is provided so that the audience can fill in the blanks in their notes. Not only does the audience have to pay attention in order to compile a complete set of notes, they may also remember the important concepts better by having to write them down.

In PowerPoint, a handout is essentially a printout of the slides in your presentation. As with the notes pages, you can add text and art—such as your company logo—to all of the handout pages. You also choose whether to include two, three, or six slides on a handout page. Another option to consider is leaving space on the handout so that your audience can take notes during the presentation. In the following sections, you create a handout for the "Computer Training" presentation that is stored on the Advantage Diskette.

MODIFYING THE HANDOUT MASTER

You add text and graphics to a handout by modifying the Handout Master. Unlike notes pages, handouts cannot be edited individually. In fact, you see them only after they are printed.

Perform the following steps.

1. Ensure that the first slide of the "Computer Training" presentation appears in the presentation window.
2. CHOOSE: View, Master, Handout Master
3. To see the entire handout page:
   CLICK: down arrow beside the *Zoom Control* drop-down list box
   SELECT: 50% (or another zoom factor to resemble Figure 5.4)
   Your screen should now appear similar to Figure 5.4.

FIGURE 5.4 HANDOUT MASTER WITH OUTLINES SHOWING WHERE TWO, THREE, AND SIX SLIDES WILL PRINT

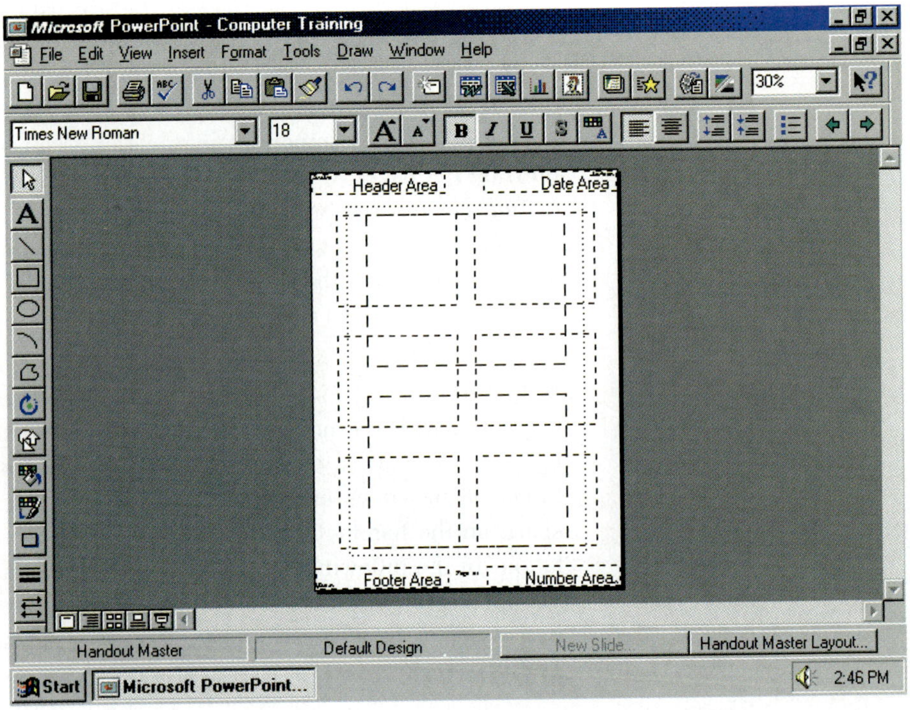

4. To enlarge your view of the handout page:
   CLICK: down arrow beside the *Zoom Control* drop-down list
   SELECT: 75%
5. DRAG: the elevator scroll box to the top of the vertical scroll bar
6. In this step, you insert a title in the header. Do the following:
   CLICK: the mouse pointer in the upper left-hand corner of the page (in the Header Area text box)
   (*Note:* It doesn't matter whether the insertion point is before or after the <header> code. Like the <footer> code, the <header> placeholder is non-printing.)
7. To change the point size of the text:
   CLICK: down arrow beside the *Font Size* drop-down list box
   SELECT: 18
8. TYPE: `MPC College:`
   PRESS: ENTER
   TYPE: `Computer Training Center`
   Your screen should now appear similar to Figure 5.5.

FIGURE 5.5 TEXT INSERTED IN THE HEADER OF THE HANDOUT MASTER

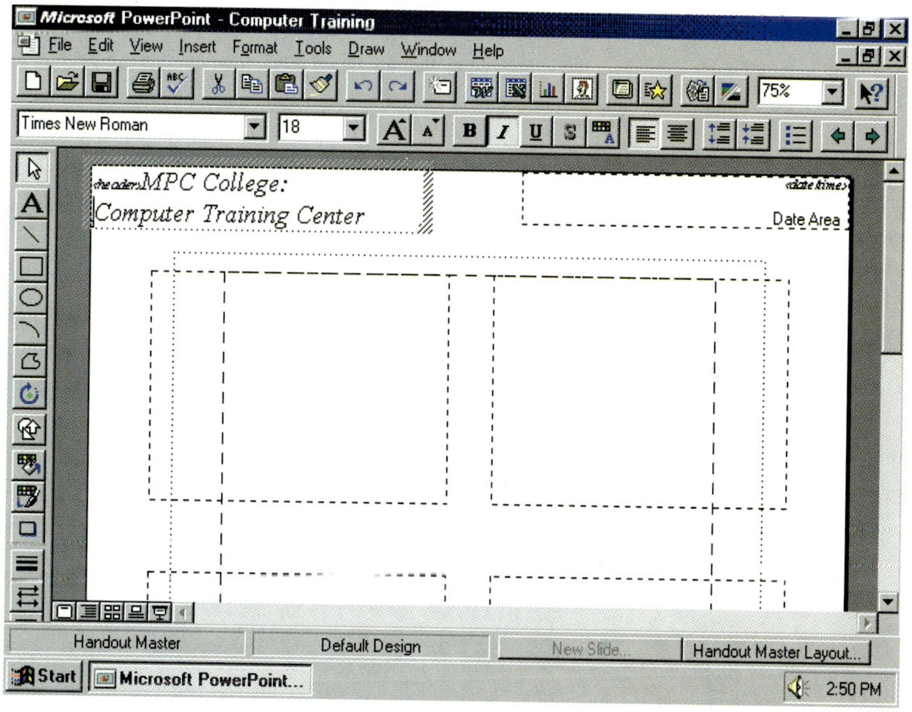

QUICK REFERENCE Modifying the Handout Master	1. **CHOOSE: View, Master, Handout Master** 2. **Modify the formatting specifications of the Text placeholder or add text and graphics to the Handout Master.**

PRINTING AUDIENCE HANDOUTS

To print audience handouts for the "Computer Training" presentation, perform the following steps.

1. CHOOSE: File, Print
   CLICK: down arrow beside the *Print what* drop-down list box
   SELECT: Handouts (6 slides per page)
2. To print the entire presentation:
   SELECT: All option button in the *Print range* area
   PRESS: ENTER or CLICK: OK
3. To prepare for the next section:
   CHOOSE: View, Slides

QUICK REFERENCE
Printing Audience Handout Pages

1. **CHOOSE: File, Print**
2. **SELECT: Handouts (number of slides per page) from the *Print what* drop-down list box**
3. **SELECT: the desired handouts to print in the *Print range* area**
4. **PRESS: ENTER or CLICK: OK**

PRINT OPTIONS FOR SLIDES

As you've seen throughout this learning guide, the process of printing involves first opening the presentation you want to print, identifying what you want to print (slides, outline, notes pages, audience handouts) and then specifying the range of slides to print.

In the following sections, we describe some additional options that you should be familiar with when printing your presentations.

SETTING UP THE SLIDE FORMAT

The size of your printed slides is determined by the settings in the Slide Setup box (Figure 5.6). If you don't want to use the default settings, you should choose File, Slide Setup to establish the settings before you begin creating slides. Review the options in Table 5.1 for more information. Landscape orientation means that what you print will print across the length of the paper. In portrait orientation, a slide image would appear taller than in landscape orientation.

TABLE 5.1
Slide Dimensions

Slide Output	*Width*	*Height*	*Orientation*
On-Screen Show	10 inches	7.5 inches	Landscape
Letter Paper (8.5 × 11 inches)	10 inches	7.5 inches	Landscape
A4 Paper (210 mm × 297 mm)	10.83 inches	7.5 inches	Landscape
35 mm slide	11.25 inches	7.5 inches	Landscape
Overhead	10 inches	7.5 inches	Landscape
Custom (your own settings)			

Perform the following steps.

1. Ensure that the first slide of the "Computer Training" presentation appears in the presentation window.

2. To display the Slide Setup dialog box:
   CHOOSE: File, Slide Setup
   Your screen should now appear similar to Figure 5.6.

FIGURE 5.6 SLIDE SETUP DIALOG BOX

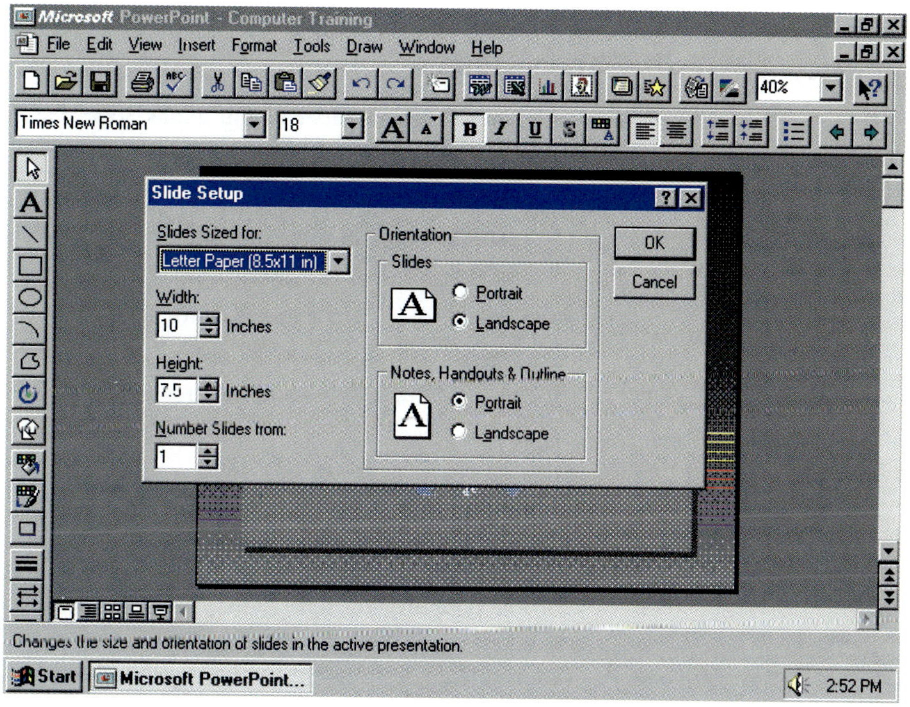

3. CLICK: down arrow beside the *Slides Sized for* drop-down list box
4. Review the options in the drop-down list box and do the following:
   SELECT: Cancel command button to leave the dialog box
5. Save the "Computer Training" presentation back to the Advantage Diskette.
6. Close the presentation and exit Microsoft PowerPoint.

35mm SLIDES

If you will be creating 35mm slides of your presentation, make sure to first select 35mm slides in the Slide Setup dialog box (described in the previous section). Then you choose File, Print to display the Print dialog box. Select the *Scale to Fit Paper* check box to have PowerPoint scale your slides so they will fit. Select the *Print to File* check box, in order to create a file that can be turned over to an outside service bureau for the creation of 35mm slides. (*Note:* After you press ENTER, PowerPoint prompts you for the name of the slide file.)

For more convenience, if you are in North America and have a modem in your computer, you can send your presentation directly from PowerPoint to Genigraphics, a company that specializes in the output of color 35mm slides and other types of color output. Choose the File, Send to Genigraphics command from the Menu bar and then follow the instructions presented by the Genigraphics wizard. (*Note:* If the "Send to Genigraphics" option doesn't appear in the File menu, then this option wasn't installed on your computer.)

QUICK REFERENCE
Creating 35mm Slides

1. **CHOOSE: File, Slide Setup**
   SELECT: 35mm slides in the *Slides Sized for* drop-down list box
   PRESS: ENTER or CLICK: OK
2. **CHOOSE: File, Print**
   SELECT: Slides in the *Print what* drop-down list box
   SELECT: *Print to File* check box
   SELECT: *Scale to Fit Paper* check box
   PRESS: ENTER or CLICK: OK
3. **PowerPoint will prompt you for the name of the output file.**

PACKAGING YOUR PRESENTATION

If you typically present PowerPoint presentations on different computers, you need to know about the Pack And Go Wizard. This helpful wizard packages your entire presentation, including the PowerPoint Viewer program (if desired), into a single file. In fact, you can even package multiple presentations together on the same diskette or across several diskettes. For an added sense of security and to ensure that the presentation looks the same on another computer, the Pack And Go Wizard lets you include linked files and embed TrueType fonts. Lastly, the wizard compresses the presentation so that it takes fewer diskettes to take your show on the road! For more information on this topic, refer to the PowerPoint on-line Help facility or run the command by choosing File, Pack And Go Wizard.

SUMMARY

In this session, you learned how to create and print notes pages and audience handouts. You used the Notes Master and the Handout Master to include text or other objects in the headers and footers of every notes or handout page. The session concluded by showing you how to use the Slide Setup dialog box and how to print 35mm slides.

COMMAND SUMMARY

Many of the commands and procedures appearing in this session are provided in Table 5.2 below.

TABLE 5.2
Command Summary

Task Description	*Menu Command*
Display the Notes Master	View, Master, Notes Master
Display the Handout Master	View, Master, Handout Master
Display the Slide Setup dialog box	File, Slide Setup
Print 35mm slides	File, Print
Package a presentation for delivery on another computer	File, Pack And Go Wizard

KEY TERMS

Handout Master
The slide you edit to change every page in an audience handout.

landscape orientation
In this mode, your slides print across the length of the page.

Notes Master
The slide you edit to change every notes page.

notes page
A notes page, used by the presenter, that includes a smaller printed version of a slide on the top of the page and an area for notes below.

portrait orientation
In this mode, your slides print across the width of the page.

EXERCISES

SHORT ANSWER

1. What is the Notes Master used for?
2. What is the Handout Master used for?
3. What are the dotted lines that appear on the Handout Master?
4. What is the *Zoom Control* drop-down list box used for?
5. How do you change the orientation of the slides you print?
6. What is meant by landscape orientation? portrait orientation?

7. If you want all your notes pages to print with a larger notes area and a smaller screen image, what should you do?
8. How do you create 35mm slides?
9. What does a notes page look like? What does a handout look like?
10. How do you include text on an audience handout?

HANDS-ON

(*Note:* Before working through the following exercises, make sure the Advantage Diskette is in drive A: or drive B:.)

1. Open the "Applications Software" presentation that is stored on the Advantage Diskette. Perform the following steps.
   a. Display slide 1 in Notes Pages view.
   b. Type in a few sentences of notes that would be helpful when presenting this slide.
   c. Print the notes page you created in Step *b*.
   d. Display the Handout Master.
   e. Type the current date in the upper right-hand corner of the page.
   f. Print the audience handouts.
   g. Save the "Applications Software" presentation.
   h. Close the presentation.
2. Print audience handouts for the presentation that you created in Session 2 called "Session 2 Exercise." Make sure to include your name in the footer of the handouts.

CASE PROBLEMS

SPRINGS COLLEGE, COLORADO

(*Note:* In the following case problems, assume the role of the primary character or characters and perform the same steps that they identify.)

1. Ten days pass before Bradley receives an e-mail from Gayle. After perusing the information, he determines that the content fits nicely with an upcoming lecture he is giving on the general steps involved in conducting market research. After printing the message, Bradley highlights the points that he wants to include on the slides. The remaining information will have to go into his speaker's notes. He proceeds to create a presentation consisting of seven slides: five content slides, an introduction slide, and a summary slide. After adding some clip art images, transitions, and build slides to the presentation, he saves his work as "Marketing" onto the

Advantage Diskette. As the final step, Bradley prints the slides, speaker's notes pages, and audience handouts.

Date: Nov. 15, 1996
To: Bradley Neumann
From: Gayle Fanning
Subject: Steps in Marketing Research
cc:

A marketing research project involves the following steps:

1. ***Specify Your Objectives***
   As a marketing researcher, you must know the ***reasons for conducting the research.*** *Also, you must* ***properly define the process*** *to ensure that you will gather information on which you can base decisions. Don't let managers request unnecessary research based on their own excitement.*

2. ***Determine the Data Sources***
   You must determine whether the information can and should be gathered from ***internal sources*** *or from* ***external sources.*** *Internal sources are a company's financial statements and management information system reports. External sources include newspapers, trade journals, and government or industry reports.*

3. ***Define the Sample***
   To provide information of any use, you must find a representative population sample. Issues that you must take into consideration include the ***size of the sample*** *and the* ***data collection methods*** *you will use.*

4. ***Collect, Process, and Analyze the Data***
   Data collection consumes a large portion of the research budget. The processing of data involves ***reviewing the data for accuracy and completeness*** *and then* ***tabulating or coding the results.*** *Most data analysis is conducted using computers.*

5. ***Present the Results***
   At the end of the research process, you communicate your results to management through an ***oral presentation*** *and/or a* ***written report.*** *Ensure that you keep the presentation simple—your audience is there to be informed, not won over by your technical prowess.*

2. Bradley has been asked to deliver his "Marketing" presentation to the local chapter of the AASP (Association of Advertising and Sales Professionals), and Gayle and her client have agreed. The association has rented the lecture theater on the Springs College campus for an expected attendance of 200 members. They've also asked Bradley to produce a copy of his presentation on 35mm slides so they can send it to their head office in Atlanta. Bradley decides to change the presentation's template for use as a 35mm slide and add a copyright notice to the bottom of the audience handouts. The notice reads, "Copyright © 1996 by Gayle

Fanning and Bradley Neumann." He outputs the presentation for 35mm slides to a print file called "Marketing-35mm" on the Advantage Diskette.

3. Wally Fong had to dodge several people and trays to make it safely to where Bradley was sitting in the cafeteria. He politely asked to join Bradley and quickly took the seat across from him at the small round table. "I understand that you're the new guy who is taking over for Gayle. I'm Wally Fong, an instructor in computer sciences. I was communicating with Gayle over the Net and she mentioned that you had done some outstanding work in PowerPoint." Bradley smiled shyly and went back to his half-eaten salad. "I'd like to get your help on developing a PowerPoint presentation that reviews some of the newest operating system software." After further clarification and two espressos, Bradley agreed to help Wally with his project.

   Given that Bradley's time was limited, he encouraged Wally to develop the content for the presentation using the AutoContent Wizard. He would then take Wally's work and add clip art images, slide timings, transitions, and build slides. To get Wally started, the two men developed an outline for the presentation together, as provided below:

General	Operating System Software Review • Prepared by Wally Fong, Computer Sciences, and Bradley Neumann, Business Admin.
Introduction	This presentation reviews the strengths and weaknesses of operating system software currently available for the personal computer.
Topics of Discussion	The main ideas to be discussed include looking at three operating system software solutions: Windows 95, OS/2 Warp, and System 7.5.
Topic One	Windows 95 • Graphical user interface (GUI) • 32-bit, preemptive multitasking • Plug and Play technology • Access to the Internet and the Microsoft Online Network
Topic Two	OS/2 Warp • Graphical user interface (GUI) based on System Object Model (SOM) • 32-bit, preemptive multitasking • Runs DOS, Windows, and OS/2 applications software in separate sessions

Topic Three	System 7.5 • Most mature and developed of all graphical user interfaces (GUI) • 32-bit preemptive multitasking • Excellent for graphics and multimedia • Runs on new PowerPC platform
Real Life	The User's Perspective • Will it run the applications I need to use? • Will it provide a more stable environment? • What are the real costs of switching from my current operating system software?
What This Means	Learn to review the features of operating system software with respect to your computing needs. Do not get consumed by the advertisements pervading every trade journal that promise the world for only $99. The real costs are much greater than this!
Next Steps	1. Build a checklist of the features you require in operating system software. 2. Review each operating system based on this checklist. 3. Consider all the costs associated with switching or upgrading your system software.

As Wally, create a presentation using the AutoContent Wizard. Next, assume the role of Bradley and apply an on-screen template and special visual effects to the presentation. Save your work as "Operating Systems" onto the Advantage Diskette and then print the presentation.

Microsoft PowerPoint 7.0 for Windows 95

Toolbar Summary

STANDARD

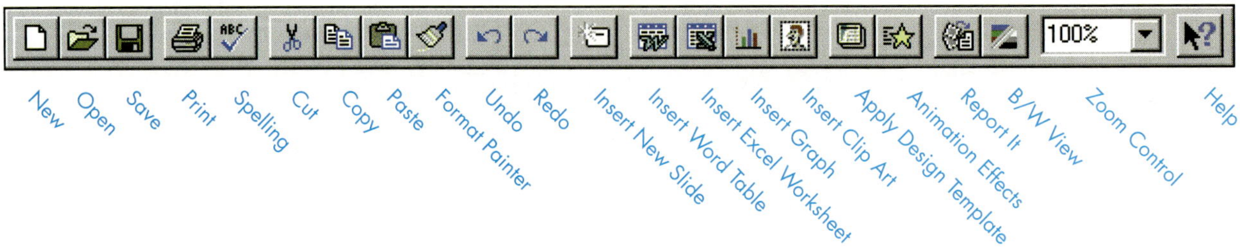

FORMATTING

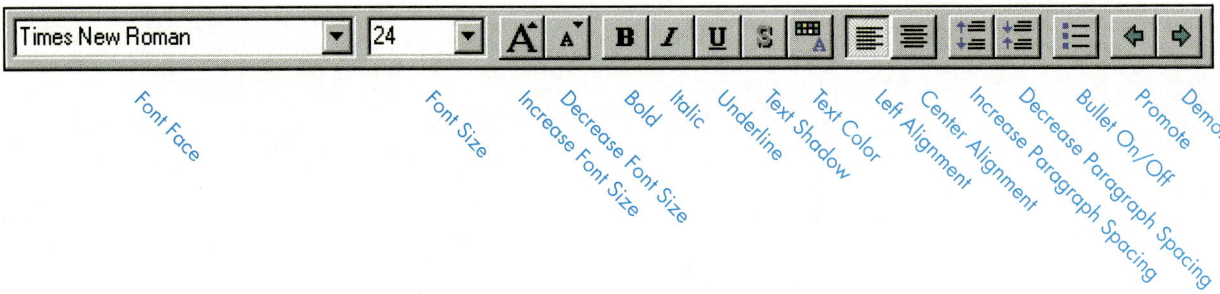

DRAWING

DRAWING+

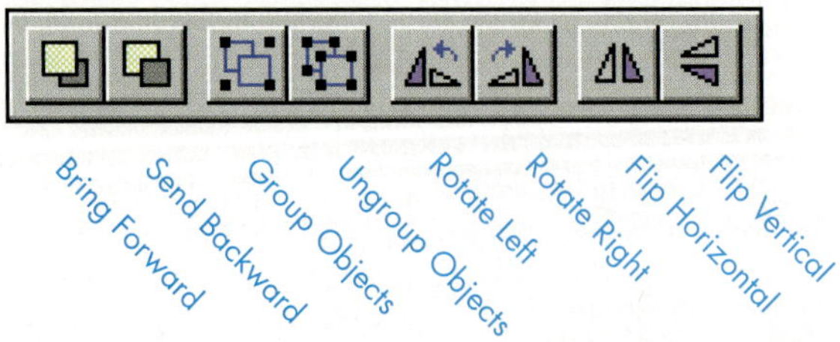

DRAWING+

AUTOSHAPES

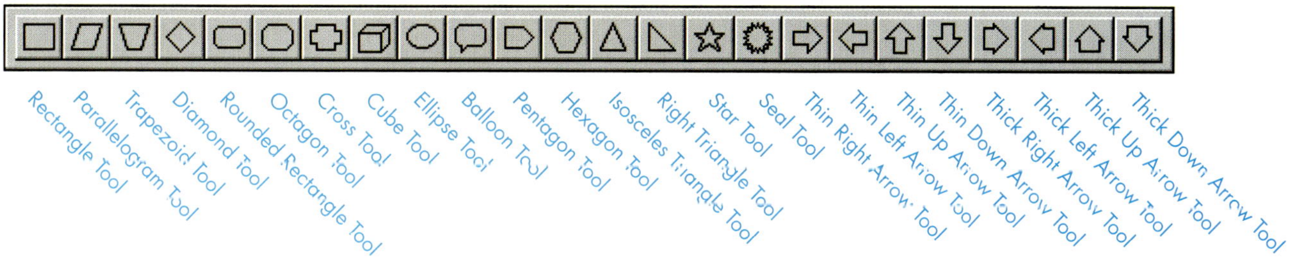

ANIMATION EFFECTS

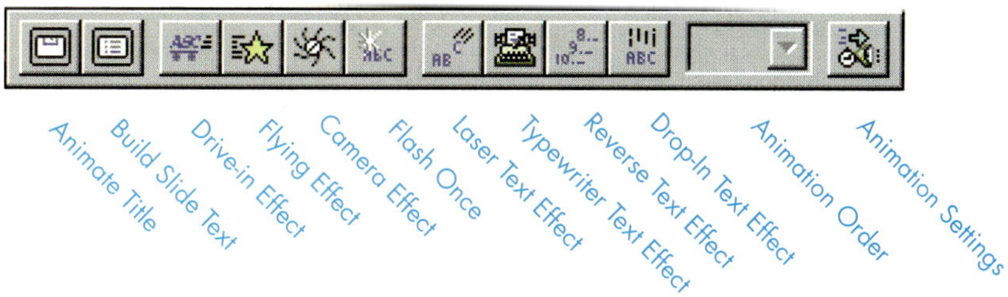

Index

A

Animation, 144–146

Animation Effects toolbar, 8

Application window, 15–16, 39

AutoClipArt, 7

AutoContent Wizard, 7, 48, 80
  using the, 50–56

AutoCorrect, 7

AutoLayout, 62, 80

B

Black and White View, 8, 102–103

Build slide, 49, 80
  creating a, 143–144

Bullets, 66–67, 114
  text, 104–106

C

Case studies and problems. See also Exercises
  Session 1, 3, 42–43
  Session 2, 47, 86–88
  Session 3, 91, 116–120
  Session 4, 123, 152–154
  Session 5, 157, 170–173

ClipArt Gallery, 71, 80, 124
  adding art from the, to slides, 74–76
  finding art in the, 126–129
  inserting clip art using, 125–126
  moving and resizing clip art using, 130–131

Color scheme, 99, 100–102, 114

Command summaries, 39, 80, 113, 146, 169

D

Default presentation format, 50, 80

Design template, 49–50, 80
  using a, 57–60

Dialog box, 20–21

E

Equation Editor, 124

Exercises. See also Case studies and problems
  Session 1, 40–42
  Session 2, 81–85
  Session 3, 114–116
  Session 4, 147–151
  Session 5, 169–170

F

Footer, 161

Formatting text, 67–70

G

Graphic file, 132, 147

Graphs, 125, 132–135

H

Handout Master, 163–165, 169

Handouts, audience, 5, 39, 163–166

Header, 161

Help, 22–27

K

Keyboard, 10

Key terms, 39, 80–81, 114, 147, 169

L

Landscape orientation, 166, 169

M

Masters, 50, 81

Meeting Minder, 8

Menu bar, 16, 18

Microsoft Graph, 132, 147

Microsoft Organization Chart, 136, 147

Microsoft PowerPoint 7.0. See PowerPoint

Microsoft Windows 95. See Windows 95

Mini-apps, 123–125, 147

Mouse, 9

Multitasking, 7, 39

N

Notes
  creating and printing, 158–161
  modifying, 161–162

Notes Master, 161–162, 169

Notes pages, 5–6, 158, 169

Notes pages view, 32

O

Organization charts, 125, 136–139, 147

Outline, 6

Outline view, 31

P

Placeholders, 62, 81

Portrait orientation, 166, 169

PowerPoint
  describing, 3–6
  features of, 7–8
  getting help in, 22–27
  the guided tour of, 14–22
  leaving, 38
  presentations in, See Presentation
  starting, 10–14
  summary of, 38
  working with, 8–10

PowerPoint viewer, 4

Presentation, 4, 39
  closing a, 37
  editing a, 71–76
  the importance of color in a, 99–102
  manipulating text in a, 107–110
  an on-screen, 32
  opening a, 27–29
  overview of creating a, 47–50
  packaging a, 168
  printing a, See Printing
  reviewing a, 71
  saving a, 60–61
  text bullets in a, 104–106
  using slides in a, See Slides
  using templates in a, See Templates
  using the text tool in a, 110–113, 114
  using Wizards in a, See Wizard
  views in a, See View(s)
  visual effects in a, See Visual effects

Presentation Conferencing, 8

Presentation template, 50, 81

Presentation window, 15, 16–17, 39

Printing
  audience handouts, 165–166
  creating and, speaker's notes, 158–161
  options for, slides, 166–168
  a presentation, 78–79

Public speaking
  notes for, See Notes
  tips for, 157–158

R

Run-time version, 4, 39

S

Scanner, 132, 147

Scroll bar, 17

Shortcut menus, 18–19

Slide Master, 95–97, 98, 114

Slides, 4–5, 40 See also Slide Master; Slide shows
- adding text to, 63–65
- build, 49, 80, 143–144
- changing the layout of, 72–74
- creating 35 mm, 167–168
- editing individual, 97–98
- formatting text on, 67–70
- inserting ClipArt to, 74–76
- introduction to adding, 62
- manipulating bullets on, 66–67
- print options for, 166–168
- setting up the format for, 166–167

Slide shows. See also Slides
- adding animation for, 144–146
- creating a build slide for, 143–144
- incorporating transitions in, 141–143
- introduction to running, 139
- setting timings for, 139–141

Slide show view, 32

Slide sorter view, 31

Slide view, 30

Slide work area, 16

Status bar, 16

Style Checker, 7, 76–78, 81

T

Taskbar, 21

Templates, 3, 40
- applying, 91–94
- design, 49–50, 80
- presentation, 50, 81

Terminology. See Key terms

Text. See Presentation; Slides; View(s)

Text tool, 110–113, 114

Timings, setting, 139–141

Title bar, 16

Title Master, 95, 114

Toolbar(s), 19–20
- Animation Effects, 8
- Drawing, 16
- Formatting, 16
- Standard, 16

Transition, 49, 81

V

View(s)
- black and white, 8, 102–103
- manipulating text in outline, 107–110
- notes pages, 32
- outline, 31
- slide, 30
- slide show, 32
- slide sorter, 31
- switching among the, 33–37

Visual effects
- animation as, 144–146
- clip art as, See ClipArt Gallery
- graphs as, 125, 132–135
- organization charts as, 125, 136–139, 147
- pictures as, 132
- and slide shows. See Slide shows
- by working with objects, 123–125

W

Window
- application, 15–16, 39
- presentation, 15, 16–17, 39

Windows 95
- the advantage of working in, 6–7
- loading applications in, 11–12

Windows Taskbar, 21

Wizard, 3, 40
- AutoContent, See AutoContent Wizard
- Pack And Go, 4, 7, 168

WordArt, 125

WYSIWYG, 7, 40